Nirvana for Sale?

Nirvana for Sale?

Buddhism, Wealth, and the Dhammakāya
Temple in Contemporary Thailand

Rachelle M. Scott

Cover image: A picture of the top of the Mahadhammakaya Chedi with individual Phra Dhammakāya images. Courtesy of the Dhammakāya Foundation.

Published by State University of New York Press, Albany

© 2009 State University of New York

For information, contact State University of New York Press, Albany, NY
www.sunypress.edu

Production by Eileen Meehan
Marketing by Fran Keneston

Library of Congress Cataloging-in-Publication Data

Scott, Rachelle M.
    Nirvana for sale? : Buddhism, wealth, and the Dhammakaya Temple in contemporary Thailand / Rachelle M. Scott.
        p.   cm.
    Includes bibliographical references and index.
    ISBN 978-1-4384-2783-6 (hardcover : alk. paper)—ISBN 978-1-4384-2784-3 (pbk. : alk. paper)
    1. Wat Phrathammakai (Khlong Luang, Thailand)   2. Wealth—Religious aspects—Buddhism.   3. Buddhism—Thailand—Customs and practices.   I. Title.
BQ6337.K452W3636 2009
294.3'9109593—dc22   2008051369

10 9 8 7 6 5 4 3 2 1

For Ian and Phoebe

Contents

List of Illustrations

Acknowledgments

I am indebted to a number of people who helped to make this book a reality. This book reflects the insight, support, and generosity of my teachers, my advisors, my family, and my dear friends. First and foremost, I am forever indebted to my professors at Lawrence University, Arizona State University, and Northwestern University who taught me to examine religion through the eyes of practitioners—from listening to the stories of Jain nuns in Pune, India, to cataloging newspapers from Burma during the turbulent year of 1988, to hearing stories of debates in West Africa over the proper way to pray. Collectively, my teachers have shown me how religions are inherently diverse, dynamic, and deeply connected to their broader societies.

This book stems from my dissertation, which I completed at Northwestern University under the tutelage of two exceptional scholars, Dr. George Bond, who fostered my understanding of the Theravāda tradition in South and Southeast Asia, and Dr. Robert Launay, who pushed me to think critically about the anthropological study of religion. I am deeply indebted to them and to Dr. Brook Ziporyn, Dr. Jacob Kinnard, and Dr. Ananda Abeyesekere for their invaluable insights and suggestions at different phases of this project. I must also thank my colleagues in the Department of Religious Studies at the University of Tennessee, who have offered tremendous support to me as I transformed my dissertation into a book for publication, and the three anonymous readers whose astute criticisms and suggestions greatly aided in that endeavor.

This book also would not have been possible without the generosity of countless individuals in Thailand whose assistance formed the backbone of my exploration of religion in Thailand during my research years of 1998, 1999, and January to February of 2001. First, I must thank my dear friend, Duangtip Seeluangsawat, who so generously offered her time and assistance to me while I was living in Thailand. She is an invaluable friend and person, and my debt to her is immeasurable. In the same spirit, I must thank Dr. Phramaha Phairoh Kritsanavadee of MahaChulalongkornrajavidyalaya University for his generous offerings of wisdom and for his commitment to showing me the many dimensions of Buddhism in Thailand. At the Dhammakāya Temple in Pathum Thani and the Dhammakāya center in Chicago, I am grateful to a number of individuals who graciously listened to my questions and spent innumerable hours talking with me about their lives and experiences at the Temple. I am also grateful to the Dhammakāya Foundation for granting me permission to use a number of their images and to quote extensively from their publications. I must also thank the following individuals and institutions for granting me permission to reproduce their materials in this book: Suwanna Satha-Anand, Phra Phaisan Wisalo, Jonathon Watts, *Matichon* magazine, *The Nation*, University of South Carolina Press, State University of New York Press, and *The Journal of the Siam Society*. I would also like to thank Dr. Suwanna Satha-Anand of Chulalongkorn University, Navachai Kiartkorkuaa, and Pawinee Petch-sawang for their assistance at different points in this project. I must also thank my Thai language instructors at Arizona State University, the University of Wisconsin–Madison, and the American University Association in Bangkok who opened a new world of language to me. I am also deeply grateful to the Ford Foundation, the Social Science Research Council, and Northwestern University for generously supporting my research in Thailand.

Last, but certainly not least, I must thank my family for their patience and support throughout this process. I am grateful to my parents, Katherine Kuzniar and William Jacobs, who have fostered my love for exploring the historical, cultural, and personal dimensions of religion. I am also deeply grateful to David and Kathleen Scott who have read countless versions of this book, who have offered insightful suggestions, and whose own standards of excellence have served as a model for what my work should be. Finally, I want to extend a special thanks to my husband, Kelvin, who has provided me with seemingly limitless amounts of support, who took time away from his violin making to listen to me talk about Buddhism and all things Thai, and who encouraged me as I juggled writing with teaching and raising a family. I also want to give one last and most special thanks to my beloved children, Ian and Phoebe, who remind me daily of the value of living and loving.

Note on Transliteration and Terminology

In general, I have used the Royal Institute of Thailand's guide for romanizing Thai words. This method of transliteration does not have tone markers nor does it indicate vowel length. In the case of proper names, I generally have used conventional romanizations, such as Prawase Wasi rather than Prawet Wasi and Bhikkhu Buddhadāsa rather than Phra Phutthatat. When referring to Buddhist concepts, such as merit, I have tended to use the Pāli (such as *puñña*) or Thai (*bun*) versions of the word, with a couple of notable exceptions. I frequently use the Sanskrit words *nirvāṇa* and *stūpa* instead of their Pāli equivalents (*nibbāna* and *thūpa*) because of the familiarity of the former within the English language. As for the name of the Dhammakāya Temple, I have chosen to refer to it as the Dhammakāya Temple (Pāli/English) instead of Wat Phra Thammakai (the Thai version) for the purpose of readability and because the Temple uses the Pāli word, Dhammakāya, in its English-language materials. When referring to the specific practice of meditation, I use the lower-case version of dhammakāya. In some cases, however, I have maintained the Thai form of the word. For instance, I have used the Thai version of Mahathammakai Chedi, instead of the Pāli/English MahaDhammakāya Cetiya, because of the frequent use of the Thai word *chedi* in both English and Thai materials.

Introduction

> Don't overlook the chance of [a] lifetime.... It has been the tradition of
> Buddhists since ancient times to build Buddha images in temple grounds
> as an act of devotion and in homage and recollection of the supreme vir-
> tues of the Lord Buddha.... Creating a Buddha image is now no longer
> the realm of royalty and the aristocracy—but a gesture of devotion through
> which you can be one part of the Mahathammakai Chedi and the Mahat-
> hammakai Chedi can be a part of you!
>
> —From a pamphlet distributed at the Dhammakāya Temple
> in Pathum Thani, Thailand, 1999

In the spring of 2000, after a decade of arduous planning and construction, the
Dhammakāya Temple completed its Mahathammakai Chedi, a massive monument that honored the Buddhist tradition and the Dhammakāya community.[1] Temple publications presented the *chedi* as a *sunruamphlangsattha* (a
center for the power of faith) that would foster both inner peace and world
peace.[2] The Temple engraved the names of the donors on individually commissioned Buddha images, which were cast by Dhammakāya monks in merit making ceremonies and subsequently affixed to the exterior of the chedi or housed
within its interior. For one visiting the Temple today, the sight of these Phra
Dhammakāya images reflecting and scattering the sun's light leaves an indeli-
ble impression, as does the sheer size of the monument—it occupies a space of
one square kilometer and purportedly accommodates up to one million people
on the grounds around its circumference. The chedi has become a focal point
for pilgrims who travel to the Temple in Pathum Thani, Thailand each year to
practice meditation and to participate in the Temple's numerous religious and
social activities.

The building of a memorial monument (*chedi*, Thai; *stūpa*, Sanskrit) as a
container for the Buddha's physical and symbolic relics has a long history in
the Buddhist tradition.[3] While the origins of the stūpa cult remain the subject
of much speculation, it is clear that the construction of reliquaries played an
important role in the first few centuries of Buddhist history. The *Mahāvaṃsa*,
one of the Sinhalese chronicles, connects the founding of the Buddhist religion

1

Mahathammakai Chedi. (Photo courtesy of the Dhammakāya Foundation.)

in Sri Lanka with the building of a stūpa for the Buddha's relics.[4] In the *Mahāparinibbāna-sutta*, which recounts the Buddha's final days, the Buddha instructs his followers on how to enshrine his relics: "A [stūpa] should be erected at the crossroads for the Tathāgatha. And whoever lays wreaths or puts sweet perfumes and colours there with a devout heart, will reap benefit and happiness for a long time."[5] In South and Southeast Asia, offerings made for the building of a stūpa are considered especially fruitful for the generation of merit (*bun*, Thai; *puñña*, Pāli). As a result, the history of Theravāda Buddhism recounts numerous stories of the building of stūpas and the donors who made them possible.

Given the long history of stūpa building in South Asia and Southeast Asia, it is intriguing that the construction of the Mahathammakai Chedi became the subject of a heated controversy in Thailand in 1998 and 1999. This controversy assumed center stage in Thai public discourse when the national media reported on the Temple's publicizing of miraculous events at the site of the chedi. The Temple reported that on September 6, 1998, as thousands of Dhammakāya practitioners meditated in front of the chedi, the sun appeared to be "sucked out of the sky." It subsequently was replaced by an image of Luang Pho Sot of Wat Paknam, the late founder of the meditation method used at the Temple. Some individuals saw him in the form of a golden statue, whereas others pictured him as a giant crystal. Not long after the event, the Temple published testimonials of eyewitnesses in their pamphlets and in newspapers.

Accompanying these testimonials were digitally rendered montages of the reported miraculous sightings.[6]

Critics quickly denounced the Temple's marketing of the "miracle in the sky" as a means to procure more donations for the construction of the chedi. After meeting with the Temple's abbot, Deputy Education Minister Arkom Engchuan told the press that he had informed the abbot that "[b]illboards picturing the miracle that are used to invite donations are not suitable. Instead, they should be used to invite the public to study the teachings of Lord Buddha at the temple."[7] Criticism of the Temple's marketing of the "miracle in the sky" quickly merged with criticisms of the Temple's purported materialism and its distribution of amulets thought to attract wealth and prosperity (*dut sap*, literally to "suck material assets"). This situation, in turn, generated more discussion of the purported widespread commercialization and corruption of Buddhism in contemporary Thailand, as well as the inability of the monastic establishment—namely the Mahatherasamakhom (the Supreme Saṅgha Council)—to curtail it.

While it is tempting to reduce the controversy to yet another story of "a big temple gone bad"—the characterization that dominated the Thai and International press—far more than the purported materialism of a suburban Thai temple was at issue. Observing the tide of public opinion while living in Bangkok in 1998 and 1999, I was struck by the breadth and scope of the controversy: It literally dominated the headlines from November of 1998 to August of 1999. Its pervasiveness and longevity indicated to me that it raised broader questions about the state of "Thai Buddhism." Local debates over the Dhammakāya Temple's wealth, its construction of the Mahathammakai Chedi, its marketing and distribution of amulets, and its advertising of the "miracle in the sky," became a discursive site for an extensive discussion of Buddhist orthodoxy, orthopraxy, and identity at a critical moment in Thai history.

The controversy erupted in the midst of the Asian economic crisis of 1997 to 1999. During this time, many Thais reevaluated notions of prosperity, development, progress, and "Thai values." As the Dhammakāya Temple marketed its new religious monument, two populist discourses emerged within the public sphere that questioned the effects of global capitalism on Thai society. A new form of Thai nationalism blamed Western capitalism, especially the institutions of the IMF and World Bank, for Thailand's economic woes, and a new form of Thai localism urged Thais to reject Western development models and return to their agrarian roots.[8] The critique of the Dhammakāya Temple's wealth and alleged heretical teachings and practices fit within this broader discussion of the erosion of Thai values and the disastrous effects of global capitalism on Thai society.

Today, Buddhists are redefining Buddhist religiosity within contexts of dramatic social, economic, and political change. This atmosphere breeds discussions regarding the "state of Buddhism" and the integrity of the saṅgha in the contemporary world. The integrity of the saṅgha has long been a central issue within Buddhist communities because members of the saṅgha are the principal preservers of the tradition through their orthodox teachings and purity of practice. But the modern period has ushered in an unprecedented number of challenges to the institution of Buddhist monasticism around the globe. Over the past two centuries, the integrity of the saṅgha has come under scrutiny as the dramatic forces of colonialism, modernization, secularization, and most recently, globalization have affected monastic institutions. In Sri Lanka, Burma, Laos, and Cambodia, European colonialism fostered the destabilization of the monastic community, which in turn laid the foundation for new forms of monastic and lay practice.[9] In Thailand, the nineteenth and twentieth centuries witnessed the centralization of religious authority and the homogenization of Buddhist teaching and practice under the guise of modern saṅgha reform.[10] In China and Tibet, Buddhist monks and nuns faced the serious challenge of political opposition to institutional religion.[11] In Japan, during the Meiji period (1868–1912), Buddhist institutions lost their privileged status when nationalists increasingly identified Buddhism as a "foreign religion."[12] And in the West, as convert Buddhist communities arose, individual practice and religious thought were privileged over the establishment and maintenance of Buddhist monasticism.[13]

The effects of these challenges to the saṅgha continue to shape Buddhist practice in countries across the globe, but the postcolonial world offers new challenges to Buddhist communities as they navigate their religious paths within the culture of global capitalism. This culture provides new avenues for religious expression and critique, particularly in relation to ideas concerning consumption, the sine qua non of capitalism. Consumption is *"the* factor, *the* principle, held to determine definitions of value, the construction of identities, and even the shape of the global 'ecumene.'"[14] As such, contemporary religious identities are often constructed either in synergy with consumption or in direct opposition to it. Consumption can be viewed either as a vehicle for the enjoyment of the fruits of religious piety or as the mechanism of its destruction. At the forefront of these debates over contemporary religious identity are varying appraisals of the proper relationship between wealth and piety.

The correlation between wealth and piety has engaged religious thinkers throughout history. At the heart of many of these religious discourses is a discussion of "worldliness": To what degree does a particular religious perspective embrace or reject this-worldly values such as wealth, health, and an abundant number of sons. For religious persons who posit a theory of the ultimate as distinct from the world, the act of being religious often entails strategies of rejection—discourses and practices aimed at separating one's self from this-worldly values and goals. The disciplinary practices of monastic communities, for instance, aim to create new selves through the renunciation of familial roles and obligations. Some monastic communities may view renunciation as an absolute rejection of the world (the Christian anchorite tradition is one example), but not all monastic traditions possess an ethos of radical rejection. In some cases, renunciation may be better viewed as akin to basic training in the military, where the focus is on the creation of new ways of being. Other religious orientations recommend ideals of selflessness and simplicity within families and communities. Still other modes of religiosity embrace this-worldly benefits, such as health and wealth, as signs of religious piety and as a legitimate aim of religious practice. In this case, religiosity is deeply embedded in the material fruits of everyday life.

While we commonly label particular religious traditions as other-worldly or this-worldly in orientation, the reality is far more complex than such simple categorizations suggest. Religious traditions are dynamic and encompass a wide variety of perspectives, many of which are influenced by the power relations and historical circumstances of a given community at a particular moment in time. Specific religious assessments of the "world," therefore, do not simply reproduce a given religious orthodoxy; they also reflect broader assessments of the state of society at a particular historical moment.

Today, debates over the relationship between wealth and piety reflect differing orientations towards global capitalism, as it redefines communal and individual identities and promotes consumption-oriented markers of success. In the United States, the signs of global capitalism are readily apparent on the grounds of mega-churches, with their McDonald's and coffee shops, day spas and recreational climbing walls. Their leaders commonly preach a religious message of self-improvement or personal fulfillment that mirrors the discourses of prominent self-help gurus. An example is Joel Osteen, the senior pastor of Lakewood Church in Houston, Texas. He spreads a message of personal fulfillment that is explicitly couched in this-worldly terms. The titles of some of his sermons include, "Enlarge Your Vision," "Financial Prosperity," "Do All You Can Do to Make Your Dreams Come True," and "Developing Your Potential."[15] In his best-selling book, *Your Best Life Now: 7 Steps to Living at Your Full Potential,* he merges standard discourses on divine relationships with practical advice on personal success.[16] This fusion of religion with self-improvement, health, and prosperity is, of course, not limited to the United States. It is a global phenomenon, from Sweden and West Africa to Australia and Chile.[17] While all of these forms of "prosperity-religiosity" share common features, such as the use of new media for the dissemination of the message, there are significant differences as well. Joel Osteen preaches his message of "religious self-improvement" within a relatively affluent and stable cultural context, whereas religious persons in other parts of the world, such as in Africa or Latin America, embrace the "prosperity gospel" as they grapple with radically shifting, and sometimes devastating, socio-economic and political realities.

As self-help gurus and prosperity-gospel preachers seek to merge the values of late modern capitalism with religion, their critics insist on the centrality of simplicity and renunciation in religious worldviews over and against that of modern, consumer-oriented, hedonistic materialism. In fact, contemporary debates over religion and worldliness are often framed in reference to questions concerning the relationship between religion and our contemporary culture of consumerism: Should religions co-opt the language and models of consumerism? Is religion a product that can be sold with Madison Avenue marketing techniques? Or should religion be used as a vehicle for critiquing the market and our contemporary culture of consumerism? Some commentators even posit the possibility that consumerism itself is a religion that is competing with the values of other religions. This argument is put forth by David Loy, an outspoken Buddhist, social critic, and academic who argues that consumerism is perhaps the first truly global religion.[18] He identifies consumerism as the most influential value system in late capitalism. As such, he suggests that consumerism should be viewed as a religion with its own conception of the divine (the Market) and its own soteriology (the consumption of consumer goods). He insists that if we view consumerism as a "secular" ideology, we miss the depth of its impact on contemporary values.

When debates emerge within religious communities over the relationship between religion and wealth or religion and consumerism, they typically extend to broader issues involving religious identity, belief, and practice. This is especially true in the case of religious scandals, which tend to recast religious difference as simply sensationalized stories of the faults and indiscretions of wayward individuals. In an instructive essay on the analytical value of religious scandals, Frances Fitzgerald argues that the case of Jim Bakker, the former PTL (Praise the Lord) head and founder of Heritage USA, was more than simply an investigation into Bakker's alleged embezzlement of church donations.[19] The scandal played into an existing debate within Pentecostal and charismatic circles over the relationship between God and personal and corporate finance. To reduce the scandal to a tale of Bakker's personal shortcomings fails to recognize this larger debate over conceptions of contemporary Pentecostalism. While the popular press may reduce religious controversies such as those involving the Dhammakāya Temple and Jim Bakker to stories of corruption, materialism, and greed, these stories shed light on important debates concerning orthodox religiosity within religious communities.

Orientalism and the Study of Theravāda Buddhism

Contemporary debates over the Dhammakāya Temple's purported commercialization of Buddhism reflect internal struggles over the representation of

Thai Buddhism, particularly the question of whether so-called popular religious practices reflect authentic Buddhist piety and practice. For over two centuries, reformers within the Buddhist tradition have sought to extricate and banish permanently those elements of "cultural Buddhism" that reflect animistic, magical, and mundane concerns. Practices that were particularly abhorrent to these reformers included astrology, the chanting of Buddhist *sutta*s for protection and blessing, and the veneration of Buddha images, to name only a few. Reformed Buddhism, on the other hand, represented the pristine and authentic religion of the founder, Siddhattha Gotama (Siddhartha Gautama, Sanskrit), which emphasized the perfection of ethics and wisdom. Contemporary debates over Dhammakāya amulets, miracles, and the construction of impressive (and costly) pieces of art and architecture are an extension of this modernist debate within both Buddhist and academic circles.

The Buddhist modernism of the nineteenth century, which sought to distinguish authentic Buddhism from its popular forms, emerged within contexts of colonialism, Christian proselytization, and emergent discourses on the nature of religion, reason, and progress. The presentation of Buddhism as inherently rational and consistent with modern science was not merely a statement of religious orthodoxy, it was a discourse that countered the portrayal of Buddhists as backward, primitive, and entrenched within superstition and magic. Like Hindu Modernists in India who promoted pristine versions of Hinduism (such as Ram Mohan Roy, 1772–1833), Buddhist modernists perceived a disparity between authentic Buddhism and the religion of the masses that in their opinion led to mischaracterizations of the tradition as a whole. To repair the image of the religion and its practitioners, reform was necessary, and the heart of this reform was aimed, as in the past, at the saṅgha. In Sri Lanka, Anagarika Dharmapala (1864–1933) argued that Buddhist monks should become "a spiritual army" whose task it was to eliminate traditional ritualism from popular Buddhism and reform the practice of errant monks.[20] In a similar manner, the reformed monastic lineage of King Mongkut (Rama IV, r. 1851–1868) in Thailand, the Thammayut order, embodied a renewed commitment to discipline and orthodoxy, and was used as a vehicle by the government for religious reform and the centralization of authority.[21]

These internal discourses of reform promoted a rational, textually based, philosophical Buddhism. It constituted a form of indigenous Orientalism or an "Orientalism of the Orientals," which informed and was informed by the emergent study of Asian languages and religion in the West.[22] As a category, the term Orientalism initially referred to the study of the "Orient" by European philologists and historians, but since the publication of Edward Said's exceedingly influential study, *Orientalism*, the term has been embedded within critiques of power and representation, the dichotomy between the East and the West, and the construction of the "Other."[23]

In the case of Buddhism, several studies have focused on the European construction of Buddhism as an object of study. One of the most influential and controversial of these studies is Philip Almond's *The British Discovery of Buddhism*.[24] Following Said's assessment of Western representations of Islam, Phillip Almond has argued that "Buddhism" as an object of discourse (and hence of analysis and comparison) was created by the Victorian culture in which it emerged. As a result, this "construction and interpretation of Buddhism reveals much about nineteenth century concerns and can be read as an important sign of crucial sociocultural aspects of the Victorian period."[25] The product, according to Almond, is a textually based form of Buddhism that emphasizes philosophy and ethics. Within this Victorian construction, the Buddha, is portrayed as a great historical figure (similar to the historical Jesus), a liberator of the masses, and an "enlightened" being.

More recently, Richard S. Cohen has convincingly demonstrated how the usage of "enlightenment" as a translation for *nirvāṇa* became popularized in the nineteenth century. He argues that by the mid-1870s "it had become commonplace to call the buddha 'enlightened,' and by the end of the 1880s, the terminologies of 'enlightened' and 'enlightenment' dominated the English-language literature on Buddhism."[26] This was due, in part, to the efforts of Max Müller, who consistently used it in his analysis of the Buddha and the Buddhist tradition. Cohen argues that the word enlightened fits perfectly within Müller's science of religion, which sought to uncover the pristine forms of religion and ultimately prove the superiority of Christianity. According to Cohen, Müller's use of the terms enlightened and enlightenment made Buddhism more religious and universal by making it more comparable to Christianity (which provided a basis for the comparison of religions). The presentation of the Buddha as a rational philosopher who succeeded in becoming fully enlightened fit nicely within the context of Europe's own Enlightenment. This envisioning of the tradition was subsequently transported to America through such media as European scholarship and literature, the Theosophical Society and other new movements, as well as through various forms of Buddhist modernism. In both Europe and America, "enlightened Buddhism" was viewed as consistent with modern science. Paul Carus (1852–1919), the editor of Open Court Publishing Company and avid student of comparative religion, wrote in a letter to Anagarika Dharmapala that in his opinion "Buddha's intention was nothing else than to establish what we call a Religion of Science. 'Enlightenment' and 'Science' are interchangeable words."[27]

For early European scholars of Theravāda Buddhism, this "enlightened" Buddhism was located within the Pāli canon since they believed that it contained the earliest and hence purest form of the historical Buddha's teachings. The locating of "pure Buddhism" within the Pāli canon reflected not only the Protestant preoccupation with texts,[28] but also the modern emphasis on historical religious figures. As Christian theologians embarked upon the search for the historical Jesus, European and American Orientalists sought to reconstruct a biography of the Buddha based upon historical facts, not religious myth. Within this framework, they portrayed the Buddha as a great reformer and egalitarian, who rejected caste and Hindu ritualism and preached an inherently agnostic, ethical, and rational religious message. Aspects of his biography that did not fit this paradigm, such as the tales of miraculous events in his numerous lives, were reduced to examples of "the love of exaggeration and of mystery universal among rude peoples" rather than viewed as key components of his sacred biography.[29]

This nineteenth-century focus on the life of the historical Buddha led to the general assessment within Orientalist scholarship on Buddhism that the Theravāda tradition in its ideal practice (i.e., Pāli canon Buddhism) was the most authentic form of Buddhism. Some commentators viewed other forms of Buddhism as appealing, such as Marquis Lafayette Gordon, a missionary to Japan who wrote that the Pure Land tradition was the best "gospel" of Buddhism. But all concluded that these later forms were less "purely Buddhist" since they did not emphasize the teachings of the historical Buddha.[30] Within European Orientalism, therefore, Theravāda became known as the most orthodox school of Buddhism. As a result, the Theravāda tradition, despite significant diversity within it, has been labeled by many commentators as the most conservative branch of Buddhism and hence closest to the original teachings of the Buddha. Pāli-canon Buddhism then became synonymous with early Indian Buddhism. Little attention was paid to commentarial or vernacular texts within distinctive local forms of Buddhism.[31] These Theravāda texts, along with the entire corpus of Mahāyāna and Vajrayāna texts, were viewed at best as significant alterations of the tradition, and at worst as signs of the tradition's decay.

The valorization of Pāli-canon Buddhism as the true embodiment of the historical Buddha's rational and ethical religion inevitably set up a marked distinction between so-called pure Pāli Buddhism and the corrupted local forms of the Theravāda tradition. Whether this contrast was viewed as the result of natural decay[32] or of the lamentable devolution of a great tradition,[33] it reified the distinction between the rational and ethical Buddhism "preserved" within the Pāli canon and the ritual-oriented, cosmologically rich Buddhism of the masses (both lay and monastic). The sharp distinction was one that led to the championing of reform by both European sympathizers such as Colonel Henry Steel Olcott (1832–1907) and reform-oriented Buddhists such as Anagarika Dharmapala and King Mongkut.

While calls for reform have existed within the Theravāda tradition throughout its history, especially when new political authorities sought legitimacy and centralized power, modern calls for reform were unique in that they were, in part, embedded within a global conversation about the nature and character of orthodox Buddhism. This is not to say that Western constructions of Buddhism determined how Buddhists conceived of their tradition, but rather that they constituted part of a dialogue about authentic Buddhist doctrine and practice and the need for reform in Theravāda countries. One instance of this exchange is King Chulalongkorn's 1904 essay on the *jātaka*s, in which he relied heavily on the work of T. W. Rhys Davids (the founder of the Pāli Text Society). In this essay, King Chulalongkorn (r. 1868–1910) dramatically redefined the jātakas as examples of pre-Buddhist folklore, rather than as stories told by the Buddha about his former lives. This served to rationalize the tradition, undermine the focus on jātakas within the Buddhist tradition, and reinterpret the life of the Buddha in modern historical terms.[34]

A common theme in both Western and Asian discourses of reform was the need to eliminate the "magical" and overly "ritualistic" elements of the tradition—to redirect the focus away from mundane concerns (health, happiness, and prosperity in this and future lives) to the ultimate concern of *nirvāṇa* with its focus on the perfection of ethics and wisdom. Take, for instance, the case of the miraculous powers (*iddhi*) of meditation adepts. Stories of these abound within vernacular texts such as the stories of Phra Malai in Thailand and within anthropological portraits of "living Buddhism," but few references are made to them in canonical-based descriptions of Theravāda Buddhism. Winston King's classic examination of meditation in the Theravāda tradition, *Theravāda Meditation: The Buddhist Transformation of Yoga*, makes only one reference to the miraculous powers of meditation adepts. In that comment, he states that while the "magical and psychic powers that accompany meditative achievement probably have always been a part of the Buddhist schema . . . [t]heir casual, self-serving manifestation, as their direct pursuit, has always been condemned in the mainstream teaching."[35] This sentiment is echoed by many modernist Buddhists today; when referencing miracles in the tradition, they tend to focus on the canonical proscription found in the *Kevatta-sutta* against seeking miraculous powers and against using them to procure support.

While not being the dominant theme within these modern discourses of reform, the topic of monastic wealth and the desire for wealth among the laity was clearly present in early modern Orientalist and Asian critiques of contemporary popular Buddhism. The image of the ideal otherworldly renunciant was contrasted with the reality that many monks were the recipients of lavish gifts. In T. W. Rhys Davids' historical overview of Buddhism, he describes Buddhist monasticism as embracing the spirit of poverty with its admonition against various forms of personal property, an ideal that becomes "swallowed up by the permission given to the community to possess not only books and other personal property, but even lands and houses. Gautama himself is related to have received such gifts on behalf of the Sangha, which, at the time when it flourished in India, must have rivaled in wealth the most powerful orders of the Middle Ages; and in Buddhist countries at the present day the church is often as wealthy as it is among ourselves."[36] In European scholarship, such "excesses" were often characterized as representative of the general decline of the religion since the time of the Buddha. Monastic wealth, merit-seeking laypersons, and Buddhist ritualism were all viewed as the corruption of a once pure, and in many cases, highly rational religion.

This portrait of Buddhism and Buddhist history that was created by nineteenth-century European Indologists provided the basis for Max Weber's famous characterization of early Buddhism as an other-worldly religion of "cultivated professional monks," aimed at the salvation of the individual.[37] This religion of the monastic "virtuoso" is distinct from the religion of the house-holder whose focus is on the procurement of "worldly goods," such as "riches, a good name, good company, death without fear, and betterment of rebirth opportunities."[38] Weber's Buddhism of the monastic virtuoso functioned as an ideal type, an example of "other-worldly" asceticism, in his typology of the world's religions. As one of the founding fathers of modern sociology, Weber's interest in the study of religion was intimately connected to his analysis of so-cial action—of how particular religious ideas might affect social behavior. In particular, Weber wanted to answer the question of why capitalism emerged in Europe rather than China or India. To this end, his portrait of Buddhism as a religion of other-worldly ascetic virtuosos provided a useful contrast to his pre-sentation of the "inner-worldly" ascetics of Protestant Christianity, whose de-sire to validate their state of salvation led to the rise of modern capitalism. Weber's analysis of early Buddhism set the stage for numerous discussions of the relationship between wealth and piety in Buddhism, especially in the an-thropological study of Buddhism.

Anthropological descriptions of Theravāda Buddhist societies commonly framed the contrast between the "original spirit of renunciation" and the reali-ties of wealthy monasteries and prosperity-seeking laypersons in terms of the distinction between the Great Tradition of Theravāda Buddhism and the little traditions of Sinhalese, Burmese, Thai, and other local Buddhisms. While many of these accounts insisted upon the importance of examining local versions of Buddhism, they continued to reify the idea of a Great Tradition that transcended local variations. In "The Great Tradition and the Little in the Perspective of Sinhalese Buddhism," the renowned anthropologist Gananath Obeyesekere contrasted the Great Tradition of Theravāda Buddhism, "with its corpus of Pāli texts, places of worship, and a great community of monks" and that of Sinha-lese Buddhism, the religion of the masses. He argued that this perspective en-abled us to acknowledge the differences among the various local religions of South and Southeast Asia, while simultaneously acknowledging their shared lineage (Theravāda Buddhism).[39] While sensitive to diversity, his perspective assumes that the Great Tradition transcends local context and history, and re-

ifies it as the essential, permanent form of the religion, in contrast to local, inherently dynamic traditions. But among those traditions identified in the
modern period as a "World Religion," every envisioning of a Great Tradition—
such as Theravāda Buddhism, Christianity, or Hinduism—[40] occurs within local contexts subject to culture, history, and relations of power. Contrasts,
therefore, between so-called transcendent Great Traditions and local religions
are acts of authorization—they identify that which is essential to the religion
and that which is subject to reinterpretation (religious change) or misinterpretation (heresy).

One result of this authorization process in the modern period has been
the separation of mundane concerns from that which is deemed to be authentic and ultimate. Obeyesekere, for instance, argued that "a monk rarely or never
participates in the rituals of the lower cults, with their purely material rewards";
whereas the shaman addresses the "gross material aspirations of the masses."
The Theravāda portion of Sinhalese Buddhism emphasizes the other-worldly
"salvation idiom," while "the rest of the system has to do with the quest for
material objectives and this-worldly goals."[41] In a similar vein, Melford Spiro
distinguishes between "normative" Buddhism, which focuses on the pursuit of
nibbāna (soteriological Buddhism), and "non-normative" forms: kammatic
Buddhism, which is focused on the improvement of one's next lives through
kamma, and apotropaic Buddhism, the religion of "man's worldly welfare" are
examples.[42] Obeyesekere's description of the Great Tradition of Theravāda and
Spiro's description of normative soteriological Buddhism sound surprisingly
similar to the descriptions of Buddhism presented by Buddhist modernists and
European Orientalists who presented orthodox Theravāda as an inherently rational and ethical religion of personal liberation.

To their credit, both Obeyesekere and Spiro directed a shift in Buddhist
studies towards the analysis of "Buddhism on the ground," which helped to lay
a foundation for the anthropological study of Buddhism. They recognized aspects of Buddhist religiosity, such as a focus on magic, miracles, and special
powers, which European Orientalists had either ignored or devalued. However, their distinction between two radically different kinds of Buddhism (great
versus little and normative versus non-normative) rests on two fundamental
errors. First, it generates a sharp divide between monastic and lay religiosity
when, in fact, the distinction between the monastic and the layperson is more
a difference of degree than of kind. On the one hand, monks and laypersons
both practice renunciation, albeit to different degrees: monks renounce their
obligations as householders; where as laypersons practice renunciation through
generous acts of giving to the saṅgha. On the other hand, not all Buddhist monks
live lives of deprivation. In fact, Buddhist monks historically have possessed
material wealth, acting as both patrons of the tradition and recipients of support. Commonly held distinctions between ascetic monks and a merit-hungry

laity, therefore, simply do not reflect the myriad of ways in which Buddhist life and practice exist within given communities.

The second problem with Obeyesekere's and Spiro's categories is their failure to recognize the polemical nature of religious categorization. The classification of a particular doctrine or practice as normative or non-normative is not simply the domain of the unbiased, objective scholar. The process of classification is fundamental to internal debates within religious communities over religious identity and authority.[43] In Buddhist societies, when critiques of monastic wealth or lay religiosity emerged within a given community, they were typically aimed at a specific group and hence reflected local power struggles.[44] The condemnations of lax, lazy, and decadent monks, therefore, were not disinterested historical assessments of the "state of the religion"; they functioned to support the authority of specific groups of monks and laypersons over others.

Today the politics of classification continues as Buddhists around the globe seek to define Buddhism within dramatically new social, political, and economic contexts. For some Buddhists in Asia and most Buddhists in the West, a new Orientalism has emerged over the past few decades. Whereas nineteenth-century European scholars viewed Buddhism as an atheistic, individualistic, and rational religion that offered a sharp contrast to Christian faith and piety, today neo-Orientalists represent Buddhism's focus on simplicity and moderation as the antithesis of Western materialism, capitalism, and consumption.[45] Buddhism, with its critique of greed, hatred, and delusion, its discourses and practices of renunciation, and its emphasis on generous giving, appears to undercut the values, processes and effects of global capitalism. This view of Buddhism dominates Western practice, and clearly informs the reformist platforms of many Buddhists throughout Asia. Because of the assumption that Buddhism is an antidote to the ills of global capitalism, neo-Orientalists tend to attack the association between wealth and piety in Buddhism with as much passion as early Orientalists lamented the corruption of rational Buddhism by magic and superstition.

Debates over the role of wealth in Buddhism, once again, are not restricted to academic circles nor are they merely the concern of Euro-American Orientalists. They are central to many discussions about Buddhist identity and practice within Buddhist communities. The Dhammakāya controversy of the late 1990s, as it emerged within the context of the Asian economic crisis, prompted many Thai Buddhists to ask, What is the role of golden stūpas, Buddha images, amulets, miracles, and merit-making within Buddhism? Critics of the Temple viewed its marketing of amulets and miracles as signs of the corruption of the Buddhist tradition by the forces of global capitalism; Temple elites and practitioners situated Dhammakāya amulets and miracles within the tradition of Theravāda Buddhism. These differing visions of Buddhism provide us with an opportunity to analyze debates over Buddhist religiosity at a new moment in Thai history, as Thais grapple with the implications of living within a global consumer culture.

Theoretical and Methodological Considerations

A primary goal of this book is to demonstrate how Buddhist interpretations of the relationship between piety and wealth are historically contingent and embedded within authorizing discourses and within relations of power. Following the suggestion of Charles Hallisey to approach Buddhist ethics historically rather than searching for a single moral theory,[46] I do not seek to identify the place of wealth in Theravāda Buddhism. This task would presuppose that the tradition has a single orientation towards wealth. Rather, I examine the relationship between wealth and piety historically: through Buddhist texts and narratives, through expressions of piety, and within the broader field of discourses about wealth and society at a specific place and time (postmodern Thailand). This approach enables us to ask, When and under what circumstances is the relationship between Buddhist piety and wealth described in favorable terms and when is it viewed critically in terms of decadence and corruption? This question moves us away from our own assumptions about the relationship between wealth and piety, and towards the historical analysis of how specific Buddhists envisioned their tradition. In this way, my approach to the topic of wealth and piety resembles Tessa Bartholemeusz' approach to the just war tradition in Sri Lanka.[47] In her book, *In Defense of Dharma: Just-War Ideology in Buddhist Sri Lanka*, Bartholemeusz effectively contextualizes both just-war and pacifistic ideologies within the tradition. She argues that many scholars of Sri Lanka have privileged the canonical narrative of pacificism in their constructions of authentic Theravāda Buddhism, "thus prompting us to accept that imagined and ultra-pacific Buddhism as the real one."[48] Rather than asking the question of why Buddhists today ignore their pacific roots, Bartholemeusz focuses on the historical construction of varying forms of authentic Buddhism—some of which justify violence, others that do not. As Talal Asad argues, anthropologists may note the conformity between the past and the present but they must also examine the "practitioners' conceptions of what is apt performance, and of how the past is related to present practices, that will be crucial for tradition, not the apparent repetition of an old form."[49]

The primary case study of this book will be the Dhammakāya Temple, which has effectively linked traditional Buddhist discourses on wealth and piety to contemporary practice and identity. On the one hand, I will argue that the Dhammakāya Temple has successfully incorporated a modern ethic of prosperity within its platform for personal and social transformation, while simultaneously emphasizing the traditional practices of meditation and merit-making (albeit in new ways). On the other hand, I will examine how the Temple's collective wealth and the wealth of its lay followers have led critics to question their motivations, the integrity of their piety, and the legitimacy of their practice. My analysis of the Dhammakāya Temple and other cases of wealth and Buddhist piety will not seek to either prove or disprove the authenticity of pro-wealth forms of religiosity. The latter claim is especially important, as there is a tendency for commentators to assume that any conflation of wealth and piety is necessarily disingenuous.

An instance of this is Lise McKean's book *Divine Enterprise: Gurus and the Hindu Nationalist Movement*, in which she argues that there is an asymmetrical exchange between renunciant gurus and their followers.[50] This exchange system, according to McKean, is supported by moral arguments that represent the gurus as disinterested and benevolent, and establishes relations that "yield handsome profits for gurus."[51]

> Exchanges between devotees and gurus, like those between patrons and Brahman ritualists, bear the promise of social use value....Those who enter into these circuits of commodity exchange and consumption seek to profit by them. The ideology of spirituality and renunciation makes it possible for gurus and their religious organizations to not only mask the drive for profits that underlies exchanges with followers but also renew the promise of value which they offer to followers.[52]

McKean's analysis of guru wealth is informed by a Marxist perspective, from which she seeks to highlight the domination and exploitation inherent within these movements, as well as their failure to address so-called real problems. In her analysis of Gayatri Parivar, a new religious movement in Hardwar, she argues that the movement portrays wealth as a product of hard work and a partnership with God, but that it presents no challenge to the problems of the unequal distribution of wealth or mass poverty.

As true as this may be, we must ask the question, Does Gayatri Parivar need to address these problems in order to be a legitimate religious organization? McKean would answer in the affirmative, as would many other critics of global capitalism. Such assessments, however, are steeped within specific ideological stances or religious beliefs about wealth and piety. The analysis of capitalism's effect on Buddhism, for instance, is usually posed in terms of the negative impact of capitalism on Buddhism—how Buddhist practices and objects become the means by which one accumulates and secures material capital rather than tools that lead to the cessation of greed, hatred, and delusion. One example of this approach is that of Phra Phaisan Wisalo, a "socially-engaged" Thai monk, who writes:

The distinction between religious faith and consumerism is becoming increasingly vague these days. Although religious worship
may involve physical objects such as Buddha images, living within
a moral discipline to keep oneself grounded in Dhamma is required in every religion. Nowadays, religious faith has been altered
to the degree that it means purchasing auspicious objects to worship. One's faith (saddha) is no longer measured by how one applies it, how one lives their life, but by how many holy or sacred
articles one possesses.[53]

This is a fascinating analysis of recent changes in Thai Buddhism, but we need
to recognize that it is a religious reaction to these changes. Phra Phaisan
Wisalo is writing as a Buddhist monk, as a representative voice of Buddhist
orthodoxy. The value of material objects within a given religious tradition is a
subject of great debate within religious discourses, and it is a topic worthy of
exploration. However, the judgments themselves—such as this passage by Phra
Phaisan Wisalo—are the subject of my inquiry, not the basis for it.

As a result, I do not begin this book with an assessment that the
Dhammakāya Temple has, in fact, commercialized Buddhism nor do I seek to
prove that this is so, for this approach requires a judgment of what constitutes
authentic Buddhist religiosity. The identification of orthodoxy and orthopraxy
is an act of power, as is its use in the critique of the teachings and practices of
others.[54] Talal Asad highlights the implications of this power in his "The Idea
of an Anthropology of Islam."[55] He states that "[o]rthodoxy is crucial to all
Islamic traditions," but anthropologists often overlook a vital component of it,
that "orthodoxy is not a mere body of opinion but a distinctive relationship—a
relationship of power. Wherever Muslims have the power to regulate, uphold,
require, or adjust *correct* practices, and to condemn, exclude, undermine, or replace *incorrect* ones, there is a domain of orthodoxy."[56] One who condemns the
Dhammakāya Temple's marketing techniques as "commercialized," therefore,
enters into the domain of the *authorization* of Buddhist orthodoxy.[57] This is not
my intent. Rather, I am concerned with the dynamics of religious traditions—
how particular religious discourses and practices are situated in reference to
real or perceived pasts in order to authenticate (or reject) their place within the
tradition. Religious persons are, in the words of Thomas Tweed, constantly engaged in processes of "crossing and dwelling" within their traditions.[58] Buddhism, as with all religions, is not a static entity; it is continually created
through space and time. Thai Buddhists today "make religious homes" or construct religious identities through interactions with a variety of textual, ritual,
artistic, and institutional traditions, personal and collective memories, and new
religious experiences. Whose voices are heard and by whom are historical questions of the utmost importance, and they require an examination of the fields

of discourses—participants, consumers, strategies, and mechanisms—in the context of their construction and dissemination.[59]

The chapters in this book provide this kind of examination. Chapter 1 sets the stage for an analysis of Dhammakāya discourses on wealth and piety by demonstrating the dynamic character of Buddhist renunciation itself, as it is constructed within specific historical and cultural contexts. Once we envision Buddhist renunciation as a construct, we can then address how varying discourses on renunciation affect attitudes towards wealth in the Buddhist tradition—how monastic wealth, for instance, can serve both as an index of prosperity and effective righteous rule and as a sign of decadence and the need for monastic reform. Chapter 2 begins my analysis of the specific case of the Dhammakāya Temple, which exemplifies the fusion of social and personal prosperity and modern piety. This chapter examines the history and success of the Temple within the context of modern urban Buddhism, and it offers several explanations for the Temple's phenomenal growth and popularity, including its lineage of charismatic leaders (Luang Pho Sot, Khun Yay Ubasika Chan, and Phra Dhammachayo) and its unique dhammakāya meditation technique. Chapter 3 examines the ways in which the Dhammakāya Temple utilizes the narratives and practices of generous giving and merit-making in its fund-raising for the Mahathammakai Chedi. One strategy is the linkage of contemporary donors to the tradition of exemplary donors; they accomplish this by inscribing the names of individual donors on the base of the Phra Dhammakāya images, by distributing Phra Mahasiriratthat amulets to these donors, and by telling the stories of donors in amulet magazines and at Temple services. Chapter 4 presents the late 1990s controversy over Dhammakāya teachings and practices as an example of a specific debate over the relationship between wealth and piety. The controversy is set within the historical context of the Asian economic crisis of the late 1990s, which spurred a heightened re-evaluation of social and cultural institutions and values. Chapter 5 relates the Dhammakāya controversy to the broader field of debate over the commercialization of Buddhism, the marketing of Buddhism as a product for consumption, and the effects of consumerism on contemporary Thai society. The principal voices within this discussion are the late Bhikkhu Buddhadāsa, the well-known promoter of dhammic socialism; Phra Payutto, the most prominent scholar-monk in Thailand today; Sulak Sivaraksa, the outspoken and controversial social critic; Samana Phothirak, who was formerly known as Phra Phothirak, the founder of the back-to-basics Santi Asok movement; Dr. Suwanna Satha-Anand, Professor of Philosophy at Chulalongkorn University; and Phra Phaisan Wisalo, abbot of Wat Pha Sukato. Finally, the Conclusion addresses how the Dhammakāya Temple controversy served as rallying cry for religious reform in postmodern Thailand.

Chapter 1

Buddhism, Renunciation, and Prosperity

Ancient Buddhism ... is a specifically unpolitical and anti-political status religion, more precisely, a religious "technology" of wandering and of intellectually-schooled mendicant monks. Like all Indian philosophy and theology it is a "salvation religion,".... Its salvation is a solely personal act of the single individual....

—Max Weber, *The Religion of India: The Sociology of Hinduism and Buddhism*

The image of the solitary Buddhist monk, with his eyes cast downward and his body in perfect meditative repose, squares well with the conception of Buddhism as a religion of renunciation. The Buddhist tradition, in fact, embraces this image in a number of ways. In Theravāda societies the Buddha's central act of renunciation is reenacted each time that a young man undertakes ordination, going forth (*pabbajjā*, Pāli) from home to homelessness, holding a clip of his hair in his hand as a senior monk shaves his head. Perhaps at no other time is the dramatic shift from lay life to monastic life more pronounced than in this initial act of ordination, for the acts of shaving the head and of donning monastic robes are the most clearly visual marks of the separation from ordinary life. In addition, Buddhists, at varying times in history, have viewed the forest monk—who adopts a stricter discipline in his path to perfection—as an exemplar of Buddhist practice and the purest source of merit for the laity.

There is no doubt that these images of renunciation also occupy a principal place in the minds of Western scholars. The classification of Buddhism as a religion of renunciation emerged in countless descriptions of Buddhism in the West, most notably in the work of Max Weber (1864–1920). In the quote that opens this chapter, he described early Buddhism as a religion of "wandering and intellectually-schooled mendicant monks," whose individual quests for religious liberation are essentially personal and distinct from the "world of rational action." This characterization of Buddhism as essentially a religion populated with ascetic philosopher-monks holds a preeminent place in Orientalist constructions of Buddhism.[1]

As early as the 1960s, however, scholars of Buddhist societies began to question the portrayal of Buddhism as essentially asocial, individualistic, and otherworldly.[2] This questioning was spearheaded by the anthropological examination of Buddhism within lived societies. From this perspective, some scholars criticized the Orientalist reliance on canonical texts, which tend to present an essentialized image of Buddhist practice. Instead, these scholars suggested that we use the full range of material available for analysis, including vernacular texts and archeological and epigraphic evidence.[3] Other critics highlighted how Weberian constructions of Buddhism ignored those aspects of the tradition that speak directly to social, political, and economic issues.[4] This critique is not only found in academic circles. It is also a common critique made by socially-engaged Buddhists, such as Bhikkhu Buddhadasa, A. T. Ariyaratne, and the fourteenth Dalai Lama, who argue that the tradition emphasizes dhamma-inspired action within society.[5] Still other critics have noted that the portrait of Buddhism as asocial, individualistic, and otherworldly has failed to represent the living traditions of Buddhism around the world with their veneration of Buddha relics and amulets and their stories of miracles and special powers.[6]

All of these critiques highlight the tendency in Western scholarship to ignore the world-engaging aspects of Buddhism in descriptions of authentic Buddhist doctrine and practice. One reason for this tendency may be our general predisposition towards viewing religion as essentially otherworldly and locating the essence of religion in canonical texts rather than in vernacular texts, material culture, and embodied practice. Gregory Schopen argues that this tendency in studies of Indian Buddhism reflects Protestant presuppositions within Buddhist studies, suppositions that have influenced our methodology and analysis of Indian Buddhism.[7] In fact, Schopen posits that "our picture of Indian Buddhism may reflect more of our own religious history and values than the history and values of Indian Buddhism."[8] Such critiques are not limited to Indian Buddhism. Ian Reader and George Tanabe argue that studies of Japanese Buddhism have similarly privileged canonical constructions of Buddhism, thereby devaluing and, in some cases, ignoring those practices that reflect a world-affirming or world-engaging ethos.[9] There is no doubt that this tendency to ignore the world-engaging aspects of the Buddhist tradition has had a profound and pervasive influence on Buddhist studies.

Having said this, our portrait of Buddhism would be equally incomplete if we failed to recognize those strains of the tradition that do, in fact, resonate with the portrait of early Buddhism as individualistic, asocial, and fundamentally otherworldly. The narrative and social histories of Theravāda Buddhism possess innumerable examples of a world-renouncing ethos within the tradition, from the celebration of the Buddha's renunciation on each Vīsakha Pūjā day[10] to the impassioned patronage of forest monks in South and Southeast Asia. Indeed, in a recent analysis of early Buddhism, Greg Bailey and Ian Mabbett insist that the original message of early Buddhism, as articulated in the *Sutta Nipāta*, focused on asceticism and otherworldliness.

> It can be called 'ascetic' because of its rejection of the world, but of course the Buddha, unlike some of his contemporaries, rejected deliberate self-mortification, or extreme asceticism; his is a middle way, espousing calm detachment. In this view monks wander constantly, rejecting all social ties. Their object is to obtain a transcendent vision of the way things really are, abandoning all attachments in every sphere. In the absence of attachment and ignorance, one will cease generating karma, and thereby become enlightened and escape the unending frustration and distress inseparable from worldly existence.[11]

While Bailey and Mabbett recognize the place of ascetic Buddhism in the *Sutta Nipāta*, they nevertheless acknowledge that ascetic Buddhism existed alongside social versions of the tradition, many of which emphasized public practice and ritual, as well as devotionalism and magical powers. One of the great strengths of their portrait of early Buddhism is that they demonstrate the presence and competition among different forms of Buddhist religiosity during this early period.

Given the diversity of religiosity that has always existed within Buddhist communities, it should not surprise us that competing groups have promoted varying ideas regarding engagement with the world (so-called this-worldly orientations) and regarding rejection of world engagement (so-called otherworldly orientations).[12] When we examine specific Buddhist communities historically, we see how multiple forms of Buddhism have competed with each other, creating a tension between those elements of the tradition that emphasized and glorified (and patronized) forms of otherworldly asceticism and those that favored domesticated monasticism and its relations to the wider society.[13] In fact, the Pāli canon itself reflects a particular reading of the tradition during a moment of increased competition between rival *nikāyas* in Sri Lanka. The *Mahāvihāra nikāya* legitimated its authority and vision of Buddhist orthodoxy and orthopraxy through the creation of the Pāli canon. In so doing it promoted its "conservative and/or reformist, text-oriented self-definition" against other lineages who privileged different texts and indices of spiritual authority.[14] In addition to recognizing the plurality of Buddhist voices, it is also important to note that specific renunciant groups rarely reflect an exclusively "this-worldly" or "other-worldly" orientation. Buddhist monks and nuns through the centuries have constructed their lives as Buddhist renunciants within a wide variety of social and cultural contexts. What constitutes a Buddhist life of renunciation, therefore, is highly dependent upon context.

This chapter seeks to highlight the dynamic character of Buddhist renunciation by examining instances of its practical construction—how renunciation itself is constituted vis-à-vis specific strategies and historical circumstances. It would be a mistake to assume that renunciation has meant the same thing to all Buddhists at all times. Most Buddhists throughout history would agree in principle that renunciation is a valuable religious act, but there have been and continue to be disagreements within Buddhist societies over the value of specific acts of renunciation. In Thailand, one of the principal differences between the two Theravāda *nikai*, the *Mahanikai* and *Thammayutnikai*, is that the latter insists upon eating only one meal a day, whereas the former permits two. Appropriate levels of renunciation are also negotiated within specific historical contexts as new situations arise outside of the parameters of the Buddhist monastic code. Many Thai monks will honor the precept against handling gold and silver by not handling paper money, but at the same time, they possess personal bank accounts and use checks and credit cards. As a result, the image of the proper Buddhist renunciant is similarly subject to interpretation. In some contexts an emaciated monk wearing a tattered robe may symbolize heightened piety, whereas in others he may be perceived as a beggar, desperate for lay generosity. It is within these varying constructions of renunciation that we may begin to see different orientations towards wealth in the Buddhist tradition.

Buddhist Discourses of Renunciation

The Pāli word that is typically translated as renunciation is *abhinikkhamana*, which connotes a departure, a moving away—hence the popularity of the phrase "moving from home to homelessness" to signify Buddhist ordination. The Buddha's own journey from the princely life of luxury to the life of a wandering mendicant is known as the *mahābhinikkhamana* (The Great Renunciation), an event central to the Buddha's hagiography. The *Mahāsaccaka-sutta* provides one version of this event:

> Before my Awakening, when I was still an unawakened Bodhisatta, the thought occurred to me: 'The household life is crowded, a dusty road. Life gone forth is the open air. It isn't easy, living in a home, to lead the holy life that is totally perfect, totally pure, a polished shell. What if I, having shaved off my hair & beard and putting on the ochre robe, were to go forth from the home life into homelessness?'

So at a later time, when I was still young, black-haired, endowed
with the blessings of youth in the first stage of life, having shaved
off my hair & beard—though though my parents wished otherwise and were grieving with tears on their faces—I put on the
ochre robe and went forth from the home life into homelessness.[15]

Buddhist renunciation, as described in the Pāli canon, places an emphasis on
the shift from a home-centered life, which includes marriage, children, and
productive labor, to a homeless life divorced from familial responsibilities and
financial obligations. In this vein, early Buddhist renunciation mirrored the
practices of other *samanas* (*śramana*, Sanskrit, literally one who strives) in
Northeast India in the sixth and fifth centuries BCE, who rejected not only
the householder's life but also his primary mode of religiosity—the fire sacri-
fice that defined a householder's ritual life.

In moving outside of the ritual sphere of the home, Buddhist renouncers
and other samanas redefined religious practice. They focused on personal discipline through the perfection of technologies of asceticism and meditation. For
these groups, renunciation was not the summum bonum of religious practice
but rather the vehicle for the acquisition of religious truth and the catalyst for
a transformative ontological experience. The path of early Pāli Buddhism, commonly referred to as the middle path (*majjhimā paṭipadā*), emphasizes the perfection of ethics (*sīla*), concentration (*samādhi*), and wisdom (*paññā*) over ritual
orthopraxy. In this version of Buddhist practice, renunciation is viewed not as a
necessary prerequisite to religious perfection but rather as a mode of practice
that is most conducive to religious perfection. It is possible in theory for a layperson to experience Buddhist perfection, but it is deemed to be highly un-
likely: Lay life is far too encumbered by familial and social responsibilities to
facilitate the perfection of ethics, concentration, and wisdom.

The description of renunciation as a form of liberation from lay life is, in
fact, a dominant theme in Pāli literature. One example is the story of the Venerable Bhaddiya Kaligodha who continually exclaimed, "What bliss, What
bliss!" whenever he left society for a secluded tree or empty dwelling.[16] When
the Buddha questioned the monk about his unusual behavior, Bhaddhiya stated
that his life as a king required him to guard his kingdom constantly. This was a
state of existence that created great fear and agitation within him. His life as a
monk, on the other hand, allowed him to dwell in peace, without the mental
disturbance of trying to secure his belongings. We can also locate the theme of
liberation in some of the verses in the *Therīgāthā*, which describes the experiences of nuns in the early community. The verse of Sumangala's mother, for
instance, contrasts the bliss of renunciation with the life of a dutiful housewife,
who is tied to her pestle, pot, and husband.[17] The stories of Bhaddhiya Kaligodha

and Sumangala's mother describe renunciation as an act of liberation from lives that promote the mental states of fear, greed, passion, and aversion. These states are undesirable not simply because they make our lives unpleasant, but also because they bind us to multiple rebirths, and therefore are linked to the generation of suffering.

Scholars agree that renunciation in general was viewed as a positive and effective practice for the religious path in early Indian Buddhism. Indeed, when we look at the expanse of Buddhism's history over the past 2,500 years, we can say with some certainty that renunciation was and has remained a central feature in expressions of Buddhist piety, albeit not the primary one, since most Buddhists remain within lay life. When, however, we question specific acts of renunciation vis-à-vis the tradition, in so far as what does and does not constitute an authentic act of renunciation, we need to do more than simply state that renunciation is a central Buddhist practice. We must investigate the contexts in which these acts of renunciation take place in order to understand better how renunciation functions within specific Buddhist communities.

In the early Buddhist community in India, Buddhist acts of renunciation need to be placed alongside the religious practices of other renouncers and brahmins with whom the Buddhist monks and nuns were competing for patronage. Comparisons and contrasts of varying types of religiosity are replete in the Pāli canon, including myriad references to other forms of asceticism and religious practice. Discourses on renunciation in the Pāli canon are highly context sensitive in that they seek to prove the superiority of the Buddha's practice above all others. In the canon there are descriptions of religious persons who renounced too much (the excessive asceticism of Jain renouncers was a common theme in early Pāli texts) and those who renounced too little (brahmins were depicted as greedy, wealthy, and corrupt). The followers of Gotama Buddha, in contrast, renounced just enough, according to Buddhist texts, in order to progress along on the path to *nirvāṇa* without becoming overly attached to specific practices.

But what is "just enough renunciation"? To answer this question, many scholars have turned to the *Pāli-vinaya*. It is within the *Sutta-vibhaṅga* of the *Vinaya* that we find the *pāṭimokkha*, which lists the 227 rules of the *bhikkhu* order (311 for *bhikkhunīs*). But rules, however detailed, are always subject to interpretation. Let us take, for instance, the injunction in the *Vinaya* against the handling of gold and silver by Buddhist renunciants.[18] Should one interpret this rule to simply mean that a Buddhist renunciant should not touch currency? Does it mean that renunciants should not be actively engaged in trade? Or does it mean that members of the saṅgha should embody a virtue of simplicity by lacking personal possessions? Scholars who rely exclusively on the *Pāli-vinaya* as the exclusive source for answers to these questions, will inevitably present a picture of Buddhist monasticism as one that embodies a spirit of poverty and simplicity. In a description of the general principles of the *Vinaya*, Richard Gombrich, for instance, writes that "[t]he key to this life is that victory over craving which results in 'being content with little.' This is the attitude which must be cultivated, the attitude which lies at the heart of the simple life. In practice, the simple life is based on owning the minimum of property . . . and also on that drastic simplification which results from cutting the normal social ties to family and community."[19] The answers to these questions become less straightforward, however, if we examine them historically. Gunawardana's impressive analysis of the political economy of the saṅgha in medieval Sri Lanka unequivocally demonstrates that some Buddhist renunciants did not interpret the precept against handling gold and silver as a ban against owning land and accumulating enormous wealth as landlords.[20]

Gregory Schopen's analysis of the *Mūlasarvāstivādin-vinaya* also raises a number of questions regarding our interpretation of renunciation in Indian Buddhism.[21] In this *Vinaya*, which was utilized in northern India during the Kuṣān period (fifth to sixth centuries CE), Buddhist monasticism looks very different from its portrait in the Pāli canon. It is commonly assumed that monastic ordination requires the renunciation of all personal property. Schopen notes, however, that the *Mūlasarvāstivādin-vinaya* assumes that monks had the resources to pay debts and taxes and compensate others for the destruction of property. Moreover, this *Vinaya* refers to seals that distinguish personal (*paudgalika*) property from communal (*sāṃgkika*) property, as well as detailed descriptions regarding the proper management of a monk's property following his death. From this analysis, Schopen concludes:

> A great deal of the *Mūlasarvāstivādin-vinaya* takes for granted that the monks it was meant to govern had and were expected—even required to have personal property and private wealth. If Buddhist monks were ever required to renounce personal property—and there are good reasons for doubting this—they certainly were not by the time the *Mūlasarvāstivādin-vinaya* was redacted. Some Mūlasarvāstivāda monk, those who were "well known and of great merit," were even expected to be quite wealthy. Rather than suggest that such wealth should be renounced or avoided, this *Vinaya* redacted detailed rules to transmit that wealth to other monks and to shelter it from the state.[22]

Given this evidence, we should begin to rethink Buddhist monasticism in India and our general assumptions regarding Buddhist renunciation.

Such descriptions of monastic life are nothing new for scholars of Chinese Buddhism. Monks in China have amassed personal wealth, cultivated crops on monastic land, and engaged in business activities for centuries. Yet, scholars have tended to attribute these worldly practices to a general Chinese dislike of religious renunciation and a result of the pervasive influence of Confucian ideals on Buddhist practice, rather than to see them as intrinsically "Buddhist." While there is undoubtedly some truth in this assessment, we should not attribute all world-engaging aspects of Buddhist monasticism to outside forces. After all, Schopen's analysis of Buddhist monasticism in northern India presents similar images of world-engaging monks. At the same time, we must recognize that these world-engaging monks did not exist without controversy. As in the Pāli canon, we find examples in Chinese history of contested visions of Buddhist renunciation. John Kieschnick provides a description of some of the criticisms leveled against world-engaged monks in medieval China:

> The contrast between the austere ideal of the monk and the material success of Buddhist monasteries was not lost on Buddhism's critics. A fifth-century monk-turned-critic questioned his former brethren, asking, "Why is it that their ideals are [so] noble and far-reaching and their activities still are [so] base and common? . . . [Monks] become merchants and engage in barter, wrangling with the masses for profit." One sixth-century critic complained of the wealth and energy "squandered" to erect "elaborate temples." For "the teaching bequeathed by the Buddha called on his followers not to cultivate the fields and not to store up wealth or grain, but to beg for their food or clothing, and to practice the dhutangas. This is no longer true." The criticism of what seemed rank hypocrisy continued into later periods. In the early seventh century, Emperor Gaozu, for instance, noted the contrast between the teachings of Buddhism that "give priority to purity, distancing oneself from filth, and cutting off greed and desire" and the "inexhaustible greed" of monks intent on "amassing ever-greater quantities of goods." Or consider a famous eighth-century memorial by Xing Tipi submitted in protest to imperial support for monastic construction that, again, contrasted the "purity" and "self-denial" of Buddhist teachings with the "vast halls, lengthy corridors" and "elaborate ornamentation" of Buddhist monasteries.[23]

As we shall see, these criticisms are remarkably similar to those leveled against the Dhammakāya Temple in contemporary Thailand. Debates over Buddhist wealth and simplicity thrive today in Thailand as dramatically different conceptions of Buddhist life collide.

In the academic study of religion, our task is not to judge whose level of renunciation is more Buddhist, but rather to acknowledge that renunciation, as a category of religious practice, is subject to debate, discussion, and reflection. The contestable character of Buddhist renunciation as an ideal and as an empirical reality is aptly highlighted in "Matsii," a short story by the Thai author Sri Dao Ruang.[24] The story concerns a young Thai woman who abandons her children alongside a road after her husband leaves her. A police officer chastises her for being an unfit mother. Matsii responds by asking why no one questions these actions when they are committed by men. When the police officer asks her who has committed such an act without censure, the young woman responds: "Phra Wetsandon did it!"

The story of Phra Wetsandon (Prince Vessantara), the penultimate birth story (*jātaka*) of the Buddha, is well-known throughout South and Southeast Asia. It relates how the bodhisatta as Prince Vessantara perfects the virtue of generous giving (*dāna*, a lay form of renunciation) through relinquishing his kingdom, his wife, and even his two children to a series of strangers who request these gifts. The story of Prince Vessantara is known as the *Mahāchāt* (the great life) in Thailand and is recited annually by monks throughout the country. Charles Keyes correctly notes that there "is probably no Buddhist in Thailand beyond the age of ten or so who could not give at least a synopsis of the story, and many people especially in villages, can quote passages in the same way English speakers can quote parts of the Bible, or selections from Shakespeare."[25] A similar familiarity with this narrative exists in other Theravāda Buddhist cultures including Burma and Sri Lanka. Its popularity may be due, in part, to the belief that hearing an entire recitation of the *Mahāchāt* will ensure a beneficial future birth—perhaps even rebirth during the time of Metteya, the next Buddha.

Sri Dao Ruang's reference to this story, however, highlights the ethical ambiguities present within it.[26] While this text is usually presented as a prescriptive tale of generous giving, Sri Dao Ruang uses it to draw a contrast between Thai views of male and female acts of renunciation. In this story we enter a world where women seldom renounce lay life and, when they do, they fall under suspicion and ridicule. Female renouncers in Thailand (*mae chi*) are rarely given the respect of a religious person and are often viewed as "abandoned" or "broken-hearted" women rather than religious virtuosos.[27] Sri Dao Ruang succeeds in linking this gendered subtext to the story of Prince Vessantara. Matsii's act of renunciation raises questions about the social implications of renunciation (for both men and women) and highlights the culturally and historically contingent character of Buddhist ideas about renunciation as a religious practice.

Buddhist renunciation, therefore, must be viewed historically. In the Pāli canon, Buddhist forms of renunciation are contrasted with the practices of other competing groups in order to demonstrate the superiority of the Buddhist path; here, Buddhist renunciation entails the rejection of both Brahmanical wealth and Jain asceticism. Descriptions of monastic practice in second-century India, in the fifth and eighth centuries in China, and in medieval Sri Lanka demonstrate that Buddhist renunciation did not entail the renunciation of *all* property, a fact of monastic life that led in some instances to the amassing of great wealth. At the same time, we have voices within the tradition that have used Buddhist teachings and narratives as a means for critiquing the accumulation of property within Buddhist monastic life. These critiques tended to emphasize the correlation between renunciation and simplicity. Finally, we must recognize that Buddhist renunciation, in all its manifestations, is not always interpreted as a pious act within the tradition. As the story "Matsii" highlights, the prejudices against eight- and ten-precept nuns in South and Southeast Asia attest to the socially contingent character of Buddhist renunciation.

Wealth and Piety in Buddhist Texts

Debates about the character of Buddhist renunciation are nowhere more pronounced than in discussions regarding the relationship between wealth and Buddhist piety, as we saw in the section on monastic property. From the idealized portrait of an itinerant monk, divorced from the world and engaged only in deep states of meditation, it is easy to conclude that Buddhism eschews materialism and wealth—after all, the Buddha himself renounced his princely fortune in his pursuit of an end to *dukkha*. As noted in the Introduction, the portrayal of Buddhism as an essentially otherworldly philosophy has led many either to ignore the place of wealth within the tradition or to undercut its presence by describing it as an unintended consequence of a devotionally driven laity. In his seminal essay on ethics and wealth in Theravāda Buddhism, however, Frank E. Reynolds effectively counters this assumption by noting that, "Theravāda interpretations of dhamma have, from the very beginning, incorporated a more or less positive valorization of wealth, including material resources, monetary resources, goods, and services."[28] Two possible reasons for the mischaracterization of Buddhist views on wealth in scholarship are the continued impact of "Protestant presuppositions" in the study of Buddhism and a selective reading of the canon based upon these presuppositions.[29]

This section, therefore, provides an overview of the many discourses on wealth in the Theravāda tradition from a variety of sources—canonical suttas as well as jātaka stories, local historical tales, and other types of vernacular literature. This is not an extensive review of all of the discourses on wealth, but rather a sampling of discourses on two recurring themes: the possession of wealth and the use of wealth. Some of the examples are philosophical and didactic in orientation, whereas others are popular tales of wealth, piety, and beneficial rewards. These stories about the possession and use of wealth do not simply relay past ideas about the relationship between wealth and piety; they also continue to serve an important function within the tradition. As Charles Hallisey and Anne Hansen argue, Buddhist narratives can have a transformative impact on the moral lives of Buddhists.[30] Stories about the possession and use of wealth are particularly important to Buddhist communities since they directly relate to everyday religiosity. In subsequent chapters, we shall see how Dhammakāya practitioners (Chapter 3) and Dhammakāya critics (Chapter 5) employ different stories of wealth in their respective views of Buddhist piety.

Discourses on the accumulation of wealth—through inheritance or one's activities in this lifetime—is one of the recurring themes in Buddhist discourses on wealth. With regards to inheritance, Buddhists typically consider a wealthy birth as an unequivocal sign of merit (bun, Thai; puñña, Pāli). Theravāda cosmology posits several realms of existence; within each, there are gradations of possible rebirths that fall along a spectrum from better to worse. Not all humans are equal, nor are gods, spirits, animals, or hell beings. A rebirth as a bat that may have occasion to hear the dhamma from a monk who is dwelling in its cave is by far a more favorable animal birth than that of a poor dung-beetle whose opportunities are severely limited due to its mode of dwelling. In the same vein, a human birth into a prosperous, healthy, and amiable family is considered to be infinitely more meritorious than a birth into a poor, sickly, and quarrelsome one. The correlation of familial wealth with past merit is evident in the biography of Gotama Buddha, who was born as a prince of great wealth in both his last and penultimate births. The wealth of the Buddha functions in his biography not only as an object to be renounced (as is often emphasized by Buddhists and scholars alike), but also as a sign of the great merit that he had accumulated over innumerable lifetimes as he gradually moved toward spiritual perfection. It is therefore not surprising that the Mahāpadāna-sutta (Dīgha Nikāya 14) describes the births of former Buddhas as sons of either kings or brahmins. These are positions of unquestionable merit.[31]

The equation of wealth with merit is also seen in the Dhammapada Nissaya, a text from Northern Thailand that was commonly used as an educational primer for monks.[32] The text describes the main character, Meṇḍaka, as a seṭṭhi (wealthy person) who has abundant merit and wealth, which exceeds the five other seṭṭhis.[33] As Justin McDaniel argues in his analysis of this text, the continual restatement of Meṇḍaka's status as a wealthy person would make it impossible for one to forget that Meṇḍaka was wealthy. McDaniel argues that this reveals a strategy for memorizing important words and the main characters in the text. For our purposes, the repetition may also reflect one reason why monks memorized the text in the first place, that is, to emphasize the association between merit and wealth, which was and continues to be a popular topic for Theravāda audiences.

If being born into a wealthy family is an unequivocal sign of merit, the same cannot be said for the accumulation of wealth in this lifetime, an act that may or may not be a sign of merit. Theravāda discourses on wealth place an emphasis on the means for acquiring wealth in the present lifetime. The *Anana-sutta* instructs that one may experience the bliss of having wealth if it is acquired through one's own efforts in a righteous way.[34] This idea is found within the vernacular texts of northern Thailand as well. Consider, for instance, the *Tamnān Doi Ang Salung*, a pre-fifteenth century northern Thai chronicle, which tells of the Buddha's miraculous journey through northern Thailand. In it, we have two vivid stories of wealth resulting from piety:

> After the Buddha spent seven days at Doi Kung he came down from the mountain and journeyed north through a forest for a distance of approximately 20,000 meters to the Mae Ping River. There he met a Lawa farmer who was using a water wheel to irrigate a field. When he saw the Buddha approach, he farmer unwound the turban from his head, it miraculously turned into gold. Amazed, the farmer said to the Buddha, "O, Blessed One, by your kindness please reside here in the north with us."

> The Buddha acceded to this request and stayed at a mountain to the south of the Lawa village. The Lawa farmers offered the Buddha two pots of rice curry. After the Buddha had eaten, the arahant monks who accompanied him consumed the remainder of the meal. When the Buddha and his disciples had finished eating, King Asoka, the righteous ruler, spoke to the Lawa: "My dear Lawa, there's no longer any need for you to irrigate your fields with a water wheel. If you take the precepts of the Buddha, there will be sufficient food for you to eat." The Lawa then took the five precepts from the Buddha. Upon returning to their home they found that everything had turned into gold. Amazed, they exclaimed, "In the past we worked our fingers to the bone and still didn't have enough to eat. Now that we have taken the Buddha's precepts we have found that everything has turned to gold. The Buddha's precepts are precious, indeed! We will observe them all of our lives."[35]

In this story, the farmers acquire wealth as the result of pious reverence for the Buddha and the undertaking of the five precepts.

The acquisition of wealth, however, may be the result of unrighteous activity in one's present life such as gambling, chicanery, and theft. The tradition is equally clear concerning these modes of acquisition: wealth that is acquired through unrighteous means is to be condemned. The karmic effects of such negative activities may be actualized in one's present life by the loss of wealth or in the future by an unfavorable rebirth. In the popular version of the Phra Malai story in Thailand (*Phra Malai Klon Suat*), for instance, we are instructed that, "Those who obtain the land of others through deceit and those who cheat others through inaccurate weights and measurements go to a hell where the floor is made of hot metal and a mountain of fire pursues them in all directions."[36]

Buddhist discourses concerning the use of wealth are similarly context sensitive. Those who possess wealth may use their wealth in ways that ensure continued prosperity or they may squander their merit-rich wealth in unprofitable ways. With regard to these two scenarios, the canonical texts clearly state that the proper maintenance of wealth involves a generous attitude towards the sharing of wealth with family, friends, workers, and religious persons.[37] In the *Ādiya-sutta*, we are explicitly told that acts of generous giving (*dāna*) ultimately lead to our happiness and a heavenly rebirth.[38] The correlation between generous giving and a heavenly rebirth is also, by far, one of the most common themes in vernacular Buddhist literature. The *Jinakālamālīpakaraṇaṃ*, for instance, contains many references to kings who secured heavenly rebirths for their acts of generous giving, such as "[t]he mighty King Abhaya who had accumulated great merit had a magnificent reign of fully twenty-four years and then reached the excellent heavenly city of Tidiva."[39] In the *Cāmadevīvaṃsa*, we are similarly informed of the fate of Queen Cāmadevī: "She performed numerous meritorious deeds (*puññāni*) such as the three righteous actions (*sucaritaṃ*), and upon her death she was born into the realm of the gods (*devaloke*)."[40] As we shall see in Chapter 3, the benefits of giving are numerous, and the tradition has a long history of linking these benefits to generous donors who are memorialized in textual narratives and in inscriptions on Buddha images, stūpas, and temples.

At the same time, Buddhist literature abounds in examples of wealthy individuals who fail to give generously in their lifetime: Their hoarding always leads to an unfavorable rebirth. The Buddhist texts are, in fact, replete with stories relating the karmic effects of greed. In the *Aggañña-sutta* (Dīgha Nikāya 27), the Buddha tells the Brahmin Vāseṭṭha about the role of greed in the evolution (or devolution?) of the world,[41] which reinforces the idea that greed fuels the processes of *saṃsāra* and hinders one's progress on the path. This negative impact of greed on future lives is a common theme in the enormously popular *jātaka* tales. In the *Saccaṃkira-jātaka*, for instance, we encounter a rat and a snake who, in their past lives, were greedy men who were fearful of losing their wealth; as a result, they suffer in the present as two of the lowest type of animals. In the *Trai Phum Phra Ruang*, a fourteenth-century text from the Siamese kingdom of Sukhothai, we are told how greed can lead to the torments of hell. One may be reborn in Vetaraṇī hell as a result of taking another's property by force. In this hell, the guardians "have clubs, large knives, lances, swords, spears, and all kinds of weapons for killing, stabbing, shooting and beating, all of which are made of fiery red iron.... These beings suffer great pain and anguish that is too much for them to bear."[42] In contemporary Thailand, stories of hungry ghosts—who are born into an existence of perpetual hunger due to greed in a past life—abound in popular literature and film.

When one examines the myriad references to wealth in Buddhist literature, it is quite apparent that the assessment of wealth in the tradition is context sensitive. In one passage we may read how wealth signifies the great stores of merit that an individual has accumulated over several lifetimes; whereas in another we are admonished not to be attached to our wealth, for such attachment will ultimately lead to suffering in this life and the next. From within the tradition, one might argue that this variability is because wealth in itself is not worthy of praise or condemnation. Wealth is not inherently morally good or bad. Rather, the tradition assesses wealth in reference to specific instances of the accumulation, maintenance, and distribution of wealth: It is only within these specific instances that one can judge whether wealth is ultimately viewed as beneficial or detrimental to one's present and future lives. Phra Payutto (Phra Rājavaramuni), for instance, writes, "It is not wealth that is praised or blamed [in Buddhist texts], but the way one acquires and uses it."[43] As we have seen, there is much truth to this characterization of canonical attitudes towards wealth, but at the same time, the chronicle traditions and recent history demonstrate that varying assessments of wealth also reflect local power relations and dramatically different understandings of Buddhist religiosity. This is evident in historical assessments of the relationship between social prosperity and monastic life at particular moments in time.

Social Prosperity and Monastic Life

Academic analyses of the reciprocal relationship between the saṅgha and the laity often include statements about the dangers inherent within this relationship, especially the saṅgha's amassing of wealth as a consequence of the generosity of the laity.[44] Once again, this perception of danger rests upon a view of Buddhist monastic life as essentially "otherworldly" in orientation. Buddhist history, however, demonstrates that generous giving has produced spectacular pieces of Buddhist art and architecture, has supported the creation and maintenance of Buddhist universities, and, most importantly, has provided an environment conducive to renunciation.

One of the greatest ironies of the Buddhist path is that renunciation requires economic prosperity. A monk cannot abandon his economic role in the family unless the family can sustain itself without him; and, more practically, the monk cannot live the life of a renunciant without receiving material patronage from the laity. The viability of Theravāda monasticism, therefore, is intimately connected to the prosperity of the social community that serves as its principal patron. In the *Cakkavattisīhanāda-sutta*, which describes the qualities of an ideal king, a righteous ruler must ensure that poverty is alleviated within his kingdom, for poverty inevitably leads to theft, the breakdown of civil order, and a crippling of the monastic community. Thus, the stories of generous kings in the South and Southeast Asian chronicles are not merely statements on royal piety and patronage, they are also stories about the fate of the *saṅgha*, whose very existence is intimately connected to the rise and fall of powerful kingdoms.

Buddhist history is peppered with stories of how the saṅgha declined in its purity as a result of the lack of economic and political prosperity. One example is the fate of the Thai saṅgha following the destruction of Ayutthaya by Burmese forces in the eighteenth century. Craig Reynolds describes the saṅgha during this period as in a state of complete disarray, a condition that was only improved by the economic prosperity ushered in under the rule of King Rama I:

> Amidst such impoverished conditions, what monk could maintain a pure asceticism? Adherence to the Vinaya depended on prosperous lay people whose alms would allow monks to live free from care for their livelihood. Asceticism was possible only in prosperous times, and Rama I fostered prosperity in agriculture and commerce by restoring political order. At the same time, he issued a series of laws that defined ascetic life and reminded both monk and layman that there could be no merit without a pure Sangha.[45]

Reynolds alludes to the idea that the amount of merit generated through acts of generosity to the saṅgha depends upon the *saṅgha's* level of purity (*visuddhi*).[46] The purer the saṅgha, the more merit one accrues through patronage. The purity of the saṅgha may be measured in terms of the adherence to the code of discipline or to the perfections of *sīla* (ethics), *samādhi* (concentration), and *paññā* (wisdom), but this purity is impossible without a lay society willing and able to support the *saṅgha*. One index, therefore, of the *saṅgha's* purity is the material state of the society in which the saṅgha dwells, not only the level of adherence to the code of discipline (as in the *Vinaya*) by individual monks.

Debates over the possession of monastic wealth and the accumulation and use of land, buildings, and monetary abundance by individual monks and the saṅgha as a whole reveal differing conceptions about the relationship between wealth, piety, and society. If we look at the South and Southeast Asian chronicles, we see how monastic wealth can serve as both an index of social and religious prosperity and an index of decadence; the latter can function as an impetus for monastic reform and revival. In a review of attitudes towards wealth in the Sinhalese chronicle tradition, Steven Kemper argues that the *Mahāvaṃsa* and *Cūlavaṃsa* "never scorn wealth, but they condemn wealth as an end in itself."[47] Individuals who possess wealth and who use it wisely to maintain order and prosperity within the saṅgha and society are praised within the chronicle tradition. This is especially true for kings, who are instructed to increase the wealth of the kingdom. "The greater the amount of available wealth, the greater the potential for doing good with it and for cultivating the virtue of non-attachment."[48] According to Kemper, when monks are chastised within the chronicles, it is not for their possession of wealth *per se*, but rather because they are deemed to be undisciplined, corrupt, and immoral. "The desired quality is discipline, not poverty."[49]

The process for identifying monastic abuses, however, is not always straightforward since judgments of another's self-control and discipline are highly influenced by the relations of power between the judge and the judged. Take, for instance, the saṅgha law issued in 1783 by King Rama I (r. 1782–1809), which discouraged lay people from leaving material wealth to individual monks. This law, like the other nine issued by King Rama I, sought to establish "norms of conduct befitting the mutual relationship between monk and layman."[50] One might assume that this law represents a condemnation of monastic wealth by the new king, but the reality is far more complicated. In this 1783 case, the king was responding to an incident when a female rebel, upon her execution, left her possessions to an individual monk. Without informing his superiors, this monk retained possession of the property, which normally would have gone to the crown. Craig Reynolds argues that the king "used this incident to urge monks not to accept riches from lay people," and that, while the king could not stand in judgment of monks who received these gifts, he could "exhort lay people to respect the world of the monastery with its special code, and clarify the line between the monarch's domain and the Buddha's domain."[51]

One could place the creation of these laws in the context of King Rama I's attempts to restore the integrity of the saṅgha after years of laxity and corruption. Klaus Wenk, for instance, describes the ten saṅgha laws issued by King Rama I as attempts to "raise the moral level of this class and to restore its prestige and authority."[52] While this may be true, we might also interpret the law as a response to rebel insurgents who left their possessions to sympathetic monks rather than allowing the crown to garnish them. The ability of the state to take the lives of rebels along with their possessions demonstrated the state's power and authority. In this specific case, these actions legitimized the rule of King Rama I, who himself assumed the throne after the forced abdication and eventual execution of King Taksin (reigned 1767–1782). King Taksin had endorsed a mystical form of Buddhism that divided the saṅgha between those who supported his claims to religious authority and those who did not. Monks who aided Taksin in his personal practice were granted high positions within the saṅgha administration, while those who questioned his spiritual prowess were demoted or defrocked. After Rama I became king, he sought to restore normalcy to the *saṅgha*. To this end, he demoted and defrocked monastic supporters of Taksin and reinstated those who had been "unfairly" punished.[53] Rama I's admonition against rebels leaving their possessions to the saṅgha, may then also be read as an act that placed the saṅgha with its mixed allegiances under his supervision and legitimated his authority as king. The central issue may not have been an individual monk's reception of property or possessions from laypersons, but rather rebel money remaining outside of the control of the crown. I am not suggesting that these saṅgha laws only had political motivation or implications: They occurred within a saṅgha reform framework that employed discourses on moral and ethical laxity, *Vinaya* violations, revisions of the *Tipiṭaka*, and the blurring of distinctions between monks and laypersons. I am suggesting, however, that the wealth of an individual monk became an issue for religious and political authorities when it was deemed improper for a political rebel to leave possessions to a particular monk.

In South and Southeast Asia there is a long tradition of individual monks receiving personal gifts from lay patrons. In fact, the Sinhalese Chronicles recount many instances whereby kings offered lavish gifts to monks, and the "more accomplished the monk, the more lavish the gift (*Mahāvaṃsa* 24.21–22, n.2; *Cūlavaṃsa* 1.44–47).[54] In one instance, King Mahinda IV is reported to have fed monks from the Āraññika sect with "abundant and costly food with various kinds of curries."[55] In Thailand, one of the inscriptions by King Ram-Khamhaeng (reigned 1279–1317) of Sukhothai reads, "The people of Sukhothai are charitable, pious and devoted to alms-giving. King Ram Khamhaeng, the ruler of Sukhothai, as well as princes and princesses, gentlemen and ladies of the nobility, men and women, all have faith in the Buddhist religion."[56]

In conclusion, it is fair to say that at times generous giving to the saṅgha was not deemed problematic by the religious and political establishments. At other times, such acts were interpreted as corrupt and indicative of a decadent saṅgha. Frank Reynolds succinctly captures the varying appraisals of wealth and generous giving in his analysis of ethics and wealth in Theravāda Buddhism:

> In various Theravāda countries there has been a continuing, cyclic oscillation between periods of monastic accumulation supported by the justification of monastic wealth and periods of monastic reform accompanied by the condemnation of wealth. It is not surprising that the accumulation of and justification of monastic

wealth has often come to the fore in situations in which the monastic leadership has been closely affiliated, often by kinship, with
the political and economic elite. It is also not surprising that monastic reforms and the condemnation of monastic wealth have
often been initiated and supported by kings seeking to return monastic lands to the tax rolls.[57]

When it was considered to be a problem, as during the reign of King Rama I,
the political and saṅgha establishments emphasized those aspects of the tradition that stressed voluntary poverty or collective ownership over and against
the traditional equation of wealth or patronage with merit. As we shall see, this
kind of thinking characterized the critique of the Dhammakāya Temple during the Asian economic crisis. When generous patronage served the larger interest of the establishment as a sign of the establishment's legitimacy and
profitable rule, however, a vibrant and materially thriving saṅgha was lauded as
a sign of social well-being and religious righteousness.

Renunciation, Economic Ethics, and Social Action in Modern Buddhism

These varying appraisals of monastic wealth demonstrate how religious discourses on wealth and prosperity are fundamentally linked to broader social,
political, and economic discourses within societies at specific historical moments. In order to reconstruct the economic ethics of the early Buddhist community, for instance, we must consider canonical discourses on wealth and
prosperity in the light of relations between Buddhist monks and potential patrons as well as between Buddhist monks and their religious competitors. This
allows us to assess the positive value of wealthy patrons—in whose ranks the
wealthy king is a patron par excellence—not only as a religious statement on
the nature of karma (wealth equals merit), but also as a powerful strategy for
securing patronage for the Buddhist saṅgha in a highly competitive religious
market. Buddhist evaluations of wealth, whether affirming or critical, are situ-
ational and embedded within power relations.

Buddhist views of wealth, prosperity, and development in the modern era,
therefore, reflect the historical realities of life in the nineteenth and twentieth
centuries. This was a period of European and Japanese colonialism and imperialism, global Christian proselytization, nation-building, and religious reform.
As Asian societies have encountered the forces of modernization, a plethora of
Buddhist voices have engaged in debates over national, social, and personal
prosperity; economic issues; and social justice. The contours of these debates in
Buddhist societies have variously been informed by historical circumstances

(for instance, whether or not the country was subject to colonial rule), the strength of the polity, and the internal dynamics of the social structure. In the modern era, monks have often stood at the forefront of these discussions, assessing not only the state of Buddhism in a given society but also how a particular social, political, and economic system either reinforces or undermines Buddhist values and goals. Sometimes the injection of monastic voices into social debates is welcomed with overwhelming support by the government and civil society; at other times such interjections by monks considered to have renounced "worldly" concerns are viewed as corrupt practices, as violations of the *Vinaya*.[58] Once again, specific historical and cultural contexts influence the ways Buddhist economic ethics and the role of the monk in promoting them are defined.[59]

Buddhist socialism in twentieth-century Burma provides one example of a modern Buddhist economic ethic. While Burmese socialists drew narratives and ideals from the Buddhist tradition, their platform of Buddhist socialism emerged from within the historical circumstances of modern Burma. As with other countries in the region, Burma had been subject to British colonial rule and hence deeply affected by the political, social, and economic changes fostered by European colonialism. It facilitated international commerce, which connected Burma and other Southeast Asian states to an emergent capitalist system in Europe. The supply of Southeast Asian goods to the world market was profitable for the European colonial powers, but it destabilized local economies.[60] Modern economic "reforms," did not benefit the average Burmese farmer; one could argue that these reforms made Burmese farmers more, rather than less, economically destitute.[61] British colonialism coupled with Japanese occupation during World War II left the Burmese economy in ruins by the middle of the twentieth century. It is within this colonial context that we must situate the voices of Buddhist millenarian groups, such as the followers of Saya San, who believed that the next Buddha, Metteya, would soon restore order and prosperity to Burma, as well as the voices of Buddhist socialists who combined central themes in Buddhist philosophy with the powerful discourse of Marxism.[62]

One representative of Buddhist socialism in Burma was U Ba Swe, the second Prime Minister of Burma (1956–57), who supported a synthesis of key Buddhist principles with Marxism. U Ba Swe viewed Marxism as an interpretive framework for understanding the "political economic conditions of suffering that must precede the Buddhist quest for ultimate liberation from suffering."[63] By extension, the creation of a Marxist society would lead to the elimination of injustice and poverty and create a society conducive to following the path.

This social order was called *pyidawtha* or "Happy Land," and it drew upon discourses of the relationship between social prosperity and religious attainment.[64] This ideology was supported and promoted by U Nu, the popular Prime Minister of Burma from 1948–1956, 1957–1958, and 1960–1962. In his essay, "Kyan-to Buthama," U Nu argued that greed, hatred, and delusion (*kilesa*) are economic inequalities, and economic reform was the only way to eliminate them. He criticized capitalism for turning people away from Buddhism and underlined how socialism could provide an environment conducive to meditating on the impermanence of all things (*anicca*). He viewed the renewal of society as a return to a more perfect past and used ideal images from the canon as a charter for his own reform.[65]

As Buddhist socialism was emerging in Burma, the government-sponsored saṅgha in Thailand had a radically different orientation towards economic development. Far from being an impediment, the Thai establishment placed the saṅgha at the forefront of ushering in economic reform.[66] The co-option of the Thai saṅgha by capitalist forces occurred within a context of aggressive nation building by the political establishment. The government not only exerted tight control over the saṅgha as evidenced in the passing of the 1962 Saṅgha Act, but also used the saṅgha as a messenger of Thai nationalism, as a force against communist and ethnic separatism.

During this time, the saṅgha was involved in two government programs whose aims were to foster a sense of national identity and strengthen ties to the centralized political establishment.[67] The first program, established by the Department of Religious Affairs in 1965, was the *thammathut* (dhamma messenger) program, which sent monks to north and northeast Thailand with a message of national development. The thammathut monks described development projects, such as building schools, improving roads, and constructing bridges, as merit making activities. This positive message of social-uplift was meant to counter the influence of dangerous insurgencies. The second program was the *thammacarik* (*dhammacarika*, Pāli; dhamma travellers) program, which was started in 1964, aimed to convert tribal groups, such as the Meo, Yao, Lisu, Lahu, Akha, Karen, and T'in peoples, to Buddhism. The religious aims of the program were directly linked to the government's desire to foster a sense of national community among these disparate groups, which could then serve economic and political ends.[68] While some observers questioned the effectiveness of this program because of the difficulties of language and cultural translation, the program nevertheless stood as a symbol of the government's use of the centralized saṅgha as a means for promoting national interests.

During the turbulent 1960s and 1970s, there was tension within the country between those who viewed communism as a tool against western imperialism and those who viewed it as a threat to national survival. Monks were embroiled on both sides of these debates. One of the most vocal advocates of the conservative, anticommunist side was Phra Kitthiwuttho: He cofounded Nawapol, an extreme right-wing movement with close ties to the military elite; and founded Chittapawan Buddhist College, which was rumored to be a training camp for right-wing Khmer rebels. He became infamous for allegedly claiming that the act of killing communists produces no negative karmic effects. In one interview Phra Kitthiwuttho explained his stance on communism by stating that Buddhism may be tolerant of other religious views, "but the Lord Buddha also said that people should not associate themselves with incorrect thoughts."[69] Phra Kitthiwuttho's right-wing political ideology accompanied a view of Buddhism that emphasized the relationship between material and spiritual development. Like his more liberal contemporaries, he urged members of the saṅgha to become more active in social and economic development. At Chittapawan College he established a rice-milling operation that he saw as a solution for economically depressed farmers who were losing too much money through the avaricious involvement of middlemen. In response to the question of whether monks should be actively involved in development endeavors, Phra Kitthiwuttho stated: "In many developed societies of the West and in Japan, religion is nothing but ceremony, empty of meaning . . . Is there a danger of this happening in Thailand, with its speedily developing economy and higher education? Certainly not, technology and science will further Buddhism as the guiding light."[70] As Phra Kitthiwuttho espoused the compatibility of the Buddhism with technology, science, and capitalism, other monks were equally vocal about the dangers of modern capitalism to Buddhism and Thai society as a whole. Those monks who dared to question the direction of the government were labeled as communist sympathizers, the most notable being Bhikkhu Buddhadāsa (Phra Phutthathat) and Phra Phimontham. Both of these monks criticized the rigid anti-democratic structure of the saṅgha and, by extension (though not directly), the authoritarian government of General Sarit Thanarat.

Phra Phimontham was a pro-democratic monk who faced persecution by the government and saṅgha establishment for his political views and promotion of religious reform. In the 1940s he criticized Prime Minister Phibun Songkhram for initiating a policy barring communists from being ordained as monks, arguing that this ban was not in accordance with Buddhist principles. He eventually faced persecution under the ecclesiastical authority of *Saṅgharāja* Plot Kittisophana and his cabinet (*Khana Sangkhamontri*). The charges leveled against him included allegations of violations of the *Vinaya*'s prohibition against sexual conduct, but serious doubts surrounded these allegations. Phra Phimontham was not disrobed, but he was removed as abbot of Wat Mahatat. Two years later he was arrested "on charges of being a communist and a threat to national security," was forced to disrobe, and was held in jail for four years (1962–1966) until a military court cleared him all of the charges.[71]

Bhikkhu Buddhadāsa (Phra Phutthathat), who was arguably Thailand's most well-known modern reformist monk, was similarly criticized for his alleged support of communism during the regime of Sarit Thanarat. It was especially Buddhadāsa's formulation of "dhammic socialism"—which emphasized "the

good of the whole, restraint and generosity, respect and loving-kindness"[72]—
that was taken by some to be communist in orientation, even though Buddhadāsa
himself emphasized the need for a centralized government (a dictatorial form
of dhammic socialism). In fact, Buddhadāsa explicitly stated that Buddhism
was neither capitalist nor communist in orientation,[73] but given the political
climate of Southeast Asia in the 1960s and 1970s, his "revolutionary" reinter-
pretations of the dhamma and his critique of contemporary society led some to
question his political allegiances.

The political establishment labeled both Phra Phimontham and Bhikkhu Buddhadāsa communist sympathizers because they challenged the status
quo during a period of tumultuous unrest in Southeast Asia. Phra Phothirak's
critique of the religious and political establishment in the 1970s and 1980s,
however, emerged in a different social context: He attacked the culture of capitalism in modern Thailand and the effects of Western imperialism during a
period of unprecedented growth and prosperity. As the government was es-
pousing the rhetoric of developmental capitalism, Phra Phothirak openly criticized the effects of materialism on Thai society. He created an alternative
community called Santi Asok that embodied moderation, interdependent living, and selflessness. The "back to basics" ideology of Santi Asok has led some
commentators to compare the Santi Asok movement to fundamentalistic
trends in other religious traditions.[74] Swearer argues that this movement
"strives to strip away the 'chaff' and return to the 'fundamentals' or essence of
Buddhism,"[75] a posture that distinguishes Santi Asok monks from what some
Thai Buddhists view as an "extremely lax and commercialized clergy."[76]

Phra Phothirak's vision of a new counter-community led him to condemn many common social and religious practices that signal ethical laxity and
excessive consumption. Santi Asok members, for instance, abstain from eating
meat, from using stimulants such as alcohol, cigarettes, and coffee, and from
engaging in sexually promiscuous behavior. Phra Phothirak also rejects those
religious practices that in his opinion are based on magic and superstition, such
as image veneration and the sprinkling of Buddhist "holy" water. These practices, in his opinion, run counter to the ethos of Buddhist practice and foster
the trade of money for merit. In the same vein, Santi Asok has a strict policy
regarding the reception of donations. Potential donors must visit the Santi
Asok center at least seven times before their offerings are accepted; this is done
in order to separate what Phra Phothirak considers to be genuine donations
from those that are merely inspired by a desire for making merit.[77]

As with Phra Phimontham and Phra Phutthatat, Phra Phothirak faced
persecution at the hands of the saṅgha establishment. In his case, however, he
was forced to disrobe on charges of defying and distorting the saṅgha's discipline. He remained a renouncer, initially donning the white robes of a pious
layperson rather than the standard saffron-colored robes of Thai monks, and

assumed the title, Samana Phothirak. In Chapter 5, I will revisit Bhikkhu Buddhadāsa and Phra Phothirak's interpretations of Buddhist thought and practice and their critical reading of contemporary Thai society in relation to questions about religious consumerism and the commercialism of Buddhism. At present, however, I want to emphasize that all three monks raised pointed questions about the negative influence of modernizing capitalist forces within the kingdom, the ways in which Thai society had embraced the global ideology of progress and prosperity, and its reliance upon a Western platform of development.

More recently, this Buddhist critique of modernism and the processes of modernization has manifested itself within ecological circles. Environmentalist monks (*phra nak anuraksa*) in Thailand have sought to raise awareness of the profound ecological impact of such processes on the environment, most notably the logging industry.[78] At the forefront of these discourses is Phra Prajak Kuttajitto, who utilizes Bhikkhu Buddhadāsa's formulation of dhammic socialism for a strategy of conservation. Phra Prajak gained national attention in 1991, when he criticized the government's plan to relocate poor settlers from degraded forest lands under the pretense of saving Thailand's forests from increased encroachment. In Phra Prajak's view, the aim of this program was to foster monoculture commercial tree farming.[79] As with other progressive voices in Thailand, however, Phra Prajak became embroiled in controversy, was arrested, and eventually disrobed.

These contemporary Buddhist discourses are critical of modernity and the processes of modernization. They stand in stark contrast to the dominant political forces that have used the saṅgha to counter the forces of communism within Southeast Asia. These radically different stances to economic policy demonstrate how the saṅgha can serve concurrently as both an index of and a counteragent to modern constructions of development and prosperity. The relationship between Buddhism and varying notions of prosperity, therefore, is intimately linked to larger social and political issues.

Cults of Prosperity in Postmodern Thailand

Today, Buddhist evaluations of wealth must be situated within the context of an ever-complex global economy as some Buddhists enjoy new forms of prosperity while others grapple with the realities of unfair wages, devalued currencies, and the exploitation of the poor. The new cults of prosperity that have grown and proliferated especially in urban areas in Thailand over the past two decades reflect this new social environment and global economy. Thailand's economic boom in the 1980s and early 1990s "created a mood of national confidence that influenced all aspects of social, cultural, and religious life."[80] A number of new religious movements and charismatic-based cults, which reinforced the correlation of spirituality with material prosperity, emerged within this context. Three of the most prominent were the cults of King Rama V, the Erawan Shrine, and Luang Pho Khun. Like many similar new-age movements that have sprung up in the latter twentieth century in the West, each "contributes to the economic well-being of the individual as a spiritually empowered producer,"[81] emphasizing the synergy between spiritual power and one's ability to succeed financially. They make no distinction between religious and this-worldly goals. With the cults of King Rama V and the Erawan shrine, lack of a distinction between religion and finance fits neatly within the ethos of a Thai civil religion that is inherently this-worldly in orientation. In the case of the cult of Luang Pho Khun, however, we see a fusion of the power of Buddhist renunciation with modern Thai capitalism.

Devotion to the spirit of King Rama V (r.1868–1910) gained prominence in the early 1990s as many middle-class urban Thais sought to access the power of prosperity associated with him. Reverence for King Rama V has occupied a predominant space in modern Thai consciousness: He is lauded as the king who created the centralized modern nation-state of Thailand and as the king whose political savvy saved the country from European colonization. In the 1990s, this portrayal of King Rama V as a national hero became linked to the quest for personal success in contemporary Thailand. Photographs and images of King Rama V adorn Thai offices, classrooms, and homes. Amulets bearing his image are distributed along with amulets of famous monks and Buddha images. Devotional acts of piety are openly displayed at his large bronze image in the center of Royal Plaza in Bangkok's old city. Devotees offer flowers, candles, incense, and bottles of Thai whiskey each Tuesday evening (the day of King Rama V's birth) with services lasting throughout the night. These acts of veneration are not merely expressions of Thai patriotism, they are acts that link devotees to the culture of success that surrounds one of their most beloved kings.

In a more overt synthesis between piety and wealth, devotees of the Erawan Shrine at the Grand Hyatt Erawan hotel seek to have their wishes granted and gain tangible wealth, success, and power through their offerings and acts of devotions to the image of Brahmā (Phra Phrom), a Hindu deity associated with acts of creation. The shrine was first built in the early 1950s after a series of misfortunes plagued the construction of the Union Thai Hotel. When the workers at the site refused to continue their building efforts, an astrologer was consulted. He argued that the name Erawan (the name of the three-headed elephant upon whom Brahmā rides) had come to him in a vision and indicated that the construction project needed to be under the protective powers of the god Brahmā. As a result, the builders erected an image of Brahmā on the grounds. After its erection, the hotel became an enormous success, and years later when the hotel became the Grand Hyatt Erawan hotel, the Brahmā shrine became even more associated with Thailand's modernization and prosperity.[82]

What is particularly striking about the cult of the Erawan shrine is that its power is intimately connected to the hotel and its astounding success. While other images of Brahmā are located in Bangkok, most notably at the World Trade Center, they are not patronized by Thais in the manner at the Erawan shrine. Thais who pass by the shrine often show reverence to the image by *wai*-ing it (placing their hands together and bowing their heads), which is a common scene on buses and in cars at the intersection of Ratchaprarop and Ploenchit roads, or by purchasing small wooded elephants that are offered to it. Dancers who are proficient in *ram thai* (traditional Thai dance) perform regularly at the shrine at the request of devotees whose wishes have been granted. Lottery ticket vendors line the outside of the shrine as do beggars, street performers, and large numbers of tourists.

The cult of Luang Pho Khun Pharisuttho, abbot of Wat Ban Rai, similarly reflects the growth of prosperity movements in late twentieth-century Thailand, but unlike the cults of Rama V and the Erawan Shrine, it combines contemporary economics with traditional discourses of charismatic power. In Southeast Asia, tales abound of monks who develop miraculous powers such as prophecy, healing, and protection as the result of their advanced meditation and ascetic practice.[83] Those whose powers are especially potent often become the object of cultic adoration. This is the case with Luang Pho Khun, who "has become the focus of a national cult which emphasizes the acquisition of wealth and power."[84] One cannot go very far in Thailand without seeing an image of Luang Pho Khun. Stories about him abound in popular magazines, glossy photographs of him are on display in stores and taxis, and his image is reproduced on amulets that adorn the necks of many pious Buddhists. Luang Pho Khun's transformation from local monk to "a cultural icon, approaching the status of a living patron saint of the Thai economic boom"[85] is due to a number of factors, including traditional ideas concerning spiritual authority, the role of the media, the correlation of Luang Pho Khun with capitalism, and his relations with prominent politicians and members of the royal family. Prior to his national prominence, Luang Pho Khun was known for his strict ascetic practice in Northeast Thailand and his "down to earth" demeanor. After he was linked to miraculous rescue stories in 1993, his name achieved national recognition. The first "rescue" involved the use of one of his amulets to help free a woman from a concrete block after the collapse of the Royal Plaza Hotel in Khorat. The second story involved a young woman who jumped from the third story of a building on fire, all the while grasping her Luang Pho Khun amulet in her hand. She survived while over 200 of her coworkers perished in the disaster. Reports of the miraculous powers of the amulets spurred an incredible demand for them and created a multimillion baht industry.[86]

As we shall see in Chapter 5, Luang Pho Khun's amulets are considered not only as protective agents but also as conduits for wealth. In fact, the name "Khun" means 'to multiply,' and the ability of his amulets to multiply good luck, good fortune, and wealth is widely claimed. Ascribed with this special power, the monetary value of many of these amulets has dramatically increased. According to one report, the price of some amulets went from a mere twenty baht to a price ranging from 1,000 to 10,000 baht.[87] The names of some of these amulets include: "rich for sure," "multiplying wealth," "requesting an increase in wealth," and "paying off debts."[88]

The phenomenon of Luang Pho Khun highlights the importance of examining Buddhist conceptions of renunciation within specific historical and cultural contexts. Luang Pho Khun's amulets refer explicitly to worldly success, but his persona remains that of a detached ascetic who neither favors nor disapproves of wealth. "Khun appears to epitomize the Buddhist monastic ideal of detachment, being in but not of the world, acting as a disinterested channel for redistributing funds from often wealthy donors to the needy."[90] The fact that Luang Pho Khun receives patronage from high-ranking government and military officials and members of the royal family demonstrates how establishment forces with the kingdom legitimize Luang Pho Khun's application of Buddhist power to this-worldly spheres of activity. In fact, many politicians have sought association with Luang Pho Khun during election campaigns, including Chatichai Choonhaven and Chavalit Yongchaiyudh, two former Prime Ministers of Thailand.

The popularity of Luang Pho Khun is especially intriguing given the fact that the Dhammakāya Temple similarly links the power of traditional asceticism with worldly success in contemporary Thai society. While Luang Pho Khun's distribution of money-making amulets has spurred debate over the appropriateness of such practices (as it has in the Dhammakāya controversy), he has not yet had to bear the personal attacks leveled at the abbot and assistant abbot of the Dhammakāya Temple. One reason may be the fact that, while many of funds derived from donations have gone towards buildings at Wat Ban Rai, many more have also been directed towards charities and the poor, a fact which tempers criticisms of his own personal interest in donations. In addition, and perhaps more importantly, the visit of the King and Queen to Wat Ban Rai in 1995 quashed many criticisms of Luang Pho Khun in the press. Their public patronage legitimated his sanctity.

Conclusion

This chapter has examined multiple constructions of Buddhist renunciation in Buddhist texts and practices. Rather than positing an orthodox rendering of renunciation and using this reified concept as a means to gauge the practices of monks and nuns at specific historical moments, it is far more fruitful and historically accurate to approach renunciation as a constructed practice heavily dependent on context. Buddhist communities debate the merits of different acts of renunciation within specific historical and cultural contexts; these acts are not self-evident reflections of authentic Buddhist piety.

It is within these constructions of renunciation that we may begin to see the varying attitudes towards wealth in the Buddhist tradition. Buddhist discourses concerning the accumulation or renunciation of wealth do not simply refer to this-worldly or otherworldly orientations but rather to broader interpretations of wealth within society. As we shall see in the ensuing chapters, the Dhammakāya Temple developed during a period of unprecedented growth and prosperity within Thailand; in contrast, the nationwide controversy over the Temple's wealth and marketing techniques emerged out of a radically different historical context—the Asian economic crisis, in which the correlation between wealth and piety assumed center stage in Thai public discourse.

Chapter 2

Modernity, Prosperity, and the Dhammakāya Temple

While many in the West envision the ideal Buddhist monk as a forest-dwelling renunciant cut off from the obligations and concerns of worldly life, the reality of Buddhist renunciation has always been and continues to be far more varied than this idealized portrait would lead us to believe. In the nineteenth and twentieth centuries, for instance, Buddhist communities debated the role of monks in political, social, and religious reform. In Sri Lanka, Anagarika Dharmapala argued that monks needed to be "a Buddhist army" to usher in necessary religious and social reforms in modern Sri Lanka;[1] whereas Balangoḍa Ānanda Maitreya, one of the dominant voices of contemporary Sinhalese Buddhism, adamantly disapproved of the politicization of the saṅgha.[2] In Burma, U Nu's socialism fostered a politically engaged saṅgha, while under his successor, General Ne Win, "[m]onks were just simply surgically removed from the body politic, like diseased flesh."[3] In modern Thailand, the *thammathut* and *thammacarik* monks were messengers of the dhamma (*dharma*, Sanskrit) in the service of political centralization, while other monks, such as Phra Achan Cha, served the nation through an exemplary life of religious piety and purity in the forest tradition.

In the contemporary postmodern period, debates over the politicization of the saṅgha have continued, but they have been accompanied by a host of other questions about the role of monks in public life, especially the relationship of the saṅgha to an ever-changing global public. In recent years a number of stories have surfaced in the international media that testify to the changing face of Buddhist monasticism in the twenty-first century. In November of 2005, *The Nation* reported on a new site for religious instruction in Thailand.

> In an attempt to bring people closer to religion, the ministry is considering a plan to provide "monk zones" in department stores where shoppers can meet monks. "The project will be called 'Meet the Monks in a Quiet Corner'," said Culture Minister Uraiwan Thienthong . . . "Nowadays people have no time to go to temples,

47

only shopping malls, so if we provide the opportunity they can get closer to religion," she said.[4]

While monks in Thailand are preaching in malls, Buddhist monks and nuns in Tokyo are taking to the fashion "runway," wearing colorful, embroidered, and elaborate robes, in an attempt to attract younger people to the religion.[5]

These remarkable examples illustrate the perceived need by some Buddhists to repackage Buddhist instruction in ways that may be appealing to new audiences. The rationale for having monks in Thai malls and on Tokyo runways is the same: to attract a new generation to the Buddhist tradition. Advocates view these new sites and methods for religious instruction as a requirement for the continuation of the tradition. As a result, we witness an enormous growth in the use of new media technologies for religious instruction throughout the world, from temple websites and television channels to religious podcasts and ringtones.

What these changes represent and how they are received within a given society depend on how they are marketed to their respective publics and the broader historical contexts out of which they emerge. In this chapter, the emergence and success of the Dhammakāya Temple is analyzed within the context of postmodern Thai Buddhism, a context that reflects the institutional and educational saṅgha reforms of the nineteenth and twentieth centuries as well as the vibrant diversity of contemporary Buddhist practice and popular Thai religion. Exploring the growth of the Dhammakāya Temple through its history, lineages of authority, and distinctive practices reveals several reasons for its phenomenal material success, especially the fusion of its meditation practice with an ethic of personal and social prosperity. The Dhammakāya Temple identifies itself as a "modern temple for a modern age," but it does not entirely reinvent the dhammic wheel. As with other modern religious movements, it chooses to present itself as modern in select ways, whether by employing a contemporary aesthetic, using new technologies, or reinterpreting key doctrines and practices through a modern lens. At the same time, however, the Temple is always engaged in a dialogue with the past, as it repackages Buddhism for a new public in the present.

The fact that modern religious movements reflect their traditional pasts as well as their current contexts is evident in the case of two other new Buddhist movements in Asia, Soka Gakkai in Japan and Foguang Shan in Taiwan, both of which share striking similarities with the Dhammakāya Temple in Thailand. All three groups have grown exponentially in the postmodern period as they have sought to make Buddhism relevant to the contemporary world. This shared goal may be one reason why the Dhammakāya Temple and Foguang Shan have maintained close relations for over a decade; in fact, Dhammakāya publications refer to Foguang Shan as a "sister temple." The active and highly effective proselytization of all three groups has fostered criticism concerning their teachings, methods of instruction and proselytization, and impressive size and material wealth. At the same time, while all three groups make claims of modern relevancy, they simultaneously emphasize the continuity of their doctrine and practice with the traditions of Buddhism from which they emerged.

Soka Gakkai (the Value-creating Society) emerged in 1930 as a social movement devoted to the educational theories of Makiguchi Tsunesaburo (1871–1944), who promoted the cultivation of happiness through "goodness, beauty, benefit or gain."[6] As Makiguchi became increasingly devoted to Nichiren Buddhism in the 1930s, Soka Gakkai began to adopt a more religious focus.[7] The fact that Makiguchi and his disciple, Toda Josei (1900–1958), were imprisoned for failing to embrace the nationalistic Shinto of the state testifies to their high level of commitment to Nichiren Buddhism. Although Makiguchi died in prison, Toda used his prison experience to strengthen his commitment to Nichiren Shoshu. Following his release, he dramatically transformed Soka Gakkai into a "new religious movement" with an active agenda of proselytization. According to Metraux, this revamped Soka Gakkai "promised happiness, meaning in life, and the comfort of close group membership to the restless, rootless, searching, and deeply frustrated people of postwar Japan."[8] Soka Gakkai's enormous growth in the 1950s and 1960s demonstrates how this optimistic religious message of prosperity appealed to many in postwar Japan. At the same time, the religious organization faced criticism in Japan for its antagonistic stance towards other religions, its controversial method of proselytization (*shakubuku*), its support of the Komeito party, and its tense relations with the Nichiren Shoshu priesthood. Following a series of controversies in Japan, the president of Soka Gakkai, Ikeda Daisaku, resigned his post in 1979 and created Soka Gakkai International (SGI) in order to focus on global proselytization.

SGI now has a significant international presence, with centers around the world. It has been particularly successful in the United States, drawing support from both immigrant and convert communities. One reason for its global success is its effective use of modern technology and marketing techniques, and the popularity of its religious message: Through the power of religious chanting ("namu-myo-ho renge-kyo"—Praise to the Wonderful Dharma of the Lotus Sutra) one can gain this-worldly benefits that range from health and wealth to world peace.[9] This stance towards contemporary prosperity strikes a popular chord with SGI practitioners; at the same time, it sounds a warning bell to critics who question the motives and religious integrity of the organization as it amasses substantial material resources. Barrett argues that this type of "materialistic philosophy" can be summed up as, "Chant 'Nam myoho renge kyo' and ask for a new car."[10] Critics reject this mechanistic form of Buddhist practice outright, while SGI members nuance the power of the chant by stressing that through religious practice one might "receive inner peace and understanding of why you don't actually need a car."[11] Like other so-called this-worldly religious organizations, SGI promotes a varied religious orientation that combines traditional discourses on non-violence, compassion, and selfless action with modern discourses on the promotion of "peace, culture and education through personal change and social contribution."[12]

Foguang Shan (Buddha's Light Mountain) is another example of a popular Buddhist organization that has adopted a positive stance towards modernity, but unlike Soka Gakkai, it began as a Buddhist temple and has retained a significant monastic component. Since 1967, when construction of the temple began, Foguang Shan has grown into one of the most prominent temples in Taiwan with over 100,000 members. Stuart Chandler estimates that between 8 and 12 percent of Taiwan's population has some affiliation with Foguang Shan.[13] Foguang Shan has an impressive international presence as well, with organizations in over 170 countries. Its popularity is due, in great part, to the charismatic power of its founder, Master Xingyun, and his promotion of a form of "Humanistic Buddhism," which focuses attention on the creation of a this-worldly Pure Land through religious education, acts of charity, and social programs.[14] In traditional forms of Pure Land Buddhism, Buddhist practitioners seek to be reborn in Sukhavati, the Pure Land of Amitabha Buddha, which they view as a place that is perfectly conducive to awakening and liberation. Here the focus on an otherworldly Pure Land is premised on the belief that the present world is so corrupted and steeped in delusion that beings are unable to progress on the path to awakening through their own efforts. Modern Humanistic Buddhism, in contrast, is far less critical of our present age. Rather than focusing on rebirth in another realm, they champion the idea of creating a Pure Land on earth today through the fostering of democracy, human rights, moral responsibility, and concern for the environment. Their discourses focus on progress rather than degeneration.[15]

Foguang Shan's positivist and activist stance towards the present era includes, as in the case of Soka Gakkai, the embracing of modern technology—especially modern communication and transportation. According to its members, Master Xingyun "was among the first Buddhist monastics to use an automobile, slide projector, and radio and television transmission."[16] Today, Foguang Shan also makes use of the Internet for the dissemination of information about the organization and its teachings. While many Buddhists in Taiwan accept the adoption of new technologies for Buddhist instruction, some are critical of the use of modern conveniences by Foguang Shan clerics, in particular, the use of air conditioners in temples. For the critics, the use of air conditioning undermines the spirit of renunciation and simplicity; practitioners, however, insist that the Buddha himself adopted new technologies.

Foguang Shan apologists further insist that the monastic life is just as austere, if not more, than other monastic residences in Taiwan.[17]

These criticisms of Foguang Shan's use of air conditioners are no doubt a reaction to the organization's overall positivist stance toward modernity and the current capitalist economy. Chandler argues that Master Xingyun's understanding of true equity (*zhenzheng de gongping*) emphasizes individual talents and hard work, and therefore promotes a this-worldly asceticism reminiscent of Weber's Protestant ethic (which of course runs counter to Weber's assessment of Buddhism and Chinese religions). "Master Xingyun sees nothing wrong with making money and becoming rich, so long as one has done so in a moral way and shares the benefits of one's property with others."[18] According to Chandler, "Master Xingyun in particular and the Foguang monastic community in general serve as a paradigm of Buddhist capitalism . . . Foguang clerics exemplify the capitalist spirit at its very best: they are a highly organized, diligent labor force, remaining fugal in personal life, but daring to expand the horizons of their "occupation."[19] As in the cases of other pro-capitalist religious figures and organization, detractors question the motives of Foguang Shan and its rapid accumulation of wealth and power. Supporters, however, view the accumulation of material resources as a means for continued growth and ability to spread the message of "Humanistic Buddhism" around the globe. In fact, while many Buddhists in Taiwan view positive assessments of wealth in mechanistic terms—the better Buddhist you are the more wealth you accumulate— Master Xingyun criticizes this interpretation as a misinterpretation of the law of cause and effect and the centrality of intention.[20]

Master Xingyun's clarification of his views on wealth is instructive for our analysis of the relationship between piety and wealth in the modern era. His emphasis on intention is perfectly consistent with the normative Buddhist interpretation of the laws of karma. So, while his positive stance towards capitalism is a reflection of his contemporary historical context, his views on wealth direct our attention back to normative ideas within the tradition. In examinations of "new religious movements" there is a great tendency to overstate the newness of these movements in order to highlight the current dramatic social, political, and economic changes that seem to have produced new forms of religion. In so doing, we often fail to see the myriad of ways in which modern religious organizations are actually bearers of their traditions. In the case of Foguang Shan, this is one of its "selling points." Foguang Shan presents itself as a carrier of traditional Chinese culture, which appeals to Buddhists living in Taiwan—especially those who suffer from a "mainland complex" (*dalu qingjie*) and those who live abroad in non-Chinese dominant cultures.[21]

Soka Gakkai and Foguang Shan share a vision of transforming this world through a stance of engagement with modernity. Both movements are "modern" but they offer a sophisticated balance between traditional discourses and practices, and modern technologies, values, aesthetics, and lifestyles. Despite these similarities, their respective platforms of religious truth and activism reflect the historical particulars of each movement. Soka Gakkai in Japan emerged out of a post–World War II context, in which the power of prosperity resonated with many against the devastation of losing a war. Foguang Shan materialized in Taiwan in a cultural context that embraced democracy, capitalism, and material progress over the communist ideals of mainland China. In both cases, material prosperity is viewed as a sign of social, cultural, and religious regeneration.

The Dhammakāya Temple and Modernity

The Dhammakāya Temple resembles Soka Gakkai and Foguang Shan in its positive orientation towards modernity. As the Thai economy transitioned from a traditional agricultural society to an export-oriented, industrialized, modern society in the 1970s and 1980s, the Dhammakāya Temple emerged as one of Thailand's largest and wealthiest temples by drawing its base from the urban and educated communities that benefited financially from this economic transition. While other new Thai Buddhist groups, such as Suan Mokh and Santi Asok, sought to foster an ethos of simplicity and moderation during this period of unprecedented economic prosperity and development, the Dhammakāya Temple embraced an ethos of modernity, prosperity, and personal transformation. This ethos resonates throughout the Dhammakāya Temple, through its massive, contemporary structures that occupy an impressive 2000 rai (800 acres); the unabashed display of wealth by its monastic leaders, who travel in luxury automobiles and wear imported Swiss robes; and its conspicuous honoring of generous donors with titles and special perks.

The Dhammakāya Temple began in 1970 as a satellite *samnak* (meditation center) of Wat Paknam, a well-known Mahanikāi temple in Thonburi. The founder of the Dhammakāya meditation group was Khun Yay Ubasika Chandra Khonnokyoong (1909–2000), a student of Luang Pho Sot (1884–1959), the popular and much respected abbot of Wat Paknam in Thonburi who "rediscovered" the meditation technique that leads to "knowledge of the dhammakāya" (*wicha thammakai*). In 1977, the samnak became an official *wat* (temple) within the Mahanikāi ordination lineage. Khun Yay's star meditation pupil, Phra Dhammachayo, became the Temple's first abbot, and together with Phra Tattacheevo, the assistant abbot, they helped the Temple to grow from a small off-shoot meditation center to Thailand's fastest growing temple. On Buddhist holy days, such as MakhaBucha and Wan Kathin, the Temple has drawn over 100,000 people from across the country and from around the world, and it has opened over twenty international centers in Europe, North America, the Middle East, and East Asia.

Scholars have described the Dhammakāya Temple variously as a middle-class reform movement with ties to the establishment,[22] a fundamentalistic form of Theravāda Buddhism,[23] a reaction to changing socioeconomic conditions and the conservatism of the saṅgha establishment,[24] and even a new urban religious cult.[25] Although each description has its own emphasis, they all share an approach that links the Dhammakāya Temple to a broader discussion of the emergence of new Buddhist reform movements in modern Thailand.[26] Some attribute the growth of reformist movements to the "pressures of modernization, secularization, and the integration of local societies into a worldwide economic and communications network,"[27] whereas others suggest that this growth is linked to the emergence of groups "outside of and in opposition to the traditional political establishment."[28]

Given this paradigm of change and opposition, the literature tends to emphasize the "new-ness" of the Dhammakāya Temple. For this reason the Temple is commonly classified as a new religious movement in contrast to normative Theravāda Buddhism.[29] The Dhammakāya Temple clearly resembles other new religious movements in its focus on a specialized form of practice, in this case, dhammakāya meditation.[30] The visualization method and its object, the dhammakāya, set the Temple apart from the mainstream saṅgha, which promotes standardized versions of *samatha* and *vipassanā* meditation and which endorses a traditional Theravāda interpretation of dhammakāya as the body of dhamma (the teachings of the Buddha or the sum of his perfections as a *Sammāsambuddha*, a perfectly awakened one). The Dhammakāya Temple aggressively markets its distinctive practice in Thailand and around the globe. Through the Dhammakāya Foundation, the Temple promotes its activities on the radio, television, and the Internet; on billboards; in newspapers; and through mass mailings. The Temple's proactive marketing has proven to be a resounding success as evidenced by the number of people who attend its services from around the country and the world.

While the classification of the Dhammakāya Temple as a new religious movement highlights its unique message and style, this designation brings with it two significant problems.[31] First, the classification of a religious movement as *new* necessarily infers a departure from what the community deems to be normative. This can lead to the perception that the "new religious movement" is a deviant form of the religion.[32] The Dhammakāya Temple recognizes this tendency and adamantly opposes the use of the term "new religious movement" to define it. Such a label is, moreover, inherently political for it not only classifies particular expressions of a religion as "inauthentic," but also creates a divide between that which is deemed as representative of the tradition and the

Ceremony Inside the Dhammakāya Meditation Hall. (Courtesy of the Dhammakāya Foundation.)

new religious movement. In the case of the Dhammakāya Temple, this labeling runs counter to its identity and stated goals. As we shall see, the Temple has taken great strides to ensure that it remains within the Mahanikāi fold and thereby maintains favorable relations with the establishment. The second problem created by a distinction between new religious movements and the mainstream is an obfuscation of those elements of the movement that do in fact resemble what we might classify as normative.[33] As seen in the following quote, the Dhammakāya Temple markets itself as both traditional and modern.

> The Buddhist temple traditionally has a significant role in the Thai community. The temple is a centre to teach and exemplify ethical practice that is an implicit part of everyday life.... This temple perpetuates the temple's traditional role but is characterized by adherence to the Dhammakaya tradition of meditation and adaption of traditional values to modern society.[34]

The Temple at once embraces modern technology and aesthetics while simultaneously cultivating what it considers to be *traditional* values.[35] In fact, it is this effective blending of the traditional with the modern, as seen in the Temple's meditation practice (this chapter) and merit-making (Chapter 3), that has attracted thousands upon thousands of middle-class, college-educated urban-ites to the Temple's teachings and practices.

The Dhammakāya Temple does not overtly use the language of reform, but it does seek to advance its distinctive form of Buddhist practice "to im-prove the lives of [its] followers, to strengthen the religion, and to bring pros-perity to the nation."[36] In a manner similar to Soka Gakkai and Foguang Shan, as well as to the prosperity gospels of prominent Christian evangelicals and the "health and wealth movement,"[37] the Temple links personal and communal success to the application of Buddhist truths to one's everyday activities. Tem-ple publications are replete with stories of how dhammakāya practice can help students to prepare for college entrance exams, transform wayward teens, cul-tivate confidence in professionals, and bring families together. In short, the Temple emphasizes its ability to address issues central to modern life. Temple representatives argue that while other temples in Thailand are losing support due to the inability of their monks to address the needs of a modern populace, the Dhammakāya Temple has undergone unprecedented growth.

The Dhammakāya Temple embodies modernity in its art, architecture, and marketing techniques. The Buddha image, Phra Dhammakāya, which is displayed in the Ubosot and on the Dhammakāya chedi, is distinctively

Phra Dhammakāya Image, Ubosot Hall, Dhammakāya Temple. (Photograph by Rachelle M. Scott.)

modern. It lacks the typical Thai features and styles of dress that are commonly found on Thai images. Its buildings and landscaping embrace a contemporary aesthetic, from its clean, quiet, and orderly appearance to the absence of meandering stray dogs and cats or monks smoking cigarettes openly in public.[38] The organization of the Temple's administration employs current business practices, using state-of-the-art media in its advertising campaigns. And unlike other Thai temples, lay practitioners dress in distinctive uniforms with Dhammakāya insignia or in T-shirts imprinted with popular slogans such as "world peace through inner peace."[39] The phenomenal growth of the Dhammakāya Temple effectively demonstrates how one Thai temple's efforts to "adapt traditional values to modern society" have made it central to the lives of its practitioners.

The roles and functions of Buddhist monasteries in modern Thailand have often been linked to the dramatic social, political, and economic changes of the twentieth century. Some commentators describe these changes in terms

Ubosot Hall, Dhammakāya Temple (Photograph by Rachelle M. Scott.)

A Dhammakāya Foundation Promotional Image. (Courtesy of the Dhammakāya Foundation.)

of the processes of secularization—that monasteries are increasingly being consigned to the private sphere and are therefore losing their influence in such areas as education and local politics.[40] Others emphasize that these changes reflect the renewed spirit or reformist ethos of modern Thai Buddhism.[41] Whether these changes are viewed in a negative or positive light, there is no doubt that substantial institutional changes have occurred within the Thai saṅgha over the past century and a half, and that these changes have had a profound influence on the roles and functions of temples within their broader communities. Richard O'Connor describes the institutional change in modern Thai Buddhism in terms of a shift from the influence of local temples (*wat,* Thai) within distinct communities to a saṅgha-centered religion.[42] With this institutional shift, local temples no longer serve as the educational and social

, have been superceded by national Bud-
Ays, and national rankings; and popular
exemplars but rather national icons who re-

, trend over the past few decades, it is now
mples and religious organizations such as the
o reestablish the wat-as-community model.[43] The
ouilt an international World Dhammakāya Center,
ands of practitioners within and outside of Thailand
by r̄   aditional Thai Buddhism" with an ethos of prosperity
that is per̄   to this new society. Its vision is to create a temple community in the t̄   onal sense of a *wat* as the "moral, social and symbolic
centre of a community."[44] In so doing, it partially distinguishes itself from the
saṅgha-centered mainstream by promoting its distinct practice and authorizing tradition.

Modern Reform and Religious Authority

Historians typically trace modern religious reform in Thailand back to middle
of the nineteenth century, to the reforms of King Mongkut, Rama IV (reigned
1851–68). King Mongkut spearheaded this reform through the creation of a
new ordination lineage in the Thai saṅgha, the Thammayutnikai (adhering to
the dhamma order), which was modeled after the strict practice of the Mon
tradition. As its name implies, the Thammayutnikai was founded as an alternative to the Mahanikai, the order that Mongkut characterized as those of long-
standing habit.[45] The Thammayutnikai represented a more *authentic* form of
Buddhist practice since it adhered more strictly to the monastic discipline presented in the *Vinaya*. Thammayut monks, for instance, were to eat only one
meal a day (in contrast to the two meals by Mahanikai monks), rely exclusively
on alms food, and drape their robes over both shoulders. Thammayut monks
were also expected to attain a high level of proficiency in both meditation and
scholarship, two areas where the standards among Mahanikai were thought to
be lax. In terms of preaching, Thammayut monks employed an extemporane-
ous style in the vernacular, whereas Mahanikai monks continued to use the
elite language of Pāli in standardized sermons.[46]

King Mongkut's creation of the Thammayutnikai followed an established
pattern of saṅgha reform in Theravāda Buddhism, that is, purification of the
saṅgha through a renewed adherence to the *Vinaya*. While Charles Keyes suggests that King Mongkut's reforms were "as radical a reformation of Theravada
Buddhism as that instituted by Martin Luther or John Calvin,"[47] Mongkut's
reforms were in fact consistent with the tradition's own mode of reformation,

which focused on an enhanced faithfulness to the *dhamma-vinaya*. Contrary to Keyes' implication, King Mongkut's reformist sect did not provoke the same kind of political and religious turmoil as the Protestant Reformation in Europe. In fact, the Thammayutnikai did not receive recognition as a legitimate *nikai* until the reign of King Mongkut's son, King Chulalongkorn (Rama V, reigned 1868–1910), and while the Thammayut order did grow after its founding, most men continued to be ordained as Mahanikai monks. King Mongkut's reforms did serve, however, as an impetus for the structural and educational reforms of the twentieth century, and the Thammayut order was one means for their implementation. These reforms were facilitated not only by Thammayut monks in royal temples in Bangkok, but also by Thammayut *pariyat* (scholar) monks who utilized the lineage of forest monks such as Acharn Man to establish Thammayut monasteries in northeast Thailand.[48] Their co-option of the northeastern *thutong* (*dhutanga*, Pāli) tradition by Thammayut officials, however, was not a simple or unproblematic undertaking. Regional differences and alliances made religious reform a long process, and the prejudice against regional practices did not help to facilitate the process.

The reign of King Chulalongkorn brought with it substantive changes in the religious as well as political, social, and economic spheres. This was a time of nation-building, and saṅgha reform was one index of and vehicle for the centralization of national authority and identity in Bangkok. As Tambiah notes in his analysis of modern saṅgha reform, political stabilization in the nineteenth and twentieth centuries led to the increased regulation of the saṅgha by political authorities.[49] The Saṅgha Act of 1902 "provided for a hierarchical ecclesiastical structure with positions of ecclesiastical governor generals, provincial governors, district governors, all filled by monks. This hierarchy paralleled the civil administrative structure."[50] King Chulalongkorn himself appointed the major abbots at the royal temples in Bangkok, whereas lower level government officials approved the appointments of lower abbots made by ecclesiastical officers. The Act also specified that monks were to be registered and have fixed residences. Tambiah describes this creation of a church-like organization for the regulation of the saṅgha as one indication of the trend towards political subordination of the saṅgha.[51]

In modern Thailand, as in earlier centuries, Buddhist doctrine and practice is not only diverse—it is often polemical. Since 1902 there have been attempts by the national government and ecclesiastical authorities to centralize religious authority or, rather, to homogenize Buddhist practice through a reformist platform. With the stated purpose of improving knowledge of the *dhamma-vinaya*, religious authorities implemented a national ecclesiastical exam system in 1911. This exam was based primarily on the textbooks written by Prince Wachirayan (1860–1921), the half brother of King Chulalongkorn, head of the *Thammayut* order and Supreme Patriarch.[52] These books included

Putthasatsana Suphasit (select Buddhist sayings), *Phuttaprawat* (the life of the Buddha), *Winayamuk* (entrance to the *Vinaya*), and the *Nawakowat* (instructions for newly ordained monks and novices). Prince Wachirayan's interpretation of Theravāda doctrine, therefore, functioned as a modern equivalent to Buddhaghosa's fifth century CE masterpiece, the *Visuddhimagga* (Path of Purification), which similarly standardized Buddhist orthodoxy and orthopraxy. According to one biographer, Prince Wachirayan's texts filled an important void; at that time there was a shortage of bhikkhus who possessed "a sound basis of knowledge or a reasonable faith consistent with the spirit of Buddhism." The biographer continues by describing Buddhist education at the time of Prince Wachirayan:

> Buddhist education was then rather an individual affair, with each taking the subjects he liked in the way he pleased. Most were satisfied with what had been traditionally done and were practically unable to distinguish the special characteristics of Buddhism from other faiths. Thus in many cases they preferred only the superficial aspect of the truth, with a consequent laxity in Vinaya and ignorant distortion of the Dhamma. Even the way bhikkhus preached was haphazard and the language used was generally too old or too high to appeal intelligently to the ordinary mind. The examination procedure in Buddhist education was still conducted orally and individually, there being as yet no written examination.[53]

From this biographer's perspective, Prince Wachirayan's orthodoxy rectified the heretical and decadent tendencies of the saṅgha.

As mentioned earlier, the implementation of saṅgha reforms in the countryside proved to be a daunting task for the Bangkok officials. In a book on the forest tradition in modern Thailand, Kamala Tiyavanich paints a convincing portrait of the tensions between modern establishment Buddhism and regional Buddhist traditions.[54] In the northeast, saṅgha officials from Bangkok were highly critical of the practices and way of life of most northeastern monks. "Regional monks organized festivals, worked on construction projects in the wat, tilled the fields, kept cattle or horses, carved boats, played musical instruments during the Bun Phrawet festival, taught martial arts—and still were considered respectable *bhikkhu* (monks) all the while."[55] Saṅgha officials from Bangkok viewed these practices as improper and not consistent with the mode of life outlined in the *Vinaya*. Saṅgha officials also criticized the preaching methods of many northeastern monks. In one report cited by Kamala, a saṅgha inspector reported that "most monks preach about alms giving, generosity, precepts, and moral conduct. Basically, the monks' sermons consist of jātakas, especially the Great Birth story."[56] As noted in Chapter 1, the *Mahāchat* (the

Great Birth) is the penultimate birth story of the Buddha as Prince Vessantara, who perfects the virtue of generosity (*dāna*). The popularity of this jātaka, as well as the emphasis on jātaka stories in sermons, was indicative of regional Buddhism in the north, south, and central regions as well. In general, reformist saṅgha officials viewed these sermons on jātaka stories as more of a form of entertainment rather than as expositions on dhamma. Kamala notes how the reformers insisted that "sermons be sober and didactic," and she suggests that such reforms engendered sermons that were "abstract, dry, alien, and irrelevant" to the lives of lay people. The result was that attendance at sermons "dwindled to a ritual of merit making."[57]

This clash of ideas over proper monastic practice led to conflicts over the location of Buddhist authority in the twentieth century. Reformers sought to diffuse this problem by implementing a policy that forbade local abbots from ordaining novices or monks without the approval of a Bangkok-appointed preceptor; constructing a new set of symbols to judge the merits of a particular monk, including honorific fans and ecclesiastical titles; and judging the efficacy of particular abbots based on the size and cleanliness of their wats, the number of monks under their tutelage who passed the *naktham* and Pāli exams, and their adherence to the Bangkok ritual calendar.[58] Subsequent saṅgha legislation also sought to address the issues of authority. The 1941 Act democratized saṅgha authority by locating power within an assembly of monks, while the 1962 Act reverted back to a hierarchical structure with the Supreme Patriarch (*Sangharat*, Thai; *Saṅgharāja*, Pāli) as the central authority. Over the past two decades progressive monks and Thai intellectuals have increasingly called for saṅgha reform. Contemporary reformist rhetoric focuses on the feudalistic characteristics of current establishment Buddhism and its inability to address modern needs and problems. Like other reformist movements in Theravāda history, modern establishment Buddhism authorized a new Buddhist orthodoxy and a new means of propagation. In the modern Thai context, this authorizing project entailed the development of a new structure (administrative organizations), a new voice of authority (a national *Saṅgharāja*), and a new standard for measuring orthodoxy (national exams and ranking system). While pervasive, these reforms did not eradicate regional differences or bases of power. In fact, there were movements that rejected these national reforms. Critical responses to modern establishment Buddhism did not simply offer contrasting interpretations of dhamma; they endorsed alternative sources for religious authority.

In northern Thailand during the 1920s and 1930s, for example, a movement arose around Khrūbā Srivijaya (1878–1939), a well-respected monk who was thought to possess extraordinary merit (*phu mi bun*) and saintliness (*nakbun*). Khrūbā Srivijaya rejected many of the reforms instituted by the Bangkok-based national saṅgha, including the new laws regarding who was authorized to serve as a preceptor in ordinations, and favored maintaining the distinctive regional traditions of northern Thailand.[59] He eventually acquiesced to the authority of Bangkok after facing the possibility of a religious schism and regional revolt, but in exchange the Bangkok-based national saṅgha authorities "tacitly allowed the northern Thai to carry out many of their traditional practices within their local communities."[60] Similar responses to centralized authority and the homogenization of Buddhist practice occurred throughout the periphery of the country.

Postmodernity and Religion in Thailand

The religious reforms of the nineteenth and twentieth centuries, while effective in molding monastic curriculum and establishing a new bureaucracy and a new monastic ideal, could not completely eliminate distinctive doctrines, practices, styles of preaching, or sources of authority in Thailand nor could it stop new religious trends from emerging, including many that did not cater to the goals and interests of establishment Buddhism. Over the past fifty years, a number of new religious trends have emerged that reflect a postmodern orientation towards the saṅgha and Thai religion. In varying ways, these trends directly or indirectly challenge the hegemonic authority of modern establishment Buddhism and its version of Buddhist religiosity.[61] These trends, such as the cult of amulets and spirit-mediums, offer modes of religiosity that combine "tradition" with "modernity" in ways that reflect new historical circumstances. In some cases, these trends reflect a dismissal of the overly intellectualized Buddhism of the establishment in favor of the tradition's rich history of charisma, power, and this-worldly benefits.

As early as the 1960s, for instance, urban lay Buddhists began to patronize monks in the Thai periphery whose authority and supra-normal powers (*iddhi*, Pāli) stemmed from their skills in meditation and ascetic practices (a traditional source of authority within the tradition), not from their level of education or title within the centralized system. "These saints, who had lived and worked in humble circumstances on the periphery of Thai society and territory, received the adulation and prostrations of the urbanites of the country's capital, which was the hub of the Thai polity and society and the central arena where power and wealth were won and lost."[62] What is particularly interesting about this trend is that it displays a linkage between urban lay religiosity and forest monastic religiosity. Tambiah suggests that this relationship operates on two levels of discourse, "the charisma of the saint, who in transcending the world is able to shower upon it his virtue, and the gratification of desires on the part of the laymen, for whom prosperity and fortune approach the logic of a zero-sum game."[63] In their search for charismatic power, these lay urbanites patronize *patipattidhura* or practice-oriented monks rather than *pariyattidhura* or study-oriented monks. The patronage of forest monks is not a new phenomenon within the tradition (although the degree of patronage and prestige has varied in different historical contexts), but what is significantly new in contemporary Thailand is a sharp divide between the life of a typical urban lay Buddhist, which reflects Thailand's place within a new global economy, and the idealized life of the forest saint, who is "marketed" as wholly otherworldly. One reason for the popularity of contemporary forest monks may be the gradual erosion of the establishment's political power and prestige that has produced a need for external sources of authority and power.[64] Another reason may be the type of power that these monks transmit. When they or their followers distribute amulets, they become sources of power for personal and material enrichment. They facilitate better lay lives through their own acts of renunciation, and in the process become desired recipients of patronage.[65]

Urban Buddhists have not only patronized forest monks during this period of economic development and prosperity, they have also fostered the growth of urban spirit-medium cults, which draw from the long history of spirit-medium beliefs and practices in Southeast Asian societies.[66] In contemporary Thailand, these cults reflect the diversity of Thai religious belief and practice. These include the cults of Hindu gods and goddesses (Brahma is particularly popular in Thailand), Chinese deities (which are popular within the Sino-Thai population), royal spirits (King Chulalongkorn and Queen Suriyothai), local guardian and tutelary spirits, and the spirits of famous Buddhist saints.[67] While spirit beliefs and practices have had a long history in the region, the urban-based cults of today cater to the lives of individuals living in large cities with diverse populations. The cult of Chulalongkorn (Rama V), for instance, reflects the contemporary global economy of Bangkok; patrons believe that his spirit will grant them beneficial rewards, including "a profitable business, good health, and a happy family."[68] Moreover, the diversity of spirit-cults reflects the cosmopolitanism of Bangkok, with populations from all over Thailand as well as China and India. The popular cults of Guanyin, Brahma, and Ganesh have developed in part due to the ethnocultural assimilation of Chinese and Indians into the religious field of Bangkok.[69] The authority of these spirit cults relates directly to the powers of individual mediums, not to any centralized religious organization.

The enormous popularity of forest monks, amulets, and spirit mediums in contemporary Thai religion testifies to the diversity of Thai religiosity. In contemporary Thailand, many monks adhere to the vision of monastic life cultivated within the system of establishment Buddhism: They study the monastic curriculum, pass exams, and receive honorific titles. At the same time, other monks pursue alternate religious paths and goals—even while operating within modern establishment Buddhism. Within this space of the postmodern Thai saṅgha, we see multiple visions of monastic life. Phra Phayom Kalyano, the abbot of Wat Suankaew in Nonthaburi is outspoken, good humored, and gravely concerned about the poor in Thailand; his temple operates an orphanage, a flea market, and a number of other charitable projects. Phra Khru Wiboon, the abbot of Wat Hua Krabue, teaches his novices the practical skills of car mechanics and a lesson in caring for one's possessions at his temple's Mercedes Benz' restoration project.[70] Achan Cha, a famous monk in the *dhutanga* (ascetic) forest tradition in northeastern Thailand, has inspired a large following in Europe and America as well as in Thailand. These faces, among many others, offer distinctive visions of Buddhist religiosity in the postmodern period.

Sources for Dhammakāya Authority and Practice

It is against this backdrop of modern Buddhist reform and postmodern Thai religion that we must situate the emergence of the Dhammakāya Temple. The Dhammakāya Temple has had to negotiate a space for its distinctive form of Buddhist practice within a religious landscape dominated by the authorizing power of establishment Buddhism. The homogenization of religious doctrine and practice that was put forward by the establishment sought to eradicate difference in its creation of a national Thai saṅgha. The Dhammakāya Temple, however, has effectively marketed its distinctive practices, teachings, and authorizing tradition within this climate of religious homogenization. It has done so by strategically maintaining relations with the establishment, while simultaneously advancing its own distinct identity. It embraces national symbols of authority: Large billboards of the royal family are on public display in the Dhammakāya assembly hall as are photographs of Phra Dhammachayo, the Dhammakāya abbot, receiving an honorific fan and higher ecclesiastical title from the present Thai king, King Rama IX. The Dhammakāya Temple regularly invites high-ranking monks and monks from other temples to participate in Dhammakāya activities. Dhammakāya monks also actively participate in the national *naktam* examinations, thereby demonstrating their support for the establishment's authority to rank monks within the hierarchy of the modern Thai saṅgha. The Dhammakāya Temple does not overtly use the language of reform, but negotiates a delicate balance between maintaining beneficial relations with the establishment and fostering its own version of Buddhist authority, doctrine, and practice.

The success of the Dhammakāya Temple is due, in large part, to its ability to market its distinctive form of Buddhist religiosity to urban religious consumers. It taps into postmodern forms of urban religiosity by bringing the forest tradition to the suburbs. As with many meditation reform movements in South and Southeast Asia, the Temple effectively laicizes the meditation tradition of monastic practice.[71] Whereas patrons of the urban spirit cults of forest monks focus on the ascetic power of these past meditation masters, Dhammakāya practitioners cultivate their own power through meditation practice.[72] This power enables them to succeed in a variety of ways—by cultivating religious insight, procuring practical benefits, and even developing supra-normal powers. Through the exclusive emphasis on dhammakāya practice, the Temple effectively legitimizes its own lineage and indices of authority within space of contemporary Thai Buddhism.

The authorizing tradition of the Dhammakāya Temple begins with the re-discovery of the dhammakāya meditation technique and its subsequent spread through key exemplars within the tradition. Three figures occupy a prominent place in this lineage of Dhammakāya authority: Luang Pho Sot, the monk who "rediscovered" the dhammakāya meditation tradition; Khun Yay Ubasika Chan, a student of Luang Pho Sot and the creative force behind the construction of the Dhammakāya Temple; and Phra Dhammachayo, Khun Yay's most favored student and abbot of the Temple. Each of these individuals serves as a model of and for Dhammakāya perfection. Each is an exemplar of dhammakāya practice having reached the highest levels of dhammakāya meditation and attained perfect knowledge of the dhammakāya (wicha thammakai); their embodiment of perfection serves as a model for the personal development of others. The biographical narratives of Luang Pho Sot, Khun Yay, and Phra Dhammachayo emphasize their roles as influential teachers within the Dhammakāya tradition, thereby mirroring the Buddha's own career as a teacher. Their biographies also embody tales of miraculous occurrences, as well as supra-normal powers and knowledge that are at the very heart of the Thai tradition of Buddhist saints. In fact, Khun Yay's ability to travel to the various realms of existence through the power of her meditation mirrors the enormously popular tales of Phra Malai, whose stories of cosmological travels are well known throughout the country. The preeminent place of these three Dhammakāya adepts within the Dhammakāya tradition is apparent as one walks through the Temple grounds: books of their teachings line the shelves of the Dhammakāya bookstore; large memorials and golden images have been erected to honor the lives of Luang Pho Sot and Khun Yay; and the weekly sermons of Phra Dhammachayo are broadcasted over the Internet and on satellite television. Merchandise bearing the likenesses of all three is abundant and available for purchase in the Temple store and in the assembly hall on Sundays and special occasions. Dhammakāya practitioners know the biographies of these saintly figures, and these items serve as reminders and symbols of their esteemed status within the Dhammakāya tradition.

Luang Pho Sot and the Founding of the Dhammakāya Tradition

The biography of Luang Pho Sot (Phra Monkolthepmuni) tells the story of a young monk, who in his determination to realize ultimate truth, rediscovers a method of meditation taught by the Buddha that had been lost to Buddhists for centuries. While Luang Pho Sot's biography emphasizes his intellect and his mastery of Pāli, it is clear that his authority in the Dhammakāya tradition stems from the knowledge he derived from his meditation practice rather than from his formal academic studies. He died more than a decade before the foundation of the Dhammakāya Temple in Pathum Thani, but his life and teachings play a central role in the Temple's sense of its identity, history, and mandate to propagate wicha thammakai.

Luang Pho Sot was born on October 10, 1884 in the village of Songpinong in Suphanburi province in central Thailand. According to the biography published by the Dhammakāya Foundation, his birth was distinct because unlike other babies he did not cry—"Not even a whimper was to pass his lips, because he had been born to dry the tears of humanity."[73] The biography describes him as an exceptionally alert and intelligent child who possessed an uncanny aversion to being touched by women (perhaps due to previous lives as a monk). He was a determined youth who learned quickly.

> Luang [Pho] was a true auto-didact, and never needed prodding from anyone. Such ability is not a skill developed in a single lifetime but is the fruit of many lifetime's pursuit of wisdom, many lifetimes accruing the merit that purifies the mind. This same gift subsequently enabled him to discover *Vijja Dhammakāya*, lost for so many thousands of years, without any instruction or instructor and mirabile dictu, to instruct and initiate others in *Vijja Dhammakāya*![74]

He ordained as a novice in 1903 at Wat Songpinong after escaping a near fatal encounter with a group of river pirates. During these early years as a monastic, he studied Pāli, memorized verses for chanting, and practiced meditation. Eventually Luang Pho Sot desired a more profound understanding of the Buddha's teachings, which led him to study at Wat Phra Cetuphon in Bangkok. While there, he pursued Pāli studies and meditation training. On days when he was not studying, he would travel to other temples with renowned teachers of meditation in order to receive instruction in meditation. In a manner similar to the wanderings of Prince Siddhattha after his great renunciation, Luang Pho Sot would go to each teacher and learn all that he could, and then he would search for another. When he reached a high level of proficiency in his Pāli studies, he decided to devote all of his attention to meditation practice.[75]

One day, during his morning meditation practice, he vowed that he would not waiver in his practice until he had realized a portion of the ultimate truth taught by the Buddha. Having made this vow, he found his mind to be unusually agitated and the pain in his legs caused by extensive meditation more difficult to endure. When he resolved to detach himself from the pain and agitation through concentration, his mind became still and focused on the center of his body, at which point, "He perceived a bright clear shining sphere of Dhamma. The size of the sphere of Dhamma was equal to the yolk of an egg. The experience [that] filled his whole body was one of inexplicable bliss [that] rinsed away all agony."[76] Afterwards, his face beamed with the glow of spiritual success, and other monks even inquired why he continued to smile even while eating lunch. In the biography we are told that Luang Pho Sot remained in a state of bliss as the sphere of dhamma was firmly established at the center of his body. Later that evening, as he meditated on the sphere, it became clearer and brighter.

> Going yet deeper he could see within each sphere of Dhamma bodies of hidden dimensions of himself. Then, at the end of the succession covering all dimensions of himself, he recovered the key to understanding human nature through all of its countless dimensions. At the innermost part of every human being's nature, nested deep within the myriad of multi-dimensional bodies, there exists the body of the Buddha. This we call the Dhammakāya. It is of the form of the Buddha sitting deep in meditation. The topknot of the Dhammakāya is a lotus bud, beautifully clear and pure. Suddenly, this Buddha spoke in a resonant voice, "That is right!" Having spoken, the mouth of the Dhammakāya immediately closed again. The delight overwhelmed him.[77]

Shortly after his "rediscovery" of the Dhammakāya technique, he began his long career as an instructor of meditation.

In 1916, Luang Pho Sot became abbot of Wat Paknam Bhasicharoen, a royal temple in Thonburi. His first activities involved improving the discipline of monks at the temple. In his first sermon as abbot, he told the monks that while many of them had been ordained for years, they "still have insufficient knowledge to teach—all of you have done is clung like a parasite to the religion without doing anything of use to others."[78] Improving the discipline of the monks was an effort that was not universally supported by patrons of Wat Paknam. According to Luang Pho Sot's biography, those laypersons who conducted illicit business at the temple were especially resistant to the idea of monastic reform. This resistance led to an attempt on Luang Pho's life. One night an assassin tried to shoot Luang Pho Sot, but he succeeded in only piercing his robes. The biography states that it appeared as though the bullet recognized the importance of Luang Pho, and it refused to harm him.[79] While this might have frightened some, Luang Pho Sot was more determined than ever to reform the practice at Wat Paknam.

Reform at Wat Paknam included a renewed commitment to practice, especially meditation. Luang Pho Sot taught formal sessions on Sundays, Thursdays, and Buddhist holy days to the resident monks, nuns, and lay people. In order to accommodate the large number of practitioners who wanted to meditate for long periods of time, Luang Pho Sot built a meditation hall for his advanced pupils. During the Second World War, these pupils meditated in twelve-hour shifts, and after the war, they were divided into three teams that meditated in six shifts of four-hour duration. The biography states that this "perpetual meditation schedule was unprecedented in that it allowed the wisdom of Dhammakāya to be verified again and again."[80] It also states that Luang Pho Sot used the collective power of this meditation group for specific purposes including the removal of a large crystal ball from the earth and the diversion of Allied bombs during World War II. One story relates that Luang Pho Sot realized the Allies were planning on dropping an atomic bomb on Bangkok (because of the large number of Japanese in the area), but they miraculously changed their opinion after Luang Pho Sot and some of his advanced pupils meditated unceasingly for seven days.

Over the years Luang Pho Sot's reputation as an instructor of meditation grew, as did the stories of miraculous events at Wat Paknam. During the war, for instance, it was believed that the temple was immune from Allied bombings thanks to the power of Luang Pho Sot. Luang Pho also gained a reputation for performing miraculous healings. In fact, the demand for his healing services became so great that he started to conduct "long-distance healings." Rather than having each sick person visit him in person, he encouraged some of his more distant followers to send letters describing their illnesses in order to aid more people within a shorter period of time. He was also renowned for his prophesies. Through his own realization of the Dhammakāya, it was said that he was able to discern what others were thinking, the quality and quantity of their deeds, and if or when they would fully realize the Dhammakāya. Luang Pho's method of meditation and the tales of miraculous events, however, did raise questions outside of Wat Paknam. Kamala attributes most of this suspicion and criticism to the fact that, because he "sought to popularize meditation, a practice that no official temple followed at the time, he made enemies both of the higher-level administrators and local monks. His superior, a Mahānikāi elder, saw him as going against the saṅgha authorities."[81] The Dhammakāya Temple biography attributes the vehemence of the conservative criticisms of Luang Pho Sot to the profundity of his teachings—that his contemporaries had an incomplete knowledge or a vague understanding of the dhamma and were unable to recognize the truth of Luang Pho's teachings.

This strategy of emphasizing the esoteric character of truth, which is accessible only to a few exceptional adepts, is currently used by the Dhammakāya Temple to defend the teachings of Phra Dhammachayo, the current abbot of the Dhammakāya Temple, against charges of heresy. Prior to his death in 1959, Luang Pho Sot prophesied that Wat Paknam would become a popular site of Buddhist practice and ordered his attendants not to cremate his body, but embalm it so that he "could continue to ensure the prosperity of the temple—nurturing those who lived on by attracting pilgrims to visit Wat Paknam and pay homage."[82] While Luang Pho's biography and teachings play a prominent role in the Dhammakāya Temple's history, identity, and practice, many Dhammakāya practitioners have never paid respects to his body at Wat Paknam. This speaks to the tenuous relationship between Wat Paknam and the Dhammakāya Temple and to the Temple's predilection towards emphasizing the continuation of the tradition as it manifested itself through the teachings and practices of Khun Yay and Phra Dhammachayo. In order to acknowledge the centrality of Luang Pho's life to the history of the Dhammakāya Temple and the tradition of dhammakāya meditation, however, the Temple completed a large memorial hall to Luang Pho Sot in 2002.

Golden Image of Luang Pho Sot and Luang Pho Sot Memorial. (Courtesy of the Dhammakāya Foundation.)

This memorial hall is one of the three principal sites of the World Dhammakāya Center. Photographs of it are reproduced on the Foundation's website with the accompanying text:

> Also known as Luang Pu Wat Paknam[83] (the abbot of the Paknam Temple), the Most Venerable had dedicated himself to the study, practice and teaching of meditation. His famous concept that stillness of the mind is the key to material and spiritual success has helped many to discover the purpose of life and to experience inner peace and self-sustaining happiness.
>
> Equipped with state-of-the-art air- and temperature- control systems, the shrine is an oasis for calm for those seeking a refreshing retreat and spiritual relaxation—within just an hour drive from the capital city. The shrine contains seven meditation rooms enough to seat 350 people and a center chapel that can accommodate 1,500 people. At the center of the shrine is a stone altar supporting the solid gold statue of Ven. Phramongkolthepmuni, who had brought back the Dhammakaya (the body of enlightenment) lost to the world over 2,000 years, i.e., about 500 years after the Nibbana (passing) of the Lord Buddha.
>
> The golden statue is a tribute to Phramongkolthepmuni's rediscovery and dissemination of the knowledge that Dhammakaya or the body of enlightenment is naturally present in every human being. Thus, it is a source of ultimate happiness any human being can experience regardless of one's personal circumstances, race and religious belief.[84]

As with Buddha images in Thailand, the golden statue of Luang Pho Sot serves as an object of veneration and meditation, as well as a vehicle for the mediation of his power. Dhammakāya practitioners believe that he (or his Dhammakāya power) continues to influence the lives of the faithful, as when an image of Luang Pho Sot replaced the sun in the reported "miracle in the sky" in 1998. His influence also continues in the tradition of dhammakāya meditation, which was passed from him to Khun Yay Ubasika Chan.

Khun Yay Ubasika Chan: "First among Disciples, Second to None"

According to Temple publications, Khun Yay Ubasika Chan was Luang Pho Sot's most gifted disciple, and prior to his death he instructed her to carry on the tradition of dhammakāya meditation to others.[85] After his death, many of his students left Wat Paknam, but Khun Yay remained in order to continue teaching meditation and to care for Khun Yay Tong Sook, her first meditation teacher. When her accommodations became too small for all of her students, she and her most devoted pupils founded a *samnak* (meditation dwelling) in 1970 on the grounds of what was to become the Dhammakāya Temple (Wat Phra Thammakai). She wished to foster the growth of the Dhammakāya tradition by establishing a place for meditation, "a refuge in the midst of a turbulent world," a place to "train men to be truly men, to train true men to be monks, and to train monks to be truly monks...."[86]

As with the story of Luang Pho Sot, everyone at the Dhammakāya Temple knows the story of Khun Yay and her special gift for meditation.[87] She was born in 1909 in Nakornchaisri district of Nakorn Pathom province. Stories from her childhood focus on her turbulent relationship with her alcoholic father, as it was this relationship that eventually led her to dhammakāya meditation. In one of these stories we are told that Khun Yay's father cursed her with deafness for her next five hundred births after she attempted to defend her mother during an argument between her parents. Her father died before Khun Yay could formally ask for forgiveness;[88] as a result, she worried about the

Khun Yay Ubasika Chan. (Courtesy of the Dhammakāya Foundation.)

power of her father's curse to affect her present and futures lives. Her fear drove her to find a way to visit her father in his next birth and therefore grant her an opportunity to ask for his forgiveness. It was this motivation that led Khun Yay to practice dhammakāya meditation in 1927. She wanted to learn more about the dhammakāya technique because it was reputed to lead to special powers, including the ability to travel to the various levels of rebirth and to communicate with the beings that dwell there. When Khun Yay met Luang Pho Sot for the first time in 1935, she was granted access to his advanced meditation group without having to take the usual tests that measure spiritual abilities. According to her biography, Luang Pho Sot did not require her to take these tests because he immediately recognized Khun Yay's abilities: He knew that she would become his greatest disciple—"first among many, second to none."

Because of Khun Yay's inherent spiritual ability, it was not long before she attained the highest levels of dhammakāya meditation. This ability enabled her to visit her father in one of the Buddhist hells, where she asked for and received forgiveness. Following this episode, Khun Yay quickly gained a reputation as an especially skilled meditator who could assist other families in transferring merit to their deceased loved ones. If, for example, a family member was languishing in one of the realms of hell, Khun Yay would visit the suffering relative and transfer the family's accumulated merit to him or her; this act of merit transference would ensure release from the innumerable torments of hell. According to Phra Dhammachayo, the abbot of the Dhammakāya Temple, Khun Yay could move as easily among the various realms of existence as she could move from building to building within the Temple grounds.[89]

In addition to these extraordinary abilities, Khun Yay was also known to possess the gift of special knowledge (*abhiññā*, Pāli). Through her meditation practice, she could access the karmic history of other people (see their present and past lives), which helped them to understand their present circumstances. According to one story, Khun Yay told a man during his first visit to see her that he should stop gambling. This infuriated the man who reasoned that his wife had told Khun Yay about his proclivity for gambling. His wife insisted that she had not said a word to Khun Yay about his gambling or any other problem; in fact, that evening was the first time that she had ever spoken with Khun Yay. Another anecdote describes a man who came to visit Khun Yay after he had an unfathomable dream that had left him anxious and nervous. While sleeping outside on a porch, he dreamt of smoke arising from beneath the porch and transforming into a human figure. After meditating for a few minutes, Khun Yay told the man that he had seen a *preta* (a ghost). This preta was a relative named Rasamee who had been reborn as a preta because he had stolen money from a temple in his former life. The man refused to believe Khun

Yay's interpretation of his dream, insisting that he had no relative by that name. Many months later he returned to Wat Paknam and admitted to Khun Yay that he had discovered the relative she had named, who was known to have cheated a temple in the past. He apologized to her for doubting her abilities and thanked her for helping him.[90]

Khun Yay's biography also tells us that she had a far-reaching reputation as an instructor of meditation, which is what drew a young Chaiyabun Suddhipol, the future abbot of the Dhammakāya Temple, to Wat Paknam in 1963. He came because he had heard stories about an especially gifted and powerful nun. When they met, Khun Yay told the young Chaiyaboon that she had been expecting him, a statement that alluded to his role as the future heir of the Dhammakāya tradition. These initial meetings at Wat Paknam led to a thirty-year relationship as teacher and pupil and to the founding of today's Dhammakāya Temple. When the facilities at Wat Paknam became too small to accommodate Khun Yay's meditation classes, Khunying Prayad Prattayaponsavisudhadhipbodi donated 196 rai of land (approximately eighty acres) in Pathum Thani for the purpose of constructing a new meditation center. Khun Yay, together with Phra Dhammachayo, who had ordained in 1969 following his graduation from Kasetsart University, worked together to gradually transform a relatively small meditation center into the Dhammakāya Temple (Wat Phra Thammakai). The center became an official wat when Princess Maha Chakri Sirindhorn laid the foundation stone for the creation of an *ubosot* (ordination hall) in 1979. The ubosot was completed in 1982 and consecrated with the placement of *sima* (boundary) stones in 1985.

Over the next three decades, Khun Yay continued to teach meditation to her disciples and to facilitate fund-raising for Temple projects. A golden statue of her was cast in January 1998 to commemorate her contributions to the Temple and the spread of the dhammakāya method. Her biography reads:

> Khun Yay was the one who should get all the credit. She was illiterate, but knew everything. She was the best one who knew how to control all situations due to Khun Yay's capabilities and her power to manage things at the right time. Thus, she was the beloved one and the great leader to all her disciples, no one could ever be compared to her. We can proudly say that Wat Phra Dhammakaya's establishment was completed because of Khun Yay's support and guidance.[91]

In fact, when funding was in short supply, it was Khun Yay who "asked the Buddha for money" and who received it in return. In one story, Phra Tatthacheevo, the assistant abbot of the Temple, went to Khun Yay to express his concern about the lack of money for the Temple's building projects. She told him not to worry, and then she meditated for an extended period of time. When Phra Tattacheevo returned to the construction site, a man was waiting for him; he was there to donate 30,000 baht to the Temple since this was his father's dying wish. Phra Tattacheevo then declared: "Khun Yay was always right. The money she saw existed, both in meditation and reality, due to her wish."[92] Not only does this remarkable story relay the important role that Khun Yay played in fund-raising, it reflects the power of her meditation, which, as we have seen, is a dominant theme within her biography.

When Khun Yay died in September of 2000, the Temple delayed her cremation for over a year in order to allow disciples to pay their respects to her and to make merit on her behalf.[93] The Dhammakāya Foundation published articles by and about Khun Yay in their publication, *Anuphap haeng bun* (The Miracle of Merit), and when her cremation occurred on February 3, 2002, attendance at the Temple surpassed 200,000. The reverence paid to Khun Yay during her lifetime and after her death is noteworthy given the fact that she was a female renunciant in a Buddhist culture that does not recognize contemporary nuns as full-fledged members of the Buddhist monastic order. The *bhikkhunī* order was never established in Thailand and, because it had

Golden Image of Khun Yay Ubasika Chan. (Courtesy of the Dhammakāya Foundation.)

Procession of Golden Image of Khun Yay. (Courtesy of the Dhammakāya Foundation.)

disappeared from other Theravāda countries, contemporary Theravāda nuns are afforded neither the religious nor the social status granted to their male counterparts.[94] In Thailand they are not classified as "religious persons" legally; as a result they do not receive financial support from the government. It is common to see exemplary monks revered as modern-day saints in Thailand, but Khun Yay is the only female ascetic to receive such adulation from a large congregation of practitioners. Her religious status derives from both her piety and purity of mind. Practitioners highlight Khun Yay's illiteracy in order to emphasize how her extensive knowledge of the dhamma stemmed from practice, not from academic training. It was due to her exemplary meditation skills that she was the one chosen by Luang Pho Wat Paknam to pass down wicha thammakai to the next generation. From the perspective of the Dhammakāya Temple, she was both the teacher of the Temple's most beloved abbot, Phra Dhammachayo, and the impetus behind the construction of the Temple itself. To commemorate her contributions to the Dhammakāya community, the Temple constructed a memorial hall for Khun Yay from 2002 to 2003, which serves as both a memorial of her life as well as a place of meditation. As in the case of Luang Pho Sot's memorial hall, a golden image of Khun Yay has been placed there to honor her role as a teacher of wicha thammakai and to recognize her advanced skills in meditation.

Khun Yay Memorial. (Courtesy of the Dhammakāya Foundation.)

Phra Dhammachayo and the Rise of the Dhammakāya Temple

Khun Yay's dedication and meditation skills were not the only forces behind the creation of the Dhammakāya Temple. The enormous financial success of the Temple is due, in large part, to the vision of the abbot, Phra Dhammachayo, and the assistant abbot, Phra Thattacheevo. According to the Foundation's website, Phra Dhammachayo was the one who wished to create a temple large enough to accommodate practitioners from around the world. The Temple displays a photo of the young Phra Dhammachayo sitting in a lotus position, looking out upon a barren field that would eventually become the location of the Dhammakāya Temple (the photo is also published on their Web site). The caption under the photo reads, "Ven. Dhammajayo Bhikkhu envisions a future centre for World Peace (1969)."

　　　Phra Dhammachayo, the abbot of the Dhammakāya Temple, has been the face of the Temple since its creation. Like Luang Pho Sot and Khun Yay's biographies, Phra Dhammachayo's narrative reads as a religious version of a rags-to-riches story, although the young Chaiyaboon had far more opportunities for formal education than either Luang Pho Sot or Khun Yay.[95] In fact, stories of Phra Dhammachayo's childhood emphasize his exceptional intellectual abilities and determination to succeed. This dual emphasis also characterizes his early adulthood, as he studied for his bachelor's degree in business from Kesetsart University (one of Thailand's leading private universities) and simultaneously embarked upon meditation practice under the tutelage of Khun Yay. Education, therefore, played a prominent role in his biography alongside his "natural" abilities for meditation. Perhaps this helps to explain the Temple's building design: Rather than creating a traditionally inspired temple with wooden structures and Sukhothai-style images and stūpas, Phra Dhammachayo envisioned a modern temple for a modern era. His modern view of Buddhist life extended to religious practice, in that he has always focused on the practical benefits of meditation within contemporary life—helping to improve grades, facilitating harmony within families, overcoming addiction, and securing desirable employment. In this respect, Phra Dhammachayo's view of meditation practice resembles the new lay meditation movements in Sri Lanka and elsewhere, such as the popular insight meditation movement of S. N. Goenka, which focus on the health benefits of meditation.[96]

In addition to his modern education and view of Buddhist meditation, Phra Dhammachayo's life story also includes elements that suggest the traditional renderings of spiritual eminence. For instance, the abbot maintains a distance between himself and his congregation. Whereas the biographies of Luang Pho Wat Paknam and Khun Yay are full of their personal interactions with common, everyday practitioners, Phra Dhammachayo sets himself apart from the ordinary. Only a few high-ranking practitioners are able to converse directly with him. He does not eat with his fellow monks, nor does he receive ordinary guests into his living quarters. His instruction in meditation is always from a distance, and he is typically elevated and enclosed within a plastic shield. This spatial separation enhances the popular image of his being extraordinary, as does his physical appearance. One government official who, after seeing Phra Dhammachayo for the first time, stated:

> His carriage was magnificent, his complexion clear, clean, and radiantly glowing beneath the yellow robe. The attractiveness of his appearance ... filled me with such joy that tears flowed without my realizing it. ... It is because the Luang Phau has amassed such great merit that his complexion appears more radiant than that of another.[97]

Phra Dhammachayo is described as a man of "great personal attractiveness," who embodies charisma in the Weberian sense of "exceptional sanctity, heroism, or exemplary character" as well as the Thai notion of a *phu mi bun*, a person who possesses merit. In Dhammakāya terms, Phra Dhammachayo's appearance reflects his inner peace (*khwam ngiap sangop*) as well as his special status as the heir to Luang Pho Wat Paknam's teachings. The notion that one's external physical features reflect inner states of equanimity and spiritual perfection has a long history in Buddhist narratives and iconography. The Buddha's body, for instance, possessed the thirty-two marks of an extraordinary *mahāpurusha* (great person), and large images of the Buddha reflect the grandness of his dhammakāya.[98] Phra Dhammachayo's radiance, therefore, fits within this tradition of external signs of internal perfections, and he is not the only Dhammakāya practitioner to be described in this way. In Luang Pho Sot's biography, we are told that the "monks, novices, and nuns who resided at the temple benefited from daily practice" and as a result, "their complexions even glowed to the point that some critics wondered if they were powdering their faces."[99] In the Dhammakāya tradition, such physical signs are indicators of spiritual progress and one's realization of the dhammakāya within the individual.

Dhammakāya Practice

Luang Pho Sot, Khun Yay, and Phra Dhammachayo are paradigmatic figures who model Dhammakāya perfection (*pāramitā*) and who embody purity (*visuddhi*) of both character and mind. Similar to traditional descriptions of the path that emphasize the perfection of *sīla* (ethics), *samādhi* (mental concentration), and *paññā* (wisdom), the path of dhammakāya meditation facilitates the perfection of all three. One who is able to access the dhammakāya within has calmed the mind (samādhi), fully realized the dhammakāya (paññā), and naturally leads an ethical life (sīla). Somdet Phra Mahrajmangkalajahn, the present abbot of Wat Paknam, writes that Luang Pho Sot "once said that dhammakāya meditation would be known all over the country, primarily because it penetrates right to the heart of the practice of purification. Defilements such as greed, hatred, delusion, conceit, wrong view, doubt, sloth, restlessness, shamelessness, and lack of moral dread are uprooted naturally and effectively."[100] This path is the path that all Dhammakāya practitioners follow, regardless of religious status, gender, or age.

Although traditional distinctions are maintained between monks and lay people at the Dhammakāya Temple, the practice of dhammakāya meditation provides a common religious experience for Dhammakāya practitioners that creates a distinct community.[101] Dhammakāya meditation enables the practitioner to focus the mind and to "maintain a balance of mindfulness and happiness," which leads to a state of "contentment" and provides a "direction to life." From the perspective of the Temple, these results are not possible through other techniques.[102] Dhammakāya meditation, therefore, can lead to the power to transform one's life.

Dhammakāya meditation is the sine qua non of Dhammakāya practice in that it locates the present practitioners in the lineage of Luang Pho Sot, at

A Dhammakāya Foundation Photograph of Meditation. (Courtesy of the Dhammakāya Foundation.)

the same time as granting them direct access to the source of his authority. Outside observers frequently question and criticize the origins of this method, but Luang Pho Sot's followers insist that the dhammakāya technique was taught by the Buddha and practiced for hundreds of years in India. Practitioners argue that this technique has been latent in Theravāda Buddhism for the past 2500 years: References to the dhammakāya are found within the tradition's texts and visualization techniques are present within contemporary meditation practices. Buddhists over the past two millennia have simply failed to recognize or understand the full implications of these teachings.[103] Luang Pho's biography describes the rediscovery of wicha thammakai as a miraculous event with cosmic elements reminiscent of the Buddha's enlightenment: the heavy rains that fell that night and purified the temple foreshadowed the rediscovery of a tradition that had been lost for two thousand years.[104]

The technique begins with simple relaxation; practitioners are asked to close their eyes and to relax various parts of their bodies beginning with the face and then moving to the extremities, from the neck to the shoulders, arms, chest, midsection, and legs. Having achieved a state of visceral equanimity, practitioners proceed to visualize the movement of a crystal ball through the six bases of the mind (the opening of the nose, the bridge of the nose, the center of the head, the roof of the mouth, the center of the throat, at the center of the body) until it rests in the seventh base of mind, which is located two finger-widths above the navel. At this point, a practitioner imagines the body as empty of tissue, organs, and blood, devoid of anything save the crystal ball at the seventh base position. The goal is to cultivate one-pointedness of mind (samādhi) in order to reveal the true self, the true mind, the dhammakāya. As one advances in dhammakāya meditation practice, the visual image of the crystal ball undergoes several transformations before it culminates in the dhammakāya. Having reached this ultimate level, one is said to attain supreme happiness.

The ultimate goal of dhammakāya practice is the realization of the dhammakāya within one's self. Phra Sermchai, a practitioner of dhammakāya meditation who is not officially affiliated with the Dhammakāya Temple, describes the dhammakāya as the ultimate nature of the Buddha, the purest element, that which is permanent (*niccaṃ*), essential (*dhammasāraṃ*), and not composed of aggregates.[105] All people, according to Dhammakāya practitioners, possess this dhammakāya within (*thuk khon mi Phra Thammakai*).[106] The full realization of this ultimate ontology is equated by many practitioners with the attainment of nirvāṇa, the cessation of greed, hatred, and delusion, and the attainment of ultimate and permanent happiness (*nibbānaṃ paramaṃ sukhaṃ*). More often than not, it is the latter understanding of nirvāṇa as supreme happiness that is underscored in dhammakāya practice, rather than its traditional rendering as the cessation of greed, hatred, and delusion. At times, the two descriptions of nirvāṇa are combined: The cessation of greed, hatred, and delusion consequently generates states of serenity, bliss, and, ultimately, supreme happiness. The theme that the path of dhammakāya practice leads to supreme happiness is prevalent in Dhammakāya Temple publications and in public discourse at the Temple. One might argue that the description of nirvāṇa in positive terms—*nirvāṇa* as supreme happiness—rather than through a *via negativa* rendering of nirvāṇa—nirvāṇa is not saṃsāra—may be one reason for the enormous success of the movement in drawing new members to its practice.[107]

Donald Swearer describes dhammakāya meditation as a "unique method of meditation which involves a visualization technique not unlike that associated with certain yogic or tantric forms of meditation, and is easily taught to large groups of people."[108] The dhammakāya technique tends to be more representative of samatha (concentration or tranquility) forms of Buddhist meditation, than vipassanā (insight) meditation. In particular, the Dhammakāya emphasis on the positive fruits of meditation, including states of happiness, bliss, and contentment, are more commonly associated with samatha meditation practice than with vipassanā. Moreover, the Temple's use of a crystal ball as an object of visualization practice clearly correlates with the *kasiṇa* meditations, which are basic forms of focused meditation that aim to develop one-pointedness of mind. While this result is often characterized as the sole purpose of samatha practice, this is "not strictly true" in that "some of the *kasiṇa* meditations are meant to lead to supernatural powers as well."[109] Luang Pho Sot's and Khun Yay's demonstration of supernatural or supra-mundane powers, such as the ability to read minds and to levitate, for instance, clearly testifies to the advanced level of their meditation practice.

Buddhist meditation incorporates both samatha and vipassanā, but the normative traditions, especially in the modern era, tend to relegate samatha meditation to a preliminary practice aimed at developing one-pointedness of mind. These concentration skills are then employed in the ultimate practice of vipassanā that "alone brings the meditator to full and final release (*Nibbāna*) in the Buddhist view."[110] Implicit within this soteriology is the critique of methods that rely exclusively on samatha meditation since the bliss that is cultivated through the *jhānic* states is impermanent and is itself a source of possible attachment. The critique of samatha meditation, including its fruits of supranormal powers (*iddhi*) and knowledges (*abhiññā*), is common within modernist interpretations of Buddhism, which focus on discourses of awakening and dismiss or outright reject the magical dimensions of Buddhist meditation. Sayadaw U Pandita, a contemporary meditation master, writes:

> Anyone can get caught up in rapture, happiness and comfort. This attachment to what is happening within us is a manifestation of a special kind of craving, a craving not connected with ordinary, worldly sensual pleasures. Rather, such craving comes directly out of one's meditation practice. When one is unable to be aware of this craving when it arises, it will interfere with one's practice. Rather than directly noting, one wallows in pleasant phenomena unmindfully, or thinks about the further delights that might ensue from one's practice. Now we can understand the Buddha's mystifying admonition, for this attachment to the pleasant results of meditation is what he meant by stopping within.[111]

Critics of dhammakāya meditation highlight this tendency for attachment in their assessment of the method and its goal. From their perspective, the only aim of dhammakāya meditation is to produce pleasant states of being, not to develop paññā (wisdom).

Attachment to these feelings of bliss is not the only problem. Critics contend that Dhammakāya practitioners consider the object of dhammakāya meditation, the dhammakāya, to be real and permanent, an idea that undermines the normative Theravāda doctrine of *anattā* (no eternal, essential Self).[112] As we shall see in Chapter 4, the Dhammakāya Temple's interpretations of the dhammakāya , nirvāṇa, and anattā were topics of debate in the controversy of 1998 to 1999. But questions concerning the dhammakāya method of meditation and its object are not new. In Luang Pho Sot's biography, we read that many criticized his teachings as extra-canonical. In response, Luang Pho reportedly said:

> They only accuse us because they don't know Dhammakaya for
> themselves. They know neither the place where Dhammakaya exists, nor the meaning of the word itself! This ignorance can be the
> only reason why they are so misguided and complain about us who
> are forthright and sincere in teaching from our own true experience. When ignorant people who don't know the real Doctrine of
> the Lord Buddha attack our meditation technique, they cannot
> upset the truth, but will succeed only in undermining the faith of
> weak-minded people. The real jewel of the Buddha's teaching is
> ever-shining and only the wise can look upon it in true admiration.
> The results of the truth are derived entirely from the meditator's
> own experience, not from doctrinal study.[113]

The reliance on meditative experience as the primary source for knowledge of
the dhamma led Luang Pho Sot and his followers to emphasize the efficacy of
dhammakāya practice over other techniques. This exclusivist perspective has led
Donald Swearer to describe the Temple as "fundamentalistic" in orientation.[114]

Critics identify dhammakāya meditation as heretical and criticize the
goals of this technique, but practitioners emphasize its transformative efficacy.
Individuals are encouraged to develop their meditation practice at home, at work,
and at the temple. Temple publications are replete with personal testimonials of
how dhammakāya practice has transformed the lives of individuals—wayward
sons who become monks, adulterous husbands who recommit to their wives
and families, women who create *kanyanmit* (*kalyanamitta*, Pāli; *kalyanamitra*,
Sanskrit; good friends) rooms in their homes for friends and family to meditate together.[115] The focus on personal transformation within the world is
particularly attractive to lay Dhammakāya practitioners. In one text Phra Thatthacheevo, the assistant abbot, states that present social and political ills are
caused by the non-application of Buddhist ethics to daily life. As in the past,
when schools, temples, and homes all worked together to create "decent global
citizens," Dhammakāya practitioners feel the need to restore the kanyanmit
home "in every town, village, district, province and country."[116] The social platform of the Dhammakāya Temple is evident in its numerous activities aimed
at social and global transformation, from blood drives and antismoking
campaigns to Tsunami relief projects and most recently, a campaign in the
southern-most provinces to alleviate tensions between Buddhists and Muslims. While many of its activities are focused at the individual and national
levels, Temple discourses include discussions of global transformation. One of
the Temple's most often repeated slogans is, "World Peace Through Inner

Peace." And as we shall see in Chapter 3, the Temple's creation of the World Dhammakāya Center was meant, among other things, to provide a locus for global transformation.

The Temple's emphasis on transformation, which leads to personal and social happiness, is also evident in the popularity of the famous ethical sutta, the *Mahāmaṅgala-sutta*, in Dhammakāya practice and publications. In the traditions of Theravāda in South and Southeast Asia, this sutta is one of the most common ones used for the chanting of *paritta* (protection). Rather than focusing on the magical aspects of Pāli chanting, however, the Temple emphasizes how the study and understanding of the *Mahāmaṅgala-sutta* can lead to happiness, bliss, and safety. In the Introduction to *The Mongkhon Chiwit* (The Auspicious Life) the Dhammakāya author writes: "The Buddha taught the thirty-eight levels of dhamma practice in the *Mahāmaṅgala-sutta* for the progress and happiness of the world. They are simple enough to read but difficult to put into practice . . . Those who truly put into practice the steps of the *Maṅgala-sutta* will improve their lives whether they be layperson or monk. Indeed, following them leads to the very highest level of Buddhism."[117] These highest levels of Buddhism, according to the *Maṅgala-sutta*, are various forms of happiness, which derive from such things as associating with good people, honoring parents, learning the Four Noble Truths, attaining nirvāṇa, and experiencing peace and feelings of safety. The importance of this particular sutta to Dhammakāya practice is evident in the Temple's offering of annual exams on it for laypersons, an event that encourages and rewards reflection upon the text.

The Temple's significant growth over the past thirty years testifies to the success of its message of Buddhist practice for daily life. As stated previously, the practice of dhammakāya meditation enables monastics and laypersons alike to access the power of high-level meditation that is typically associated with famous forest monks. While other pious Thai Buddhists patronize forest monks in the hope of garnering merit for their generosity, Dhammakāya laypersons tap directly into the power of forest practice through their own meditation. One example of this practice is the Dhammadāyāda (*Thammathayat*, Thai) or dhamma-heir program for college-age men. It is an eight-week summer program consisting of intense meditation, dhamma lessons, and physical training.[118] Program participants adhere to the eight precepts, and sleep outside on mats under a mosquito-net-covered umbrella. One participant describes his participation in this program as a transformative experience:

> Dhammadāyāda training is the beginning of changes. Changes from comfortable habits like living in a luxurious house, surrounded by beloved ones, to dwelling under the Klod (the umbrella) in the midst of the rice field with no other shelter. Moreover, there is no sound of heavy traffic, no interference from others, only

quietness. There are no colorful clothes because we only wear white. There is also no sight or sound of dissent. Dinner is not served because Dhammadāyāda must observe 8 moral precepts. Our confused daily activities were left behind. Our only duty is to practice mindfulness with diligence.[119]

Having undergone this preliminary training, a young man is either eligible for consideration as a Dhammakāya novice or, if he chooses to remain as a layperson, he can employ the skills learned in the training session for "the benefit of himself, his society, his nation, and the world." Such training will make him "a good son, good student, good citizen and above all a good Buddhist."[120] The Temple also sponsors a training program for young women that is coterminous with the Dhammadāyāda program and has gone so far as to include young women in *samaneri* (female novice) style ordinations.[121] These spring training programs replace the traditional rainy season ordinations that used to serve as a rite of passage for a young man entering adulthood.[122] Not only do the training programs seek to produce a certain kind of individual, they also serve to create a unified body of young core participants who serve as an evangelical arm of the Dhammakāya Temple at their respective universities. It is not surprising, therefore, that Dhammakāya practitioners dominate the Buddhist clubs at most universities in central Thailand.

The Dhammakāya Temple's phenomenal growth is due to programs like these that attract young recruits along with their families, as well as an impressive organization that effectively markets Dhammakāya practice across Thailand and around the world. This would not be possible without the Dhammakāya Foundation that enables the monastic hierarchy to work closely with high-ranking lay personnel in the marketing and building of the World Dhammakāya Center.[123] At the head of the Foundation are Phra Dhammachayo, the abbot of Wat Dhammakāya, as its president, and Phra Tatthacheevo, the assistant abbot of Wat Dhammakāya, as its vice president. Subordinate to them is a select group of executive monks and an executive layperson, all of whom oversee the activities of the Foundation. Through the Dhammakāya Foundation, the Temple has established an impressive administrative hub with five satellite divisions: (1) a human resource center that handles accounts and personnel; (2) a support center that manages such activities as construction, public maintenance, ritual management, registration, receptions, bus services, flower decoration, and cleaning; (3) a fund-raising division; (4) an education division which deals with foreign affairs, the student dhamma training program, and educational materials; and (5) the propagation division which serves as the evangelical arm of the foundation.[124] According to the Foundation's website, it has seven primary objectives:

1. To propagate the Dhammakaya meditation technique to the general public regardless of races, nationalities, and religions in order to bring peace to the world.

2. To promote and support Buddhist studies.

3. To promote and support Dhamma education among monks, novices, laymen, laywomen, and the general public.

4. To provide general support for monks, novices, laymen, and laywomen of Wat Phra Dhammakaya as appropriate.

5. To build and maintain World Dhammakaya Centre.

6. To build and maintain Wat Phra Dhammakaya.

7. To build and maintain an academic institute that offers all levels of education: pre-school, elementary school, middle school, high school, vocational school, and university to provide intensive Dhamma education and training in addition to normal curriculum (in the near future).[125]

Most recently, these objectives have fueled the Temple's creation of its own satellite television network, DMC (Dhammakāya Meditation Channel), that broadcasts programming in Thailand and around the world twenty-four hours a day, seven days a week.

The Temple has established centers in provinces throughout Thailand while maintaining the locus of its authority in Pathum Thani. Through its network of satellite centers, the main temple is able to disperse information and instructional materials. It also sponsors trips to the main temple in Pathum

10,000 monks in the Great Sapha Meditation Hall. (Courtesy of the Dhammakāya Foundation.)

Thani and facilitates fund-raising activities. Donald Swearer suggests that the Dhammakāya Temple "proposes in effect to recreate the old galactic polity model and thereby to restore a vivid and dynamic past to a fragmented Thai society and a political environment continually beset by corruption and factionalism, in which the symbolic power of the monarchy is waning and the practical power of religion is virtually nonexistent."[126] Although one may not want to draw too close of an analogy between the Dhammakāya structure and the galactic polity model,[127] the Dhammakāya Temple has created a national network that operates independently of the national saṅgha organization, while simultaneously drawing non-Dhammakāya members to its events. The Temple presents an alternative method of practice and source of authority while maintaining diplomatic ties with the religious establishment.

Conclusion

This chapter situated the phenomenal success of the Dhammakāya Temple within the context of postmodern Thai Buddhism, a context that reflects modern saṅgha reforms as well as diverse forms of Buddhist and Thai religiosity. The Temple's creation of a distinct identity based upon a unique practice and lineage of authority serves as a response to the centralizing and homogenizing forces of modern Buddhism without creating dissension within the saṅgha establishment. One of the primary reasons for the Temple's phenomenal success with urban, educated Thais is its marketing of dhammakāya practice as a form of Buddhist practice that is perfectly suited to contemporary life within the context of postmodern Thai religion. One expression of this marketing is the Temple's emphasis on the personal benefits of dhammakāya meditation. Drawing on the urban trend towards patronizing forest monks, the Temple highlights the exemplary practice of the Dhammakāya founders—Luang Pho Sot, Khun Yay, and Phra Dhammachayo. Unlike the urban patronage of forest monks where laypeople tap into the *saksit* (power) of ascetics such as Achan Man and his disciples, the Dhammakāya Temple makes this power accessible to all practitioners. Laypersons are exhorted to apply the power derived from their own meditation practice to their daily lives, which can lead to greater success in business, education, and family life.

It is the Temple's creative blending of the traditional with the modern that has attracted thousands of middle-class, college-educated urban Thais to its teachings and practices. This unique practice and identity combines a number of "traditional" elements such as the equation of meditation with power and the patronage of monks, with postmodern elements such as the focus on lay meditation practice and the use of modern media for the dissemination of information about the Temple and its activities. The importance of recognizing

this creative blending of traditional ;
All too often, scholars of Thai Bud
innovation" to describe the Dhamr
validity, but it is not a complete pc
in which the Temple also reflects t
land and elsewhere. As will be se
only practice that has been repac
activity of merit-making has sin
tion, with lay practitioners mak
spiritual and material rewards.

Chapter 3

The Mahathammakai Chedi and Postmodern Merit Making

On January 31, 1999, the Dhammakāya Temple sponsored a mass *ubosok-kaew*[1] ordination for laymen in honor of King Bhumipol's birthday, an event that drew a throng of over 100,000 attendees. The activities began early in the morning with the offering of alms to Dhammakāya monks and ubosok-kaew novices. This was followed by a communal meditation session led by Phra Dhammachayo, sermons on the dhamma by Phra Thatthacheevo, and personal testimonials by lay Dhammakāya practitioners. The day's activities culminated in a mass gathering of practitioners at the work site of the Mahathammakai Chedi, which at the time was only partially completed. As the crowd posed for a group photograph, practitioners waved metallic flags that read, "Phra Mahsiriratthat phichit Mar" (the Phra Mahsiriratthat amulet will conquer Māra) and chanted, "Finish the chedi!" over and over again. At the end of the cere-mony, attendees stood in long lines to receive Phra Mahsiriratthat amulets from Dhammakāya monks.

The ubosok-kaew ceremonies marked yet another event in the Temple's calendar year, namely, the celebration of King Bhumiphol's birthday. It was not, however, an ordinary celebration, for it occurred in the midst of a turbulent controversy over the Temple's wealth, fund-raising techniques, and controver-sial teachings and practices. The participants at this particular event used the birthday celebration as an opportunity to demonstrate their continued support for the Temple and for the construction of the Mahathammakai Chedi. The thunderous chant of "Finish the chedi!" by over 100,000 Temple attendees un-derscored their unequivocal determination to finish the multimillion dollar con-struction project in the face of a national controversy.

Attendees at the Temple's ubosok-kaew ceremony, with whom I spoke, described the ordination as an auspicious event, as an opportunity to generate merit for one's self, for one's family, and for Thailand's beloved king. They com-pared this mass ordination to the individual ordinations that occur in Thailand throughout the year, when young men don saffron-colored robes and under-take the discipline in order to make merit for their families. In so doing, they linked the ubosok-kaew ceremony to the tradition of meritorious renunciation in which all acts of renunciation, from a layperson's observance of the five precepts to a bhikkhu's following of the 227 rules of the *pāṭimokkha*, are considered to be highly meritorious. Within this tradition, spectacular ordinations, such as a royal ordination, are viewed as especially meritorious. In the case of the ubosok-kaew ceremony, the sheer scale of the event and the auspiciousness of the day (honoring the King) made it a merit-making opportunity par excellence for all in attendance.

The Thai media did not view the ceremony through the same lens of religious piety. Many newspapers and magazines characterized the event as a blatant attempt by the Temple to "buy" public support by promising powerful amulets to the poor. For instance, numerous articles questioned the sincerity of the attendees, alleging that many of the participants were not in fact usual Dhammakāya practitioners—not "genuine Buddhist followers"—but rather "hill-tribe people, soldiers, farmers and students who were either paid to attend or pledged valuable Buddhist amulets or brought by supervisors affiliated with the temple."[2] The Temple regularly offers free transportation to the Temple in Pathum Thani from Bangkok and from other provinces as a means of exposing people, who might otherwise have no opportunity to travel to the suburban temple, to Dhammakāya practice and activities. In fact, I frequently used this form of transportation to travel to the Temple in 1998 and 1999. But given the context of the ubosok-kaew ceremony, the media portrayed the Temple's free transportation as an act of manipulation not of philanthropy. Questions concerning the genuineness of ubosok-kaew participants played upon already existing doubts concerning the Temple's marketing of the chedi and the miraculous events alleged to have taken place at the Temple.

Discussions and debates over the Dhammakāya Temple's technologies of fund-raising for the Mahathammakai Chedi became a discursive site for people to reexamine the role of merit making (*tam bun*, literally to make merit or *dai bun*, to receive merit), amulets, and miracles in Thai Buddhism. Similar debates have occurred throughout Buddhism's history as some groups have placed more emphasis on these aspects of the tradition than others. In the modern and contemporary periods, however, discourses on the role of merit making, amulets, and miracles have emerged out of radically new historical contexts. Buddhist modernists in nineteenth century South and Southeast Asia denounced the privileging of merit making, the ritualism of traditional Buddhism, and the participation of monks in acts of prophecy and magic in the contexts of colonization, of global Christian proselytization and education, and of modernist rationalism. Today, Buddhist (post)modernists continue to criticize ritualism and the magical elements of the tradition, but their criticisms emerge as a response to a new historical reality—the influence of global capitalism on Buddhist societies. Contemporary critics, therefore, take aim at what they perceive as the use of ritual and magic for commercial gain.

In the case of the Dhammakāya Temple, donors and their critics clashed over radically different ideas about the nature and state of contemporary Thai Buddhism. For donors at the Temple, the traditional Theravāda narratives that link acts of giving with meritorious rewards—as well as Buddhist amulets with power and protection, and Buddhist saints with miraculous abilities—played a prominent role in their constructions of Buddhist piety. Temple critics, however, found these emphases to be problematic. They questioned the integrity of the donors' intentions and whether the Mahathammakai Chedi was truly an object worthy of donation, a legitimate *puññā-khetta*, a field for the cultivation of merit. Critics, moreover, viewed the Temple's elaborate methods of fundraising as indices of the Temple's overall materialism and decadence.[3]

This chapter will examine how the Dhammakāya Temple has made use of traditional Theravāda narratives of merit-making and popular conceptions of the power of amulets and miracles in its promotion of the Mahathammakai Chedi. The Temple has successfully merged these traditional discourses with modern technology, a fusion that played into the Temple's self-identity as a modern temple and that fostered modern conceptions of merit and power in the lives of its donors. Fund-raising may be vital to the institutional survival of religious groups, but new methods tend to come under scrutiny, especially today when solicitations of support have gone high tech, employing satellite networks, credit-card donations, and glitzy complementary gifts. These technologies of fund-raising, while incredibly effective, have raised suspicions regarding the intentions of the Temple similar to those aroused by the numerous scandals involving the donation drives of popular Christian televangelists in the United States, such as Jim Bakker and Robert Tilton. This case of the Dhammakāya Temple and its fund-raising techniques is even more pronounced in that the Temple aggressively marketed its projects and solicited donations in an adverse economic climate. While the Temple erected billboards, distributed mass mailings, and employed "direct-sale" techniques, the Thai economy was in the throws of the Asian economic crisis, which began in Thailand in 1997 and then reverberated throughout Southeast Asia.

Merit Making and Power in Theravāda Buddhism

The front cover of one Dhammakāya fund-raising pamphlet reads, "merit is the cause of happiness and success in your life."[4] This statement refers to the principal Buddhist idea of merit (*bun*, Thai),[5] which is the beneficial fruit of skillful action. In the Buddhist tradition, merit and demerit (*bap*, Thai) operate within the karmic cause-and-effect laws, or, in the words of a famous Thai idiom, "Do good, receive good; do evil, receive evil."[6] These karmic relationships are emphasized within all forms of Buddhist texts, including canonical texts, commentaries, and vernacular literature. The *Dhammapada* (15–18), for instance, draws a sharp distinction between the delights of a beneficial rebirth experienced by the merit-maker and the torments experienced by the person who commits heinous acts. While only the most advanced practitioners are thought to possess a comprehensive understanding of karma, most practitioners would nevertheless make the general claim that karmic benefits can be realized in this and future lives. One reward commonly mentioned in Buddhist literature is a heavenly rebirth, where one dwells for an extended period of time experiencing the delights of merit. Descriptions of heavenly existence in the popular fourteenth-century text, the *Traibhūmikathā* (or *Trai Phum Phra Ruang, The Three Worlds According to King Ruang*), include such rewards as a flawless complexion, a youthful body, perfect health, and familial pleasures.[7] The laws of karma (*kamma*, Pāli) are not only embedded within Buddhist texts and oral traditions, they are also a popular theme in Buddhist art. Temple murals in Thailand express the laws of karma with vivid artistry showing the gods dancing in their heavenly abodes as hell beings are subjected to fire, swords, and other forms of torture.

The Dhammakāya Temple's statement that "merit is the cause of happiness and success in your life" reflects these ideas concerning the causal effects of meritorious action. This was stated in a pamphlet distributed at the Temple soliciting donations from prospective donors. It described how practitioners in the past have made merit for themselves and their families through offerings to monks. These statements are interspersed with color photographs of families offering gifts of food, clothing, and meditation aids to monks. Rather than focusing on the promise of future delights in heaven, the pamphlet assured the reader that benefits are realizable in the here and now. The emphasis on "this-life" benefits is a common theme in Dhammakāya publications. In *Chotmay Thueng Nanglek*, for instance, we are told that generous giving provides not only the foundation for ethics (sīla) and mental development (*bhāvanā*) that can lead to a favorable rebirth, it also produces tangible benefits and rewards within this lifetime, including wealth and prosperity.[8] While the temple's pamphlets and publications reflect modern fund-raising technology with the Temple's strategic use of modern graphic design, the ideas contained within these texts, namely the correlation between generous giving (dāna) and meritorious rewards, are intrinsic to the Buddhist tradition.

In the West, merit-making may not be the first activity that comes to mind when one thinks of Buddhist practice (meditation would, no doubt, be the first), but for a majority of practicing Buddhists in South and Southeast Asia, merit-making is central to their self-understanding of Buddhist religiosity, as evidenced in the vernacular literature and material culture of Theravāda Buddhism, as well as in the numerous references to merit-making in ethnographic descriptions of Buddhist ritual life.[9]

In Thailand, making merit (*tam bun*) is synonymous with being a good Buddhist: as a Buddhist, it is what you do. Its central place within ritual practice is due, in part, to its universality. Unlike other specialized practices such as meditation or *abhidhamma* studies, merit-making is a religious activity accessible to all—rich or poor, male or female, child or adult, layperson or monk. Of

Temple Mural Showing an Act of Dāna, Bangkok. (Photograph by Rachelle M. Scott.)

course, not all meritorious actions are equal. Buddhists argue that the amount of merit received depends on the type of action and the intention (*cetanā*) behind the action. Some activities are generally thought to produce more benefits than others. Beneficial actions conducted as a result of *kilesa* (greed, hatred, or delusion), for example, will theoretically not generate the same amount of merit as those same actions done with thoughts of the four *Brahma-vihāras*—loving-kindness, compassion, equanimity, and sympathetic joy. Buddhist texts outline a number of practices that lead to the cultivation of merit including generous giving (dāna), living an ethical life (sīla), developing concentration (samādhi), cultivating wisdom (paññā), and listening to and spreading the dhamma.[10] Within the realm of popular practice, these acts span a wide range of activities, from showing deference to a Buddha image and offering food to monks on their morning alms rounds to observing the eight precepts on Buddhist holy days. For many, the two most efficacious forms of merit-making are generous financial donations to the sangha and acts of ordination.

H. K. Kaufman's and S. J. Tambiah's anthropological surveys on the efficacy of specific types of merit-making activities highlight this ranking. In both cases, ordination and generous giving are considered more meritorious than leading an ethical life. Kaufman surveyed twenty-five individuals in Bangkhuad,

Donations for a Temple. (Photograph by Rachelle M. Scott.)

a village in central Thailand. Respondents ranked the act of becoming a monk as the most meritorious, followed hierarchically by contributing enough money for the construction of a *wat* (temple), having a son ordained as a monk, making excursions to the Buddhist shrines throughout Thailand, contributing towards the repair of a wat, giving food daily to monks and giving food on holy days, becoming a novice, attending a wat on holy days, observing the eight precepts and obeying the five precepts at all times, and giving money and clothing to the monks at *thaud kathin*.[11] In Tambiah's survey of seventy-nine family heads in Baan Phra Muan, a village in northeast Thailand, financing the building of an entire wat was considered to be the most meritorious, followed by becoming a monk oneself, having a son become a monk, contributing money to the repair of a wat, making gifts at a *kathin* ceremony, giving food daily to monks, observing every *wanphra* at the wat, and strict observance of the five precepts.[12] It is not surprising that acts of ordination are found at the top of Tambiah's and Kaufman's lists: Ordination is an act of renunciation modeled upon the Buddha's own journey from home to homelessness, a path that culminated in his realization of nirvāna and eventual career as a teacher of the dhamma. As members of the sangha, monks enter into a realm replete with merit-making opportunities, including teaching the dhamma, observing the 227 rules of the *Vinaya*, and fostering ethical and mental development. What perhaps is not so well known is the tradition in Southeast Asia of young men dedicating the merit earned from the act of ordination to their parents, thereby turning ordination into an act of dāna (generous giving). In fact, the reception of merit from a son's ordination is one of the principal ways for a woman to make merit, as she is unable to undertake the vows of a full-fledged nun (*bhikkhunī*).[13]

Acts of generous giving hold a prominent place in the Buddhist tradition, for they embody the Buddhist ethical virtues of compassion (*karuna*) and loving-kindness (*metta*), and they are realizable for all members of the Buddhist community. While not technically a part of the noble eight-fold path, generous giving provides the foundation for progress on the path since it sustains the Buddhist community. Reciprocal generosity typifies sangha-lay relations in South and Southeast Asia. Laypersons support the sangha through gifts of food, clothing, shelter, and other requisites, while the sangha serves as a field of merit for laypersons and a source for religious instruction. One receives merit through these acts of generosity based on a natural law of reciprocal exchange:

> The lay person-donor offers material gifts for the benefit of the monastic order (*sangha*). In return the virtuous power of the *sangha* engenders a spiritual reward of merit (*puñña*), thereby enhancing the donors' balance of kamma/karma, which in turn affects the

status of the person's rebirth on the cosmic scale. . . . Even though
the form of merit making rituals in Theravāda Buddhism in Southeast Asia varies greatly, the structure of reciprocal exchange remains constant.[14]

Given the importance of this exchange, it is perhaps not surprising that the
Buddhists whom Tambiah and Kaufman interviewed considered the financing
of an entire temple as a highly meritorious act, in that it ensures the function-
ing and sustainability of an entire Buddhist community. Most Buddhists do
not, of course, have the financial means to make such an offering, but as Tambiah points out in the case of the villagers of Baan Phraan Muan, such generous acts nevertheless are well known in Thailand and throughout the Theravāda
Buddhist world.

Those acts are known, in part, through Buddhist narratives that reinforce
the correlation between dāna, merit, and personal prosperity. Stories of generous donors abound in canonical and vernacular texts: Visākhā, the most lauded
laywoman in the Pāli canon, offered a continual supply of practical gifts, such
as food, clothing, medicine, and shelter, to the saṅgha; great kings such as King
Aśoka patronized the tradition through the building of temples and monuments for the community. Exemplary donors in the narrative traditions of
Theravāda Buddhism provide a paradigm for subsequent acts of religious giving.[15] Those who possess the highest standing within the tradition are the most
magnanimous of donors, whose great acts of dāna ensure the continuation and
fostering of the tradition. One of the most celebrated lay donors in the Pāli
canon is Anānthapiṇḍika, a wealthy and highly respected merchant. He is renowned both for his specific acts of generosity—most notably his donation
of one hundred thousand gold coins for the construction of the Jetavana
monastery—and the models his acts provide regarding wealth and piety—how
to give, to whom to give, and the benefits of giving.[16] Although Anānthapiṇḍika
does not himself seek meritorious rewards for his actions, the stories about him
abound in references to the results (*puññakiriyavatthu*) of such actions including longevity, prestige, and a heavenly rebirth.

Within Buddhist stories of great generosity is an explicit correlation between wealth and piety for, as we saw in Chapter 1, wealth is a sign of merit.
The Thai version of the story of Jōtika in the *Traibhūmikathā* provides a vernacular version of the meritorious rich man story.[17] Jōtika's wealth was renowned throughout Rājagaha. His seven-story castle was faced with precious
stones and featured wishing trees, pits full of silver, gold, and seven kinds of
gems, and stalks of golden sugarcane whose leaves were covered in jewels. His
wealth was the envy of the story's antagonist, King Ajātasattu. As a prince,
Ajājasattu asked his father, the renowned King Bimbisāra, to seize Jōtika's
great wealth, but the King declined, saying such an action would not be in

accordance with the dhamma since Jōtika's wealth was the result of his accumu-lated merit. Ajātasattu then sent an army to seize Jōtika's castle, but this attempt also failed. Finally, he confronted Jōtika directly, insisting that he turn over his wealth. Jōtika informed the king that his wealth could not be taken from him by force since it derived from his own merit. It could, however, be relinquished willingly as demonstrated by Jōtika upon his ordination. In the *Traibhūmikathā*, the Jōtika story is followed by a long exposition on various kinds of merit-making, demonstrating that the author correlated Jōtika's wealth and merit with the everyday merit-making activities of the ordinary person. The text

Pre-packaged Gifts for Monks, Bangkok. (Photograph by Rachelle M. Scott.)

states that there are 17,280 kinds of merit that can be made in the realm of sensual desire, eight of which relate to ten different kinds of merit-making: the giving of alms; observance of precepts (five, eight, or ten); the practice of meditation (which includes activities such as chanting or recollecting the Buddha); the dedication of merit to others; rejoicing in the merit of others; helping a family member or members of a temple; showing respect to one's elders; preaching the dhamma; listening to the dhamma; and having a steadfast faith in the Buddha, dhamma, and saṅgha.[18]

Exemplary donors within the chronicle traditions of South and Southeast Asia are often royal figures who, through their pious generosity, ensure prosperity for their kingdoms and the continuation of the saṅgha. In the *Jinakālamālīpakaraṇaṁ*, a sixteenth-century text compiled by Ratanapañña Thera of Chiang Mai, we find stories of the great kings of Sri Lanka and Siam who promoted the saṅgha through collecting relics, building stūpas, and commissioning Buddha images. One example is this passage that describes the construction of the Mahācetiya by King Duṭṭhagāmiṇī:

> The novice brought the relics given by the Nāga King Mahākāḷa and gave them to the King. The King, too, with diverse forms of ceremonies in honour and reverence, on the full-moon day of Āsāḷha under the influence of the planetary combination of Uttarâsāḷha, conducted a great festival enshrining the relics. And having done the enshrining, he caused above it the construction of a great thūpa called Suvaṇṇamālī 'Of Golden Garlands', 120 cubits in height. Accumulating unlimited merit, the King reigned for twenty-four years and, ever continuing to recollect his merit, he passed away having had (the disposal of) his body entrusted to the Order, and being reborn in the heavenly chariot that had come from the Tusita Abode, and being adorned in heavenly ornaments, he circumambulated, even while the populace was looking on, the Mahāthūpa thrice, saluted the Order of monks and departed to the Tusita Abode.[19]

In this selection and in others within the text, the author emphasizes the abundance of merit that one receives through generous acts of giving, especially from the construction of a stūpa. These stories also reinforce the positive impact of these acts on Buddhism. In the *Cāmadevīvaṃsa*, a fifteenth-century northern Thai text that recounts the founding of the city of Haripuñjaya, happiness, piety, and generosity go hand in hand.

> Cāmadevī, the queen mother, was held in the same high regard as her sons. She attained a state of great happiness (*mahādevīsukhaṃ*)

that anyone would envy: happy while sleeping, happy while standing, and happy while walking. Everything that she wanted was realized (*sabbaṃ samijjhati*).

Cāmadevī arose early in the morning. Upon waking she sat one her bed and recalled her virtue (*guṇam*) in the past, the future, and the present. With wealth sufficient for her needs, she offered food to monks, Brahmans, and even beggars. She lacked for nothing; money and rice were always plentiful.

She thought to herself, "Because of my previous good deeds, I have achieved success in this life. The time has come for me to perform good deeds for the future when I am old and ill (*anāgate kattabbaṃ kusalaṃ mayā*)."

In the morning with these thoughts in mind (*evaṃ jintayitvāna*), the queen mother arose from her bed, washed her face, attired herself in new clothes, and adorned herself with several kinds of jewelry. Seated upon a palanquin she circumambulated the city surrounded by a large retinue. East of the city she built the Rammakārāma, a forest temple, complete with a *vihāra* and a Buddha image. Afterward she [gave the following to the saṅghathera]: a residence for the community of monks headed by the *saṅghathera*; the Māluvārāma Monastery, including a *vihāra*, at the northern corner of the city to accommodate the monks from the four directions; the Abaddhārāma Monastery to the north of the city with a *vihāra* that she offered to the monks from Laṅkārāma; the Mahāvanārāma Monastery to the west of the city along with a *vihāra* and a monk's residence (*kuṭi*) as well as a Buddha image for the monks food and drink for the resident monks; the Mahāsattārāma Monastery to the south of the city and its vihāra with an incomparably beautiful image for the monks residing at the temple. Food and drink were also offered to the *saṅgha*. From her own resources (*sayaṃ*) the princess mother built *mahāvihāra* in the five different places ... With royal support from Queen Cāmadevī and her two sons, Buddhism (*buddhasāsana*) flourished.[20]

The *Cāmadevīvaṃsa* combines the dynastic elements of *vaṃsa* literature with the religious dimensions of *jātaka* and *tamnān* literature.[21] In so doing, this text, as with many northern Thai chronicles, intertwines the dramatic history of a specific place with the power of the Buddha and his followers. Stories of the Buddha's journeys in northern Thailand serve to establish these sites as sacred and auspicious.[22] They also demonstrate how descriptions of prosperous kingdoms go hand in hand with stories of piety, merit, and generous giving.

The correlation between piety, merit, and generous giving is also found in the material culture of Theravāda Buddhism. While canonical and vernacular texts glorify the generosity of donors through narratives of giving and receiving, the epigraphic evidence stands as a material reminder of these acts of dāna. Temple inscriptions throughout South and Southeast Asia relay stories of great generosity and the rewards of such action. The sixteenth-century inscription from Wat Khemā near Sukhothai (Sukhodaya), for instance, provides an extensive list of offerings to the temple (literally to the Buddha[23]) by Prince Cau Debaruci and other donors, as well as references to the donation of land by "his majesty the great upāsaka Cau Brañā Śrī Dharmāśokarāja."[24] The records of these donations are inscribed in stone in order "that (the record) may last as long as the Buddha's religion." Prior to listing the various gifts to the Buddha, the inscription tells us that the donors offered to the temple: an image of the Buddha, pedestals for other images, the floor of the *vihāra* (dwelling place), and two ponds for the monks. In the list of gifts for the Buddha, many of the items are listed with the price of the object along with its intended function, as we see in this inscription:

> Beginning here (is a list of) articles presented by Cau Debaruci to the (image of the) Buddha in the vihāra: One piece of peñcati cloth, costing two tāṃliṅ, for the throne; One brass almsbowl, costing one tāṃliṅ, to be an almsbowl for (the image of) the Buddha; One pedestal tray of foreign make, a cubit and four inches in diameter, costing two tāṃliṅ; One decorated large bowl and ten small accessory bowls, forming a set with the pedestal tray, to be used in making pāyśrī offerings in homage to the Buddha; One brass cover-box, costing five saliṅ, in which to put areca fruits in homage to the Buddha; One tray of gold alloy, costing one tical, for serving fermented tea-leaves in homage to the Buddha; One long-necked bottle with a lid, made of gold alloy and costing one tical, in which to put water in homage to the Buddha.[25]

The next items listed are gifts presented to the chedi, which unfortunately are not legible, followed by a list of items presented to the Buddha by other merit makers; these include silk, a lectern, embroidered cloth, texts, a canopy for the preaching chair, a gong, a teakwood drum, a plate gong, and stone slabs for monks to sit on and lean against during sermons. We are then told about land donations and slaves that were presented to the Buddha. This part ends with the following wish (*prātthana*, Pāli), "May all these things be strong and durable, (to bring) good results to all the merit makers until we reach heaven and nibbāna." The final section relays the principal donor's personal wishes:

> As for me, I earnestly desire the prerequisites of Buddhahood. As long as I go on without obtaining them, in whatever existence I may be born, I pray that I shall have wisdom and wealth born to me in every re-birth, and that no sickness will befall me. Furthermore the good results of the merit I earned by being ordained in the religion, and by making these benefactions to the Buddha's religion, I dedicate to my teachers and spiritual preceptors, to my father and mother, to my elders and relatives, to the lords, the kings and divinities, all of them, and to whatever creatures have gone to hell or have been reborn as pretas or animals. May every one of them attain happiness as a result of the merit I have earned in this way in the Buddha's religion![26]

These temple inscriptions served as testaments of piety as well as indices of social standing within the community since meritorious wealth also translates into social power and prestige as seen in a number of ethnographic studies.[27] In his seminal essay on merit and power, Lucian Hanks describes the Thai social order as comprised of individuals who exist within a hierarchy of varying abilities and quality of lives depending on merit (*bun*), virtue (*khwamdi*), and demerit (*bap*).[28] The meritorious rich man is, by far, the most powerful person within the community:

> Because of his greater merit, a rich man is more effective than a poor man and freer from suffering. . . . The rich man marries off his children with more elaborate ceremony and offers more alms at the temple. Contrary to the Christian gospel, a poor widow, giving her all to the priest, remains less blessed than the rich man; both have performed meritorious acts, but the Thai observe that the effectiveness of ten thousand baht far outweighs the widow's battered coin.[29]

In this cultural context, the more merit one has, the more one is able to generate through great acts of dāna, which, in turn, solidify one's power and prestige within the community.[30]

These social benefits provide motivation for the public displays of giving that are found throughout the Buddhist world. Acts of generosity are lauded in ceremony and ritual, and magnanimous donors are publicly acknowledged and praised. In this sense, these acts are similar to the ancient Greeks and Romans who valued the *euergetés*, a "doer of good," whose generosity was displayed through grand acts of public benefactions, as well as the early Christians bishops whose acts of giving to the poor were often conducted with maximum publicity.[31] In the Buddhist context, public giving serves to reinforce the social standing of magnanimous donors within the community while simultaneously offering an opportunity for those of lesser wealth to partake in the merit-making as witnesses of generosity. Grand public giving, therefore, has played an important sociological and religious role within the Buddhist tradition.

Dhammakāya Merit-Making

The Dhammakāya Temple drew on this rich historical correlation of wealth and prestige with merit in its campaign to transform the Dhammakāya Temple from a local wat to an international center for Dhammakāya practice that could accommodate hundreds of thousands of practitioners. At the inception of this transformation, Phra Thatthacheevo, the assistant abbot, told one Thai scholar that, "The Catholics have their Vatican, the Moslems their Mecca, we Buddhists therefore await our World Thammakaay Center."[32] According to Phra Thatthacheevo's vision, the World Dhammakāya Center would serve as a center for Buddhist study and practice that would bring people together from all over the world to cultivate, in the words of a popular Dhammakāya slogan, "world peace through inner peace." In keeping with the magnitude of this vision, Dhammakāya leaders have constructed a number of new buildings to accommodate and attract large numbers of practitioners: the Great Sapha Dhammakāya Hall, an assembly hall which covers an area of over forty acres and which is lauded as the "largest public building in the world;" the Mahathammakai Chedi (Mahā Dhammakāya Cetiya), a massive stūpa with 1,000,000 golden Buddha images, which serves as a focus for communal ritual and devotion; and a memorial hall dedicated to the beloved Luang Pho Sot, the founder of the meditation technique used by the Temple. In addition to these three buildings, the Temple has constructed a large memorial for Khun Yay, which is located in the older section of the Temple, and is currently building an enormous meditation amphitheatre that will surround the Mahathammakai Chedi.[33] The amphitheatre, according to the Temple, will allow one million people to meditate together.

As with the construction of temples throughout the history of the Buddhism, the construction of the World Dhammakāya Center depended exclusively on the generosity of donors. Because of the magnitude of this particular project, the Temple launched an aggressive fund-raising campaign in the late 1990s that targeted active practitioners as well as members of the wider community. Pamphlets were mailed to practitioners, their families, friends, and

World Dhammakāya Center. (Courtesy of the Dhammakāya Foundation.)

even remote acquaintances. Large billboards advertising these various fund-raising projects were placed in clear view throughout Bangkok. Temple staff utilized newspapers, radio programs, and television shows as a means of promoting interest in these activities. The Temple, moreover, found inventive ways to recognize publicly those who were exceptionally generous. These donors had preferential seating at Temple events and in publicity photographs; they had access to high-ranking Dhammakāya monks who were usually secluded from the massive crowds; they donned amulets, almost like military badges and medals of rank, which denoted the monetary level of their generosity, and some became members of the Temple's "millionaires' club," a special group of people who were guaranteed rebirth as a millionaire for the gift of a regular monthly donation.

At the same time that the Temple utilized modern technology to spread its message, solicit donations, and invent methods to acknowledge exceptional generosity, it also employed traditional Theravāda narratives of merit-making that correlated acts of dāna with the cultivation of merit and the reception of beneficial results. Nowhere was this more apparent than in its fund-raising campaign for the Mahathammakai Chedi, which made an effective and alluring association between Dhammakāya donors in the present and the exemplary donors of the past. The Temple linked contemporary donors to this tradition by inscribing the names of individual donors on the base of the Phra Dhammakāya images that were affixed to the chedi, which replicated the traditional donative inscriptions on Buddhist monuments throughout Asia. Stories of exceptional

generosity were told at Temple events and in Temple publications, and generous monetary gifts were exchanged for amulets renowned for their miraculous
powers. In these ways, the donors' names, acts of generosity and, in some cases,
their stories of miracles and inspiration became a part of the Temple's own
narrative of exemplary Dhammakāya piety. In so doing, the Temple effectively
utilized popular ideas concerning merit-making, amulets, and miracles in its
campaign to generate donations for the Mahathammakai Chedi.

Patronage of the Mahathammakai Chedi

The building of a stūpa is one of the most celebrated acts of Buddhist generosity within the tradition, for it venerates the life and power of the Buddha and
the continuation of his teachings. The *Mahāparinibbāna-sutta*, which details
the final days of the life of the Buddha, sanctions the building of memorial
monuments for the enshrinement of the Buddha's relics—the last physical
remains of the Buddha—in a manner befitting a *cakkavattin*, an ideal wheel-
turning monarch.

> Ānanda, the remains of a wheel-turning monarch are wrapped in a
> new linen-cloth. This they wrap in teased cotton wool, and this in
> a new cloth. . . . Then having made a funeral-pyre of all manner of
> perfumes they cremate the king's body, and they raise a stupa at a
> crossroads. That, Ānanda, is what they do with the remains of a
> wheel-turning monarch, and they should deal with the Tathāgatha's
> body in the same way. A stupa should be erected at the crossroads
> for the Tathāgatha. And whoever lays wreaths or puts sweet per-
> fumes and colours there with a devout heart, will reap benefit and
> happiness for a long time.[34]

While many scholars in the past viewed the "stūpa cult" as an exclusively lay
form of Buddhist religiosity, Gregory Schopen has offered convincing evidence to demonstrate that monks were involved in the stūpa cult at a very early
point within the tradition.[35] He cites the story of Mahinda and the king in
the *Mahāvaṃsa* to make this point.

> The king promises to build a stūpa; the Monk Mahinda appoints
> another monk to fly to India to procure relics; he succeeds; and
> Mahinda stays. The moral of this tale, written by a monk about a
> monk, seems obvious: the continuation of Buddhist monasticism
> in Sri Lanka depended on procuring a relic and building a stūpa
> so that the monks would have an object of worship. The relic and

stūpa cults were, therefore, seen by the author of the *Mahāvaṃsa* as a primary concern of the monastic community and a necessary prerequisite for its continuance.[36]

While scholars and practitioners may continue to debate the Buddha's intentions regarding his relics and stūpas,[37] there is no doubt that both have been central to the establishment and continuation of the saṅgha in South and Southeast Asia.

Chedi at Wat Phra Kaew, Bangkok. (Photograph by Rachelle M. Scott.)

As containers for the Buddha's relics, stūpas are monuments of great power.[38] These memorial monuments not only mark the presence of Buddha relics, they literally make the Buddha present.[39] In so doing, they tap into the abundant power of the Buddha, and mediate the influence of this power to the lives of Buddhist practitioners.[40] It is this power that Buddhist pilgrims hope to access as they travel from their homes to stūpas throughout the Buddhist world, from the ancient stūpa at Sañchi to new stūpas in Buddhist communities in Thailand, India, and America.

Chedi at Wat Ku Tao, Chiang Mai. (Photograph by Rachelle M. Scott.)

The popularity of stūpa veneration derives in large part from the belief that they are "fields of merit," which will bring, in the words of the *Mahāparinibbāna sutta*, well-being and happiness for a long time. Patronage of stūpa-building, therefore, became an enormously popular act of Buddhist piety, as evidenced in the legends of great stūpa-builders, such as King Aśoka (third century BCE), and the wide range of stūpas in Buddhist countries. In Thailand, the building of a stūpa is believed to be a highly meritorious act. As a result, many temples have more than one stūpa. In addition, many old stūpas are left to fall into states of disrepair as new ones are built. Restoration may have historic value, but in terms of the popular religion, it is not as fruitful of a source of merit as new construction.

The Dhammakāya Temple's construction of the Mahathammakai Chedi must be viewed within this history of stūpa building and veneration.[41] Temple publications describe the Mahathammakai Chedi as a *sunruamphlangsattha*, a center for the power of *sattha* (confidence or faith). As with the other notable pilgrimage sites across Asia, Dhammakāya practitioners envision their chedi as a focal point for the veneration of the Buddha and other acts of piety. One Dhammakāya poem describes the chedi as a place where:

There are no tears of sorrow but tears of happiness here!
There is no hunger but eternal satisfaction here!
Hot or cold weather will never interfere with the ultimate goals here!
Here people from all over the world will join hand in hand with their strong faith and will join with the [Mahathammakai Chedi].[42]

The representation of the Mahathammakai Chedi as a center for the power of *sattha* is rich with cosmological overtones, for it creates, in the words of the assistant abbot, a Buddhist center of the world akin to Mecca and the Vatican. Dhammakāya discourses do not represent the chedi as one among many but, rather, as the preeminent focal point for Buddhist piety.

The Temple's desire to create a World Dhammakāya Center that will serve as a (if not *the*) Buddhist center prompted concerns among the Dhammakāya community over the longevity of the chedi. While it is common to find stūpas in various states of disrepair, each new stūpa is built with the intention that it will stand as a lasting testament of the devotion of its patrons. For this purpose, the Dhammakāya Temple insisted that only the finest quality of materials be used in the construction of its chedi, and they chose a design that ensured effective heat, moisture, ventilation and flood control, as well as adequate earthquake protection.[43] The focus on insuring the longevity of the chedi, along with the longevity of *wicha thammakai*, reveals the Temple's progressive view of Buddhist history. Stories about the end of Gotama Buddha's dispensation do not play a role in the Temple's narratives concerning the future. On the contrary, we saw in the last chapter how the Temple leaders plan to promote the Dhammakāya method throughout the world, and thereby gather more practitioners to the Dhammakāya family (*khropkhrua thammakai*). With this progressive sense of the future, the Temple sees its rigorous campaign for the construction of the chedi as an outgrowth of the enduring notion of its central place within the Buddhist world. This view of the Dhammakāya chedi fits within a larger pattern of stūpa-building within the Theravāda tradition—

A Relic of the Buddha, Wat Saket, Bangkok. (Photograph by Rachelle M. Scott.)

Celebration in Front of the Mahathammakai Chedi. (Courtesy of the Dhammakāya Foundation.)

stūpas make sites sacred; in so doing, they reinforce the privileging of particular places over others. For this reason the Mahathammakai Chedi is called a "center for the power of faith."

The Mahathammakai Chedi, as a center for the power of faith, promotes not only Dhammakāya practice, but also Dhammakāya symbolism. According to Temple publications, the *chedi* serves as a symbol of and vehicle for world peace. This idea is expressed through the Temple's oft-repeated slogan: peace throughout the world is started within the individual.[44] People who donate money for the construction of the chedi are therefore fostering peace both within themselves by developing the perfection of dāna and within others by serving as models for admiration and emulation. Devotional songs emphasize how it will stand as a symbol of both piety and peace for generations to come. The shape and style of the Mahathammakai Chedi is a physical representation of the *tiratana*, the triple gem—the *Buddha*, the dhamma, and the saṅgha: the upper region houses relics of the Buddha along with one million individual Phra Dhammakāya images; the middle section represents the dhamma and contains the entire *tipiṭika* (the Pāli canonical texts), and the lower section is the saṅgha region, a platform base that seats up to ten thousand monks. The religious symbolism of the chedi extends to Dhammakāya exemplars since the chedi is said to represent Luang Pho Sot's purity of mind and attainment of Dhammakāya perfection as well as Khun Yay's dedication to the Temple and her teacher.

As a symbol of world peace, the triple gem, purity of mind, and dedication, the Mahathammakai Chedi functions as a preeminent field of merit for all potential donors. All gifts offered to it will, therefore, yield exceptional merit for the donor. According to one Dhammakāya text, the merit gained from these donations continues to multiply each time that the donor sees the chedi.[45] In the fund-raising campaign for the construction of the chedi, the leaders of the Temple emphasized how individual donations would benefit both Buddhism and the individual donor. Descriptions of these benefits are replete in Temple publications, pamphlets, and advertisements, as are the linkages between Dhammakāya donors and the exemplary donors of the past. One fund-raising pamphlet instructs potential donors that Buddhists have always come together to build "holy sanctuaries" in order to pass down knowledge of the triple gem to future generations and to ensure the continuation of the Buddha's dhamma in the world.[46] It is for this purpose that the Mahathammakai Chedi is being built, so that it may be a "symbol of the majestic grandeur and pricelessness of the Lord Buddha's Teaching" for generations to come. In another Dhammakāya publication, the Temple explicitly compares King Aśoka's construction of stūpas in ancient India to the contemporary construction of the Mahathammakai Chedi.[47] In referencing the legend of King Aśoka, the publication not only draws comparisons between his acts of generosity and those of Dhammakāya donors, it also places the person of Aśoka within the Dhammakāya lineage. Following the Temple's construction of the ideal lay practitioner, Aśoka is portrayed as a great patron of Buddhism and as a master of Dhammakāya meditation.

In the various fund-raising pamphlets that were disseminated at the temple and mailed to potential donors, people were instructed in how they too might become exemplary donors. Rather than financing an entire project (as exemplary donors did in the past), Dhammakāya donors could contribute to the Mahathammakai Chedi by commissioning individual Phra Dhammakāya images that would be affixed either to the exterior of the chedi or housed within its interior (prices ranged from 10,000 baht to 30,000 baht depending on location). The name of each donor would be engraved on the base of each individual image (or if the donor preferred, the names of Luang Pho Sot, Khun Yay, or Phra Dhammachayo).

This would ensure that future generations would remember the donor's generosity. The act of engraving the names of donors on pieces of Buddhist art or architecture, once again, has a long history within the tradition in South and Southeast Asia.

In addition to descriptions of the Phra Dhammakāya images, these fund-raising materials also typically listed additional benefits that a donor might receive from their acts of generous giving: wealth and prosperity, personal beauty, career success, purity and radiance of mind, and endowment with

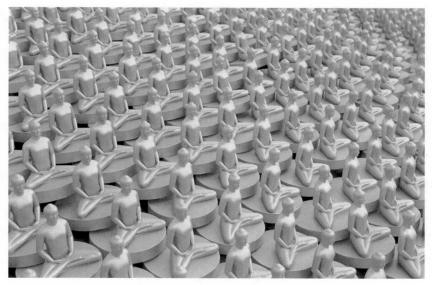

Phra Dhammakāya Images. (Courtesy of the Dhammakāya Foundation.)

Casting of Phra Dhammakāya Images. (Courtesy of the Dhammakāya Foundation.)

Casting of Phra Dhammakāya Images. (Courtesy of the Dhammakāya Foundation.)

worldly riches, heavenly riches, and the riches of nirvāṇa. This idea draws upon the narrative tradition of exemplary donors and the rewards (*ānisaṁsa*) that they received for their generosity. *Prātthanā*, the wishes that accompany acts of piety, "purport to provide the worshiper with valued material rewards—health, wealth, sensuous delight, powerful prestige, high caste status, or, if the devotee is a woman, the prospect of being reborn as a male."[48] The reception of these rewards derives from the cultivation of merit in this life and in past lives. While the actual fruits of one's merit are typically unknown,[49] many temples, including the Dhammakāya Temple, frequently refer to the "this-worldly" and spiritual benefits of generous giving.

Phra Mahsiriratthat Amulets

Fund-raising for the construction of the Mahathammakai Chedi included the distribution of amulets (*phra khruang*) to exceptionally generous donors. As with the practice of stūpa-building, the creation and distribution of sacred objects has a long history in Theravāda Buddhism. From the corporeal relics of the Buddha to votive tablets and coins imprinted with the images of meditation masters, the Buddhist tradition has long fostered the idea that power can be concentrated within objects as well as within persons. In Thailand, these objects are commonly referred to as possessing *saksit* (a compound of *śakti* and *siddhi*, Sanskrit), which highlights the tangibility of the objects' power. These power-infused objects are thought to have the ability to ward off danger, to protect one from misfortune and the influence of malevolent spirits, as well as to promote health, wealth, and good fortune.[50]

The abundance of votive tablets and *dhāranī* sealings in temples and stūpas at Nālandā and Bodh Gāya in northeast India testify to the popularity of these objects in Indian Buddhism. They were, among other things, popular items for pilgrims to collect after visiting auspicious sites. During the Pāla period (eighth to eleventh centuries BCE), for instance, when Bodh Gāya was a thriving pilgrimage center, votive tablets portraying an image of the Buddha in the "calling the earth to witness" pose (*bhūmisparśamudrā*; which recalls a pivotal moment in his awakening story) were produced in abundance, most likely for distribution to pilgrims.[51] Many of these ancient Indian votive tablets found a life outside of India in Southeast and East Asia as they moved with pilgrims, missionary monks, and traveling merchants. Art historians also note how these Indian artifacts influenced the production of similar objects throughout Asia. In the case of Thailand, there are distinctive votive tablets from each period and geographic region, and excavations at stūpas reveal the use of a number of different molds, reflecting the use of specific motifs by individual temples and monks.[52]

The contemporary "cult of amulets" in Thailand is an extension of this tradition of power-imbued objects. No one knows when it actually began, but one historian points to the reign of King Mongkut (1851–1868) during which "antique collecting" became a popular pastime among modern elites.

> Antique objects were apparently popular among the royal family and high-ranking generals. For instance, Buddha images had never before been kept inside a residence, but a trend developed wherein images were displayed on an altar in the 'Buddha-room' (*hong phra*) of each house. Because of the increased demand, many antique shops sprang up in Bangkok. To supply them, a number of archaeological sites were illegally dug up and sometimes destroyed. Burglars searched for gold caskets and Buddha images in stūpa, and in the process, often came across votive tablets that had been installed together with other valuable objects. Initially there was little interest in these small clay objects so they were discarded or sold at low prices. As the cult became more prominent, probably by the end of the reign of King Chulalongkorn (Rama V, 1868–1910), the destruction of stūpa and temple compounds expanded in the search for the tablets themselves. Since the tablets were installed in stūpa we can be certain that they were not originally used as amulets, but rather served as objects of consecration.[53]

During the modern period, it became a popular practice for these votive tablets to be worn around the neck as amulets. In its earliest phase, the focus of the cult of amulets was on antique amulets from places such as Lamphun, Lopburi, and Sukhothai, but the cult expanded to include ancient votive tablets, reproductions, and the amulets of royalty as well as living and newly diseased monks. In Stanley Tambiah's classic study of the "cult of amulets" in Thailand, he lists four classes of amulets: amulets of famous and historic Buddha images, amulets of famous Buddhist monks, miscellaneous amulets with varying images that were sacralized by monks and lay experts, and contemporary amulets that were blessed by forest-dwelling meditation masters.[54]

Phra Mahsiriratthat Amulet and Mahathammakai Chedi.
(Courtesy of the Dhammakāya Foundation.)

All of these amulets are power-laden objects that serve as symbols of Buddhist piety (a form of *Buddhānussati*—recalling the Buddha), as agents of protection and good fortune, and as indices of prestige and social standing. Amulets that portray an image of the Buddha are often interpreted as a form of a Buddha relic, an object of commemoration serving to stimulate recollections of the Buddha for the practitioner. As agents of protection and good fortune, they derive their efficacy from association with powerful materials and persons. Some amulets are miraculously created out of ordinary objects such as wood, clay, or even bullets. The latter are believed to protect the wearer from bullet wounds.[55] Other amulets derive their efficacy from acts of sacralization in which monks either informally, through the simple recitation of a formula, or formally, through a grand ceremony (*phutthaphisek*), charge them with power. There are also instances when monks confer this power without knowing it (amulets have been placed beneath their cushions). Moreover, some amulets are given their power through the expertise of lay specialists who "manipulate the more aggressive and dangerous types of magic."[56] Amulets in contemporary Thailand also serve as indices of wealth, power, and prestige within the community. Tambiah argues that the "more historic, more famous, more potent amulets are in the hands of the rulers and the wealthy, for they are sponsors of the ascetic saint as an amulet maker; these amulets confirm them in their power and act as sureties of wealth; in the words of Mauss, they are a 'magico-religious guarantee of rank and prosperity.' They reflect and legitimate, to put it in a Thai idiom, the hierarchy of merit."[57] Because these amulets function as objects of piety, power and status, it is not surprising that the distribution of amulets by temples is a common practice in Thailand, and the trade and "sale"[58] of these items constitute a booming industry in Thailand.

The Dhammakāya Temple drew upon these ideas of power, prosperity, and piety in their distribution of the Phra Mahsiriratthat amulets to donors who commissioned individual Phra Dhammakāya images for the Mahathammakai Chedi. The amulet bears an image of Phra Dhammakāya, and at its base is an inscription that reads, *dut sap* (suck wealth/property/assets). The name Mahsiriratthat means "king of all elements," referring as it does to the amulet's composition of black diamond iron, gold, and mercury. Each of these elements relates to specific benefits: Black diamond iron provides strength, gold makes one healthy, and mercury makes one's wishes come true.[59] The gold frame that accompanies the amulet also possesses special power. One advertisement describes the amulet as a *phayan*, a witness of the triple gem; it is also a vehicle for the accumulation of *bun kuson* (meritorious rewards), including *pok sap* (consumer goods), *lokiya sap* (mundane goods), and *ariya sap* (noble goods).[60] In this advertisement, readers are instructed in the method of using the amulet as an object of meditation. We are told that the amulet contains *saksit* (supernatural power) and is *khu bun* (possessed by those with merit). It should be with us at all times, and be admired and prayed to several times each day. One should cultivate feelings of love towards the image and think of it often. Rather than visualizing the crystal ball as in formal Dhammakāya meditation, one should meditate upon the amulet, repeating *samma arahang* as many times as needed until the mind is calmed.[61] At this point in the practice, one should focus on one's wishes and ask for success in future endeavors. The pamphlet informs readers that the combination of the merit generated from the commissioning of a Phra Dhammakāya image with the merit from the performance of amulet *pūja*, and faith in the triple gem will produce the following results: One will encounter happiness and prosperity frequently, his life and material possessions will be secure, he will find success in the event of an accident, and his life will be full of worldly and spiritual success.

In April of 1998, the Temple began its publication of a series of magazines entitled, *Anuphap Phra Mahasiriratthat* (the Power of the Mahsiriratthat Amulet). These magazines, which were distributed on a monthly basis at the Temple, contained inspirational stories of miraculous events in the lives of people who possessed these amulets. They reported tales of miraculous healings and stories of extraordinary rescues, as well as stories of the accumulation of wealth and prosperity. The *Anuphap Phra Mahasiriratthat* magazines resembled the glossy amulet magazines found at local newsstands in Thailand, which contain stories of renowned amulets and their effects on the lives of their "owners." Rather than selling the *Anuphap Phra Mahasiriratthat* magazines at local newsstands, however, the Dhammakāya Temple distributed them free of charge at the Temple. The magazines typically contained a number of inspirational and miraculous stories about donors who possessed the Dhammakāya amulets, as well as sermons from Phra Dhammachayo and Phra Thattacheewo, advertisements for the chedi, and the lyrics to popular Dhammakāya chants.

The stories in the first *Anuphap Phra Mahasiriratthat* magazine exemplify the general theme of miraculous power that runs throughout the other volumes.[62] The first story is of a young girl who, while dreaming, is visited by a female ghost who tells the young girl to commission a Phra Dhammakāya image at the Dhammakāya Temple on her behalf. In the midst of the dream the ghost tells the young girl her name and her age of 692. When the young girl awakes, she purchases a lottery ticket with the number 692; this leads to her winning 600,000 baht. After she gets the prize, she goes to the ghost's village. She finds the ghost's sister who, upon hearing the story, also goes to the Dhammakāya Temple and donates even more money than the young girl on behalf of her sister.

The next story tells of a young Thai woman living in England who, while visiting her family in Thailand, received a brochure about the Mahathammakai Chedi. After she had returned home with the brochure, a miraculous event occurred. She saw a beautiful light reflected in the window that she initially

Cover of *Anuphap Phra Mahasiriratthat* Magazine. (Courtesy of the Dhammakāya Foundation.)

mistook for a UFO, but upon closer inspection she realized that the light was emanating from the brochure. As she looked at the brochure, she suddenly heard a voice coming from inside her body that said, "come home, come home." The narrative informs us that she believed this to be a sign for her to return to Thailand in order to donate money to the Dhammakāya Temple. She donated

30,000 baht for an individual Phra Dhammakāya image and received a Phra Mahsiriratthat amulet in return.

Another story tells of a terminal cancer patient for whom no medical treatment, including chemotherapy, could do anything. Many years prior, he had made merit at the Dhammakāya Temple, and one day a Dhammakāya monk visited him in the hospital and told him, "You are nearly dead, but if you stay alive until your next birthday, then you will live a long time. The cancer will disappear." The man's birthday was on the sixth of December, but on the fifth of December he could no longer eat nor see, and he lost consciousness. While unconscious, he thought about the Dhammakāya Temple and all of the merit that he had made there and about how merit can make one's health improve. The story ends by telling us that he is still alive today and continues to make merit at the Dhammakāya Temple.

During the construction of the Mahathammakai Chedi, these stories were repeated at Temple events, especially on Sundays during the periods between formal meditation or teaching sessions. Practitioners spoke about their experiences at the Dhammakāya Temple, their reasons for attending, and notable events in their lives. Their voices were amplified by an array of microphones and speakers placed throughout the large assembly hall, and often were televised on the dozens of monitors mounted on pillars in the assembly hall. On one occasion, I witnessed a man stand before hundreds of practitioners and describe his association with the Temple. He explained that he started to attend services at the Temple when his mother who was wheelchair bound miraculously recovered after she had practiced Dhammakāya meditation and made merit at the Temple. Interestingly, the fact that the spokesman was a doctor added to the credibility of his statements.

Miracle in the Sky

During the construction of the Mahathammakai Chedi, reports of miraculous occurrences were not confined to the personal lives of individual Dhammakāya donors. On September 6, 1998, as more than twenty thousand of practitioners stood in front of the yet unfinished Mahathammakai Chedi, a miracle purportedly occurred. The sun disappeared from the sky and was replaced by a glowing, luminescent image of the late Luang Pho Wat Sot of Wat Pak Nam. Photographs taken by the Temple depict practitioners crying and smiling, pointing to the sky and waving reflective metallic flags with an image of Luang Pho Sot on the front.

The Temple was not reticent to advertise this event in the press. In fact, it advertised the "miracle in the sky" in the *Bangkok Post*, one of Thailand's most prominent English-language newspapers.[63] Descriptions of miraculous events abound in the daily Thai language newspapers, such as *Daily News* and *Thairath*, but it was rather unusual for a temple to advertise a miracle in the *Bangkok Post*— especially in a full-page color advertisement. At the top of the page the caption read, that while some may criticize the miracle, "it is an excellent source of inspiration to continue doing the greatest good." Underneath was a picture of the Mahathammakai Chedi with thousands of supporters around it, and in the sky is a super-imposed, computer-generated picture of a golden Luang Pho Sot. Below the chedi picture were photos of Dhammakāya practitioners in states of ecstasy and wonderment, as they gazed into the sky with tears running down their cheeks. Underneath these evocative photographs was printed the Webster's *New World Dictionary's* definition of a miracle: "An event or action that apparently contradicts known scientific laws and is hence thought to be due to supernatural causes." The advertisement continued, "Whether you believe in miracles or not, the experience of a great number of devotees at Wat Phra Dhammakāya in September this year certainly fits Webster's New World definition." There were two long testimonials describing the miracle on the bottom half of the page, while at the right-hand side there was an image of the now familiar Mahsiriratthat amulet and a description of its qualities and powers.

Finally, at the bottom of the page, there were two testimonials from witnesses who described the miracle in their own words, imploring readers to visit the Temple in order to witness such miraculous events for themselves. The first testimonial was by Dr. Somsuda Phoopat of the Education Faculty at Kasetsart University. He began his account with a reference to a previous miracle, that of Yamakapatihara, "when the Lord Buddha opens all the abodes, Preta, Asurakaya, Manussa, Devata, Brahm and Arupabrahm so that every being could see each other clearly." Although he admitted to previous skepticism, his witnessing of the miracle in the sky at the Dhammakāya Temple made him into an ardent believer.

> After the photographing of the mass devotees was completed everyone turned in the direction of the Maha Dhammakāya Cetiya [Mahathammakai Chedi]. Suddenly, a bright light was seen to our right. As we adjusted our eyes to see it even better, we could see limitless brightness in the evening sky. There in the middle of all this bright light was an image of Luang Phor Wat Pak Nam. He was clearly visible with the bright sun shining from the center of his body. The sun was clean, pure and extremely brilliant. It was a great wonder to me. I was struck speechless. All I could do was wave the flag of Luang Phor Wat Pak Nam that had been given me, with feeling of gratitude and a wish that he could somehow see me and carry me out of all suffering me and carry me out of all suffering.[64]

His testimonial continued with his description of the changing colors of the sun, tears running down his face, and others declaring the "victory of mankind" by chanting, "Chitam me, Chitam me, Chitam me."[65] As he continued to watch the sun, a golden crystal-clear Mahathammakai Chedi appeared from within it. He acknowledged the skepticism of others, but suggested that each person should "[t]ake a trip to Wat Dhammakāya and see the wonders that abound there with your own eyes!"

The second testimonial printed in the advertisement was given by Mr. Termpong Punachinda of the Thanachat Trust Company Limited. Termpong began by stating that he had heard that Luang Pho's image had appeared in the sky on August 30, but it was not until he saw the miraculous events of September 6 that he believed in the occurrence of miracles at the Temple. Unlike Dr. Somsuda, Termpong did not see Luang Pho Sot; rather, he witnessed the sun emitting flashing rays of light, and for one brief moment, he saw an image of the Buddha.

> The ray colours alternated between white, pink, and gold. My hair stood on end and I had an indescribable feeling of great happiness. My body seemed light and as if it were expanding. I had no control over my feelings, tears streamed from my eyes. The more I tried to calm myself down, the more I broke into tears. They were tears of happiness indeed, a happiness which I could not put into words. When I looked up at the Cetiya and the Sangha, they were bathed in changing lights of the sun; pink, violet and gold. Nearly all the spectators there cried with happiness. The event continued around half an hour and it definitely put me out of doubt about the "miracle" I had heard about on August 30th.

He continued his testimonial by stating that some people believed him when he relayed this story while others did not. Some asked whether it was a corona or "ring of light seen around an eclipsed sun," and others suggested that it could be attributed to mass hypnosis. He acknowledged his own doubts prior to witnessing the events of September 6, but he urged skeptics to travel to the Temple in order to develop faith.

Both testimonials end their descriptions of the "miracle in the sky" by urging individuals to go to the Temple to witness these extraordinary events for themselves. The advertisement continued this theme at the very bottom of the page with the following declaration: "Don't wait for a miracle . . . Be open to the possibility of doing a great deal of good today, even though it's late, because tomorrow might be just . . . too late!" This claim is followed by an invitation to upcoming events at the Temple, specifically the ceremonies marking the one hundred fourteenth anniversary of the late Luang Pho Sot's birthday.

We are told that although Luang Pho Sot "may have departed from us in this life. He still keeps watch over those who worship and respect him, however, we can never return his endless loving-kindness."

While modern rationalist interpretations of Buddhism deemphasize or outright denounce the role of miracles within Theravāda Buddhism, the Dhammakāya Temple's miracle in the sky is not an anomaly. Descriptions of miracles abound within the texts and oral traditions of Theravāda Buddhism, from canonical tales of the miraculous powers (*iddhi*) and miraculous knowledge (*abhiññā*) to popular stories involving the Buddha, his relics, and images. The occurrence of miracles within these narratives commonly validates the possession of supreme insight and merit by a particular individual. The foremost example of this is the Buddha's sacred biography (or rather, biographies), which is replete with miraculous events. In the *Nidānakathā*, an introduction to the *Jātakaṭṭakathā* (a collection of past life stories), there are vivid descriptions of these miraculous events. In the following passage from the *Nidānakathā*, which recounts the effects of the Bodhisattva's conception, we find a richly detailed account of miraculous occurrences.

> The moment the Bodhisatta took conception in his mother's womb the entire ten thousand world-systems quaked, trembled, and shook violently with one accord. Thirty-two portents make themselves manifest. An unlimited radiance spread in the ten thousand world-spheres. And the blind regained their sight as though to behold this wonder. The deaf regained hearing. The dumb spoke to one another. The hunch-backs stood erect. Cripples were able to walk on their feet. Creatures in bondage were released from imprisonment and fetters. The fire in all of the hells was extinguished. Hunger and thirst in the realm of the creatures subsided. All beings became affable. Horses neighed gently and so did elephants trumpet. All musical instruments echoed forth their music. Bracelets and other ornaments of human beings resounded even without striking against each other. All the directions became calm. A cool and gentle breeze blew refreshing every one. Rain fell out of season. Water spouted out from the earth and flowed around. Birds gave up their flight in the sky. The rivers stopped flowing. The great ocean turned into sweet water. Everywhere the surface was covered with the five kinds of lotuses. All varieties of flowers bloomed on land and water; flowers that bloom on creepers—all of them bloomed forth. Lotuses on stalks burst out in clusters of seven one upon the other breaking through slabs of rock on dry land. Hanging lotuses appeared in the sky. Showers of flowers came down on every side. Heavenly music resounded in the sky. The entire ten

thousand world-systems bearing of one mass garlands and fanned
vigorously with yak-tail whisks, were impregnated with the fragrance of flowers and incense and attained the highest splendour,
like a ball of flowers spun round and released, or like a wreath
of garlands tied firmly together, or like a well decorated flower-
alter.[66]

These miraculous events mark the Buddha's conception as special, as extraordinary, for it is not everyday that a future Buddha enters the world. The won-
drous detail that is found within this account is replicated throughout the text
as we read of other miraculous occurrences in the Buddha's life, including the
magical disappearance of the Buddha's earthenware bowl (which was instantly
replaced with a golden bowl by Sujata),[67] the Buddha's transformation of Mara's
swords, daggers, darts, and other weapons into heavenly flowers,[68] and his performance of a miraculous levitation to a disrespectful crowd.[69]

Similar descriptions of miraculous events in the life of the Buddha are
found in other sacred biographies, including Aśvaghoṣa's *Buddhacarita* (the Acts
of the Buddha, second century CE), and within countless tales of the Buddha
within the chronicle traditions of South and Southeast Asia. The *Tamnān Ang
Salung* (The Chronicle of [Sacred] Water Basin Mountain, a pre–fifteenth-
century text from northern Thailand), for instance, recounts numerous miracles
during the Buddha's travels in the north.[70] In one account, the Buddha proves
his majesty to a local Lawa former when "mucus dripped from the Buddha's
nose but miraculously floated up to the leaves of the Asoka tree giving the
leaves a golden hue." These leaves were then collected and honored as a Buddha relic; its power is thought to be the ability to "determine who is good and
who is evil."[71] In another account, the Buddha gives a hair relic to a group of
arahants and King Asoka, which miraculously multiplies by eight in order for
their to be eight reliquaries in that region.[72] In the *Cāmadevīvaṃsa*, a fifteenth
century text from northern Thailand, a miraculous tale leads to the founding of
the famed city of Haripuñjaya.

> The Blessed One, descending to the splendid, densely forested site
> of the future Haripuñjaya on the west bank of [Kwang] river, stood
> at the place where the relics would appear and looked for a place to
> set down his alms bowl.
>
> At that moment, a square slab smooth as a drum . . . arose from the
> earth near the tathāgata's feet. The Blessed One then placed his
> alms bowl on the stone, put his robe (*mahāpaṃsukulacīvaraṃ*) over
> one shoulder, and looked around carefully. As the governor in-
> spects a city in order to protect it, so also the Buddha inspected the

site so that the sons of the Mon would remember [the place]. While the Blessed One was so engaged, he spoke to the Mon, "O forest Ādiccarāja [Ādittarāja] will govern it. He will be of your lineage. When I have reached my parinibbāna my relics (sārīrikadhātu) will appear at this place, and the king will protect them."

Having spoken, the Blessed One took his alms bowl and after putting it in the palm of his hand, it immediately rose into the air and proceeded ahead of the Buddha. The Blessed One then ascended into the air following the alms bowl until he arrived at the Isipatana forest near Vārāṇī.

As the sons of the forest witnessed this miracle, they marveled at the power (guṇa) of the Blessed One, and then returned to their village. The white crow, hearing the words of the Buddha and telling another crow of his intention, appointed [the second crow] to guard the place and then he flew to the Himavanta forest.[73]

These tales of miraculous events from the *Tamnān Ang Salung* and the *Cāmadevīvaṃsa* not only reinforce the presence of miracles in the Buddha's biography, they serve as charter myths for stories of post-nibbanic miracles involving Buddha relics, images, manuscripts, and future meditation adepts. In the case of relics, there are numerous stories in South and Southeast Asia, which recount tales of how relics have miraculously escaped destruction by fire, by smashing, by water, and by burial.[74] Because these miraculous escapes are a sign of the power within the relic, it is not surprising that some Buddhists in Thailand believe that Buddha relics, votive tablets, and amulets possess the power to protect practitioners from misfortune, bad luck, and malevolent forces.

As we saw in the descriptions of the miraculous powers of Luang Pho Sot and Khun Yay Ubasika Chan in the last chapter, the tales of miracles in the Buddha's life also reflect the belief that skill in meditation may produce miraculous or supra-normal powers (*iddhi*) and knowledges (*abiññā*). In the *Sāmaññaphala-sutta*, for instance, the Buddha describes the possession of supra-normal powers by adept practitioners who have reached the fourth *jhāna* of *samatha* meditation; they include the ability to appear and vanish at will, to walk through barriers and on water, and to fly through the air. These powers are considered to be one fruit (*phala*) of the contemplative life. In Thailand, tales of beings with miraculous powers abound in stories of the past as well as the present. But these beings are not always monks. In the *Cāmadevīvaṃsa*, for instance, the four powerful beings who fulfill the prophesy of the Buddha are independent ascetics who have left the saṅgha but through the power of their meditation, have still developed the five higher knowledges: "psychic power (*iddhividhi*), divine ear (*dibbasotaṃ*), telepathy (*paracittavijānanaṃ*), recollection of previous lives (*pubbenivāsānussati*), and divine eye (*dibbacakkhu*)."[75] This is an important point to note, as the Dhammakāya miracle was interpreted by some as the result of the collective meditation skill of the Dhammakāya community, which included monks, nuns, and laypersons of all ages.

Today, tales of miraculous events are commonplace in contemporary Thai literature and popular discourse. The Dhammakāya Temple is far from the only temple to "advertise" miraculous occurrences or to publish magazines about the magical efficacy of particular amulets. In fact, as we shall see in Chapter 5, the sale of such stories is a thriving industry in Thailand. Stories about the history of particularly potent amulets, the monks who bless them, and their effects on the people are replete within popular "amulet" magazines. The Dhammakāya Temple's marketing of the miracle in the sky and the Mahsiriratthat amulets, should, therefore, be situated within the long-standing tradition of miracles within the Theravāda tradition as well as within contemporary beliefs about miraculous occurrences in the lives of the pious.

Debates over Dhammakāya Merit-making

Given the importance of stūpa-building in Theravāda Buddhism and the popularity of amulets and tales of miraculous powers and events in Thailand, one would not expect Dhammakāya merit-making to become the subject of a heated national debate in 1998 and 1999. But it did. As we shall see in the next chapter, critics of the Temple's teachings and practices chose to interpret the construction of the chedi as yet another sign of the corruption and commercialization of Buddhism in contemporary Thailand rather than seeing it as the product of pious Buddhists, as a field for merit-making. For some of these critics, the Temple's construction of the Mahathammakai Chedi was interpreted as an example of monastic excess, and its construction was seen as representative of a tendency within Thai Buddhism to view the "biggest as the best." Many temples throughout Thailand boast the possession of large edifices including Buddha images, temple buildings, and monuments.

For other critics, it was not the size of the chedi project that was problematic as much as the Temple's marketing techniques. These activities, according to them, were clear examples of the commercialization of Buddhism (*phuttha phanit*). In particular, critics denounced the Temple's distribution of the Phra Mahsiriratthat amulets to patrons who commissioned the individual Phra Dhammakāya images, and they criticized the Temple's advertising of miraculous events at the temple.[76]

The controversy over the Dhammakāya Temple's construction of the chedi demonstrates how acts of merit can become sites of contestation in which

Buddha Image, Wat Indrawihan, Bangkok. (Photograph by Rachelle M. Scott.)

differing groups assert competing visions of religious practice, identity, and authority. The concept of merit, while embedded within a rich history of Buddhist discourses and practices, cannot be taken as self-evident. Past studies of merit and merit-making in Thai Buddhism have asked the following kinds of questions: What is merit? How does it function in the system of Thai Buddhism?

And how does it relate to the Buddhist quest for salvation? It is clear that not all Buddhists agree on the constituent features of merit, the mechanisms for its generation, and its function within the broader sphere of Buddhist religiosity. The situation is further complicated by the fact that each act of merit-making takes place within a distinct social field, in which discourses of power, prestige, and piety influence the interpretation and assessment of Buddhist practice. Acts of dāna are especially open to disagreement, for they rest upon assumptions regarding the merit of the donors and of their recipients, the appropriateness of certain gifts, and the proper rules for exchange. Kemper argues that "gift giving has a contractual character, and customs stipulate who should give what and how it should be done,"[77] but as Bourdieu has shown us, customs are not givens. They may be reproduced "fairly accurately," but not determinatively.[78] Most Theravāda Buddhists, for instance, would agree that generosity is a key Buddhist virtue, but questions may emerge over the appropriateness of certain gifts by particular donors to particular recipients. The mechanics of giving, therefore, are subject to negotiation and contestation within history.

Katherine Bowie in a provocative revaluation of the notions of merit and charity suggests that contrary to the doctrinal emphasis on the saṅgha as a field of merit, "most villagers have a broader conception of merit making which includes charity to the poor."[79] Bowie argues that, while scholarship on merit-making generally defines it in reference to the offering of gifts to the saṅgha and temple, many "villagers generally use the phrase tham bun (to make merit) to refer to a wide range of good deeds or good actions occurring throughout everyday life, regardless of institutional setting." Her research revealed that whereas many scholars interpret the effective power of merit in reference to the amount given, many villagers "stress intention and relative ability to give." Bowie's analysis of village conceptions and acts of merit-making demonstrates how the field of merit-making, while resting upon customary ideas about merit, is not a fixed category. Merit-making is a field that is constructed through varying conceptions of efficacious action.

Rather than assuming the constituents of merit and the mechanics of merit-making, then, it is far more fruitful to examine how Thai Buddhists make use of the concept of merit, and how they relate their constructions of merit to the larger discursive tradition of Theravāda Buddhism and to their specific cultural and historical contexts.[80] Without taking this shift in orientation into account, apparent anomalous interpretations of merit (such as acts of charity to the poor) appear deviant, when they are, in fact, legitimate uses of the term within a specified context. Take, for instance, the infamous statement by Phra Kitthiwuttho that Thai soldiers would accrue no demerit for killing communists, or at the passages in the Sri Lankan *Mahāvaṃsa* that make similar claims regarding non-Buddhist "invaders." In order for us to understand why Phra Kitthiwuttho and the authors of the *Mahāvaṃsa* made use of the concept of merit in this way, we need to recognize that the economy of merit is a power-laden discourse within Buddhist societies, and, as such, it often becomes a site of debate and reflection for Buddhists at particular moments in history.

In this vein, we must recognize that the recent debates over wealth, piety, and merit-making in Thailand came to the forefront of public discourse during a period in Thailand's history when debates over prosperity and poverty were of vital interest to Thais across the kingdom. The Dhammakāya controversy "broke out" in the Thai press in 1998, in the midst of the Asian economic crisis. Thai newspapers were saturated with stories of businesses going bankrupt, engineers and accountants who were driving taxis, and abbots complaining about the decline in donations. It was also during this time that Phra Maha Bua Yanasampanno, the abbot of Wat Pa Ban Tad temple in Udon Thani and a disciple of the much beloved and admired forest monk, Phra Acharn Man, launched a "national reconstruction" donation drive to save the Thai economy. People from across the country donated currency, gold jewelry, and other valuable items to his special economic relief fund. Given this economic climate, it is not surprising that Dhammakāya critics would raise questions about the temple's marketing of the multimillion-dollar chedi. While other temples were struggling to receive enough food or to pay their monthly bills and while Phra Maha Bua campaigned to raise money to *chuay chat* (help the nation), the Dhammakāya Temple was aggressively marketing its chedi project. The disparity between these images of temple life and Thai life helped to light and fuel the flames of controversy.

In response to questions about the appropriateness of the chedi project, Temple officials defended its construction on several fronts. They stated that the chedi fund-raising campaign began during a period of unprecedented economic prosperity in Thailand—years before the economic downturn. They also cited historical precedents for the building of temples during times of economic difficulty. They compared their construction of the Mahathammakai Chedi to King Rama I's construction of Wat Phra Kaew and the Grand Palace following years of war with Burma, arguing that the construction of religious buildings during periods of economic strife serve to usher in new eras of prosperity and stability. The Temple was not alone in its discourses of prosperity during this period. In 1998, the most popular Thai New Year cards bore images of King Bhumipol on 100 baht, 500 baht, and 1000 baht Thai banknotes; the message in the cards was "Wishing you a lot of wealth (*kho hai ruay*)."[81] And finally, temple officials asked why it was so wrong for people to spend money on religion during times of economic woe, when many Thais were all too willing to spend money on luxury items such as alcohol, cigarettes, and films. In fact, they noted how the film, *Titanic*, had grossed over one million baht in Thailand over a relatively short period of time.

The Temple's response to its critics highlights a crucial point. While the critics related large public displays of merit-making to materialism in the context of the economic crisis, Temple practitioners continued to view this kind of merit-making as beneficial to the individual and to society as a whole. For Dhammakāya practitioners, the construction of the Mahathammakai Chedi, the reception of Phra Mahsiriratthat amulets, and the tales of miraculous events fit in perfectly with the tradition of merit-making at the heart of Thai Buddhism. In this tradition, the association of prosperity with merit is assumed and actively sought as one expression of Buddhist piety. The Dhammakāya Temple may have taken these practices to a new level of proselytization, but they were not fundamentally different from the long tradition of merit-making and beneficial rewards that has fostered the spread of the Buddhist tradition for centuries.

Chapter 4

The Dhammakāya Controversy: Wealth, Piety, and Authority

Embattled Dhammakāya abbot Dhammachayo vowed before thousands of his supporters at this temple yesterday that he would not allow anyone to defrock him. "I would rather die in a saffron robe," he said to big applause from his devotees, some of whom also broke into tears. In a rare speech on the controversy and the first show of defiance against religious authorities' attempts to defrock him, Dhammachayo defended himself against allegations of embezzlement and told his followers to brace themselves for the possibility that he would be removed as the Dhammakāya Temple's abbot.

—*The Nation*, May 24, 1999[1]

On the Sunday preceding Visākhā Pujā in 1999, Phra Dhammachayo announced to thousands of his disciples that he would die rather than be forced to remove his monastic robes. Having made this vow, he urged his followers to focus their attention on meditation practice and on the protection and dissemination of the Dhammakāya method. Scanning the faces of his devoted followers sitting quietly in half-lotus positions, he could see expressions ranging from immense pride to deep sadness. People were openly crying and shaking their heads. One devoted follower of the Temple walked up to the stage and addressed his fellow Dhammakāya supporters. He pleaded that they bring their families to the Temple the following weekend in order to prevent attempts by the police to disrobe the abbot. Throughout the day there were discussions about supporting and defending the abbot at all costs.

Dhammachayo's declaration of monastic commitment followed months of accusations and investigations in 1998 and 1999 into his controversial teachings, practices, and personal assets. Over the course of this controversy, Phra Dhammachayo's character became the focus of both criminal and monastic investigations. The state brought criminal charges of malfeasance and embezzlement against him, while concomitant charges were posed by high-ranking monastic officials who alleged that Phra Dhammachayo had violated the monastic code of conduct by teaching heretical views on nirvāṇa. Phra Dhammachayo's face was ubiquitous in the newspapers, news magazines, and in editorial cartoons.

On the cover of one magazine, Phra Dhammachayo's picture was encircled by a glowing haze above a picture of the golden Mahathammakai Chedi.

The Cover of *Matichon Weekly*, May 4, 1999. (Courtesy of *Matichon*.)

The caption underneath his picture read, "Nikai mai?" (A new sect?)[2] On another magazine cover, Phra Dhammachayo's portrait appeared as a criminal mug shot and the caption below it read, "WANTED!"[3] On yet another cover, Phra Dhammachayo's picture had been digitally altered to present him in a layman's suit surrounded by a burning fire; its caption read, "The End."[4]

The Cover of *Matichon Weekly*, May 11, 1999. (Courtesy of *Matichon*.)

Given the focus on Phra Dhammachayo in the press, it would be tempting to equate the Dhammakāya controversy with the *person* of Phra Dhammachayo, but the issues were actually far broader than the abbot's personal faults or merits. Debates over Phra Dhammachayo's teachings, practices, and personal wealth became occasions to reevaluate the relationship between wealth and piety in Thai Buddhism as well as the identity of Thai Buddhism itself. Arjun Appadurai argues that local knowledge is "actually knowledge of how to produce and reproduce locality under conditions of anxiety and entropy, social wear and flux, ecological uncertainty and cosmic volatility, and the always present quirkiness of kinsmen, enemies, spirits and quarks of all sorts."[5] This production of locality extends to religious identity as specific religious communities authorize and reauthorize the contours of orthodoxy and orthopraxy in times of controversy.

The Dhammakāya controversy should, then, not be interpreted as merely the story of how one of Thailand's richest temples became subject to criticism, condemnation, and ridicule. Occupying the popular imagination for over a year, the controversy was the product of and stimulus for debates over Buddhist thought, practice, and identity at a particular point in Thai history. Religious disputations provide unique windows into the fault lines of a religion at critical historical junctures: They bring into sharp relief issues facing religious communities as they respond and adapt to new challenges and social realities. This chapter analyzes the Dhammakāya controversy as an instance in history when differing views over the relationship between wealth and piety collided and became a national forum for issues of religious orthodoxy and institutional authority in postmodern Thailand. This examination of the controversy will set the stage by examining its broader context (the Asian economic crisis) and by providing a chronology of its development from November 1998 to August 1999. This overview will highlight the various modes of criticism from the government, the press, and the religious authorities, and will analyze the charges of materialism and heresy as they relate to differing critical voices within contemporary Thai Buddhism.

The Context of the Controversy: The Asian Economic Crisis

The Dhammakāya controversy emerged within the historical context of the Asian economic crisis that began in Thailand in the summer of 1997. The Asian economic crisis had a profound effect upon the economies of Southeast Asia and East Asia. The ramifications were numerous, ranging from the collapse of governments to the increase in violent crime and suicide. While I was living in Thailand in 1998 and 1999, the newspapers were full of tragic stories of how unemployment and economic despair had led formerly successful individuals to commit suicide and of how drugs and crime were invading the schools and taking over Thai youth.

Buddhist temples were not immune from the effects of the economic crisis, especially in terms of donations. In September 1998, the Thai Farmers Bank (TFB) research center conducted a poll on the amount of donations given to temples during the economic crisis; 43.5 percent of the respondents indicated that they were giving fewer donations and attending services less often.[6] One abbot reflected on these results: "People organizing funerals are cutting them down from nine or seven days to only two or three days. When new monks collect alms in the morning, they hardly receive enough for breakfast."[7] The TFB research center also received a number of complaints from local temple abbots who argued that not only were donations down, but they were also receiving a number of checks with insufficient funds. Furthermore, what little they did receive had to be directed towards monthly expenses. New construction and restoration projects were out of the question. In fact, earlier in the year the Department of Religious Affairs had requested that temples halt building projects during the economic crisis.

Given the decline in donations since the inception of the Asian economic crisis, it is not surprising that the Dhammakāya Temple's extensive fund-raising campaign for its Mahathammakai Chedi in 1998 raised serious criticisms. The adverse economic environment may also explain why, during the months preceding the Dhammakāya controversy, another religious dispute erupted in the newspapers that raised questions about the methods of the acquisition of wealth by temples. Allegations were leveled that Phra Khru Witharnsutthikij, deputy abbot of Wat Lad Prao, had overcharged for the temple's funeral services in order to increase temple profits. One woman told the press that she was forced to buy a coffin and flowers for her father's funeral at an inflated price and because she could not afford the temple's high rates for renting the funeral pavilion, she had to hold the funeral services for her father outside. Heavy rains fell on the night of the funeral. She told the press, "I implored Phra Khru Mali to let me move the coffin to an enclosed pavilion, but he said no. He even announced on loudspeakers that he would take it as a challenge if anybody helped move the coffin."[8] This story filled the headlines in all of the local papers, and it raised questions about the funeral industry in Thailand: Do temples overcharge for funeral services? How do temples manage the profits from these and other services? Should the poor be charged for religious services?[9]

More generally, the economic crisis led to a reexamination of the relationship between wealth and Buddhist piety, the rise of consumerism within popular culture, and the influences of global capitalism on Thai society. As we shall see in Chapter 5, questions concerning the appropriateness of monastic profit and the commercialization of Buddhism had circulated among the intellectual elite in Thailand over the past three decades, but the economic crisis brought these questions to the forefront of public discourse. Previously, criticism of the wealth and marketing of the Dhammakāya Temple had been restricted to the sphere of intellectual discourse. In 1998, however, questions concerning the Temple's wealth were aired by mainstream media.

Becoming a national debate, the topic of wealth attracted the attention of the religious authorities and prompted action (or at least the appearance of action) by the Supreme Saṅgha Council. In the case of the funeral controversy, Phra Khru Mali was dismissed from his administrative duties shortly after the story appeared in the press, and the Department of Religious Affairs and the Supreme Saṅgha Council agreed to institute measures that would prevent temples from seeking profits for their funeral services. These reforms took many by surprise. One observer called the investigation "unprecedented." According to him, it "is an open secret that temples charge fees for organizing funerals. Everybody knows this is improper, but they keep quiet because they don't want to quarrel with monks."[10] In periods of economic hardship and increased financial anxiety, however, accusations of the abuse of wealth by monks enter the public sphere and become forces for reform.

Historical Outline of the Controversy

Controversies concerning the integrity of monastic practice have emerged in Buddhist societies throughout the tradition's twenty-five-hundred-year history. According to the Theravāda tradition the first great schism (*saṅghabheda*) occurred in the saṅgha at the Second Council at Vesālī (330 or 320 BCE) because of the lax practice of an errant group of monks who were later called the Mahāsāṃghikas. One of their most contentious practices was the physical handling of money, a practice that appeared to violate the tenth precept against handling gold and silver.[11] From the perspective of their critics, the Sthaviravādins, these monks were to be condemned not only for their individual "defeats" (their violation of the rules of discipline), but also, and perhaps more importantly, for their collective break from the orthodox saṅgha and subsequent creation of an alternative sect. The creation of a saṅghabheda is one of the seven acts classified as a crime against the saṅgha, a crime so grievous that it bars a previously ordained person from being readmitted into the saṅgha.[12] It is also classified as one of the five heinous offenses, alongside matricide, fratricide, killing an enlightened being, and injuring a Buddha. The force with which the tradition condemns divisive behavior within the saṅgha reveals an important aspect of the Theravāda tradition, namely that the saṅgha represents the Buddha, who is no longer accessible. The Buddhist saṅgha maintains the Buddha's teachings in the world through the maintenance of orthodoxy

(*Buddhavacana*, literally the word of the Buddha) and through their purity of practice. Division strikes, therefore, at the heart of the tradition's ability to preserve the dhamma.

In Buddhist literature the most reviled divisive figure was Devadatta, the Buddha's evil cousin. According to the *Saṅghabhedakkhandhaka*, Devadatta promoted a more ascetic interpretation of monastic life than the Buddha did. He insisted that five practices were necessary for monastic integrity: first, forest dwelling bhikkhus must remain permanently in the forest; second, bhikkhus who rely on *piṇḍapāta* (alms collection) must not accept invitations to dine in a home; third, bhikkhus who wear rag robes must always wear rag robes; fourth, bhikkhus who dwell under a tree must never sleep in a structure, and finally, bhikkhus should never eat meat. Devadatta's strict application of these rules to monastic life was in opposition to the Buddha, who identified them as a matter of personal choice. Because of this disagreement, Devadatta led more than five hundred monks to Gayāsīsa district, where he established a separate order. Devadatta's story demonstrates how a saṅghabheda represents more than an individual disagreement with the Buddha. A schism may result from disparate interpretations of dhamma-vinaya, but doctrinal disputes alone do not create a schism. Richard Gombrich writes: "Splitting is a matter of vinaya, of behavior. If the split arises as the result of a disagreement, the disagreement itself is likely to be over a point of vinaya—of this recent Theravādin history furnishes us with many examples. But whatever the source of the disagreement, the result is measured in vinaya terms: holding separate pātimokkha ceremonies."[13] A schism occurs when a group of more than four monks conducts the acts of *uposatha* (ordination), *pavāraṇā* (admonishment), and *saṅghakamma* (legal act) as a separate group. The Buddhist criteria for judging whether a group adheres to the normative tradition, therefore, derive predominantly from accepted notions of orthopraxy not from orthodoxy. As a result, Buddhist communities in the past (and present) have lived under the guidance of one monastic discipline while holding radically different views on the dhamma.[14]

As we shall see, the Dhammakāya Temple controversy involves a few accusations of specific *Vinaya* violations (the standard grounds for a saṅghabheda), but the heart of the controversy stems from general questions about Buddhism in the contemporary world. One set of accusations focus on the effects of global capitalism on Buddhist practice, such as whether or not the practice of giving amulets in exchange for a specified amount of money reduces Buddhism to a "commodity," or whether the "direct sale" of personal Dhammakāya images through networks of lay disciples is an acceptable method of proselytization. Another set of accusations focuses on the Temple's controversial teachings on nirvāṇa (*nibbāna*, Pāli; *nipphan*, Thai). The issue of nirvāṇa reflects the modernist concern with issues of orthodoxy, which are the basic ingredients in the construction of an essentialized canonical text-based version of authentic

Buddhism. Both sets of questions have led critics to consider the Dhammakāya Temple as a new *nikai* (*nikāya*, Pāli)[15] and view it as a divisive threat.

The controversial character of the Dhammakāya Temple first emerged in the public sphere in the late 1980s, when the Temple purchased over 2,400 rai of land (approximately 960 acres) adjacent to the Temple. At the time, 300 local farmers were cultivating the land. When several of these farmers refused to leave, national attention was directed at the Temple. Questions were raised concerning the Temple's reasons for acquiring such a large piece land at the expense of local farmers. Although all of the farmers were eventually forced from the land (having been compensated by the Temple), the public image of the Temple was sullied by the controversy, especially by the condemnation of the Temple's appetite for wealth, prestige, and power. One elderly farmer reflected back on his imprisonment for six months for failing to follow the eviction: "I had nowhere to go then and nobody could help me. It's strange that a temple which was supposed to help people was the villain itself."[16] Another man, who had been only six years old when his family was evicted stated, "(t)hey may have a lot of rich followers and enjoy huge donations. But villagers here have no faith in the temple."[17] This dispute over land led the Dhammakāya Temple's most earnest critics to heighten their censure of the Temple's wealth in public speeches, articles, and books; nevertheless, the controversy surrounding the Temple faded from public view as other stories titillated public imagination, such as the defrocking of Phra Phothirak, the leader of Santi Asok, the sensational sex scandals of Phra Nikorn and Phra Yantra, and the environmental protests of Phra Prachak.

But the critical gaze of the Thai national media, however, was redirected back upon the Dhammakāya Temple when the ITV network aired a program in November of 1998 criticizing the Dhammakāya Temple's advertising of a miraculous event ("the miracle in the sky"); this investigative report launched a media frenzy that would last well over a year. The ITV program suggested that the Temple advertised the miracle in order to attract potential donors for its building projects. As noted in the previous chapter, the Temple publicized the miracle in several local papers, including a prominent full-page advertisement on page two of the *Bangkok Post*. The Temple also advertised the miracle on large billboards throughout Bangkok and at the temple in Pathum Thani. One sign located in the Temple's main office read, "Never before and never again," a dual reference to both the opportunity to donate funds for the building of the Mahathammakai Chedi and the miraculous occurrences. Regarding these tactics, Deputy Education Minister Arkom Engchuan stated, "Billboards picturing the miracle that are used to invite donations are not suitable. Instead, they should be used to invite the public to study the teachings of Lord Buddha at the temple. I have already told the abbot this."[18] Within a week of the ITV program, the Dhammakāya Temple was front-page news again in almost every newspaper in Thailand. While some of the reports tended to be more sensational than others, all branches of the Thai media followed the government's investigations into the Temple's "alleged unorthodox Buddhist teachings and improper fund-raising methods."[19] Following Engchuan's initial investigation, the Department of Education informed the press that they would ask the Supreme Saṅgha Council to investigate two issues, "the miracle phenomenon and the method used for fund-raising, to see whether the practices were suitable for a Buddhist temple."[20]

These allegations gained legitimacy when Phra Mettanando, an ex-Dhammakāya monk, addressed the concerns in the press. This story was particularly appealing in that he had been one of the Temple's "superstar" monks. As a Dhammakāya monk, he had received degrees in Pāli from Oxford University and in religious and medical ethics from Harvard. When he returned to Thailand, however, he discovered that the Temple had changed its focus from meditation to fund-raising and temple building. He criticized the Temple for teaching that "merit making is a solution for all personal and social problems," for luring faithful devotees into "making ever-increasing donations to fulfill the temple's aspirations," and for presenting Phra Dhammachayo as a "bodhisattva." He was especially critical of what he saw as the corruption of the abbot's character: "Dhammachayo has apparently abandoned his principle of modesty to embrace the social trappings of fame."[21] He contrasted the abbot's current activities with his stated intentions after the foundation of the Temple, "We will stop now. Our wat has 20 monks and a pavilion which can be converted into a temple. We will not build anything large."[22] Similar accusations were made by another ex-Dhammakāya monk, Phra Adisak, now residing at Wat Paknam in Thonburi. Phra Adisak criticized the Temple's emphasis on excessive merit-making at the expense of the Buddha's teachings. Like Phra Mettanando, he aired his complaints publicly through the media and faced criticism and protests by some Dhammakāya followers.[23]

In the midst of the media frenzy, the Supreme Saṅgha Council appointed one of its members, Phra Prommolee, the abbot of Wat Yannawa, to head a team that would examine these allegations. As the highest-ranking monk from region one, Phra Prommolee was the obvious choice for the monastic investigation. His investigation was conducted over several months, a period in which new allegations appeared every week. During this entire time, however, the press questioned the pace at which the investigation was being conducted, hinting at the slowness of the monastic administration's bureaucracy. Within a month of Phra Prommolee's appointment, the Department of Education even appointed a lay committee to "help Phra Prommolee speed up the investigation."[24] The fifteen-member committee, consisting of a former Religious Affairs Department chief, the current head and inspector general of the Ministry of Education, and religious experts were to examine "the temple's Buddhist teachings, fund-raising campaigns allegedly boosted by claims of miracles, outside businesses connected with the temple's operation, and reports that its abbot had several businesses run on his many land plots."[25] Several weeks later this panel concluded its investigation and asked the monastic investigator to consider eight charges: (1) misinterpretation of the Buddhist canon; (2) improper promotion of the Temple; (3) soliciting excessive donations; (4) accumulation of land; (5) expenditure of Temple funds; (6) unreasonable mobilization of massive funds for the construction of the Mahathammakai Chedi; (7) involvement in business; and (8) the style of its Dhammakāya images.[26]

The panel had based its conclusions regarding the Temple's misinterpretation of Buddhism on the opinions of several leading Thai monks. Foremost among these scholar-monks was Phra Dhammapitaka (Phra Payutto), who released a book in the midst of the Dhammakāya controversy entitled *Korani Thammakai* (the Dhammakāya Incident). In it, Phra Payutto attempted to clarify certain points of dhamma-vinaya that were in dispute, including the Dhammakāya Temple's controversial claim that "*nipphan pen atta*" (*nibbāna/* nirvāṇa is an essential self). He argued that this interpretation of nirvāṇa could not be found in the *tipiṭaka* (the Buddhist canon) and was therefore external to the Buddha's dhamma. The interpretation of nirvāṇa as *anatta* (not Self), however, could be found in many places throughout the Pāli canon.[27] *Korani Thammakai* became an overnight bestseller and served to throw more fuel on the flames of public debate.

Two months later Phra Prommolee and the Supreme Saṅgha Council concluded that the Temple had indeed misled the public through "wrong teachings" that were based upon an "imperfect understanding" of Buddhism. They issued a four-point ruling urging the Temple to align its teachings and practices with the normative Thai Theravāda tradition. The ruling ultimately strove to reaffirm the Supreme Saṅgha Council's authority as guardians of the dhamma-vinaya: (1) the Temple should provide instruction in *abhidhamma* in order to improve understanding of the finer points of dhamma (including nirvāṇa); (2) the Temple should provide vipassanā meditation practice for its followers, not simply the dhammakāya method; (3) Dhammakāya monks should follow the *Vinaya* strictly; and (4) the Temple should follow the rulings of the Supreme Patriarch and the Supreme Saṅgha Council. The council's decision was quickly released to the press and was on the front page of all of the newspapers. As critics debated the significance of the Supreme Saṅgha Council's ruling, another bombshell hit. The Supreme Patriarch purportedly submitted a ruling to the Religious Affairs Department prior to the Saṅgha Council meeting that stated that Phra Dhammachayo needed to transfer his assets, which he had acquired as a monk, to the Dhammakāya Temple; but this ruling was not forwarded by the Department of Religious Affairs to the council. Several days later another letter by the Supreme Patriarch was released to the public. This letter indirectly called for the defrocking of Phra Dhammachayo, arguing that monks who "steal" (referring to Phra Dhammachayo's reluctance to transfer land in his name to the Temple) from the saṅgha are subject to the highest penalty. In addition, the letter stated that monks who distort the Buddha's teachings and claim that the tipiṭaka has flaws would destroy Buddhism if they were not punished severely. Copies of the letter were leaked to the press, spurring a controversy over the authority of the Supreme Patriarch.

Government officials were reluctant to state that Dhammachayo should be defrocked, but the press considered this punishment imminent since previous decrees by the Supreme Patriarch had led to the defrocking of offenders within a matter of days. After much speculation over the intent of the Supreme Patriarch, however, the Council decided to defer judgment to the ecclesiastical courts. Criminal and ecclesiastical charges were laid against members of the Dhammakāya Temple in 1999. Charges of heresy (distortion of the Buddha's teaching) were filed against Phra Dhammachayo and Phra Tattacheevo by members of the Religious Affairs Department, yet no ecclesiastical trial commenced because of questions concerning the validity of the charges. Since the plaintiffs were laypersons, the Temple brought into question their right to file ecclesiastical charges against monks. As for criminal charges, the police arrested Phra Dhammachayo on August 26, 1999, on charges of embezzlement and malfeasance in a much publicized event. In the United States, reports about the arrest were heard on National Public Radio and printed in the local newspapers. The Associated Press article in the *South Bend Tribune* titled its article, "Renegade Thai Monk Surrenders," while the *New York Times* read, "Thailand: Monk Ends Standoff." After being released on bail of two million baht, the abbot released a statement to the press proclaiming his innocence and the innocence of Thavorn Promthavorn, who was charged with being an accessory to the crime of embezzlement.

While these charges led the public to expect a resolution to the controversy, it soon became apparent that this goal was still far from being reached. No central authority was able to dictate the terms of the resolution. As the saṅgha administration wavered over whether to charge the abbot and vice-abbot with theft and distortion of the dhamma, the criminal investigation slowed to a snail's pace. The failure of the saṅgha and the political authorities to bring closure to this controversy led to larger questions concerning the nature of their authority in Thailand. No where was this more apparent than in the questions surrounding the role of the Supreme Patriarch who, according to the Saṅgha Act of BE 2505 (1962), "governs the whole body of Bhikkhus and may exercise his prerogative in issuing a Patriarchal Command to the extent that it is not opposed to the law of the country, the Discipline of the Order and the Rules of the Council of Elders."[28] The Supreme Patriarch received enormous support among monastic and lay communities for his stance against Phra

Dhammachayo, but the failure of the saṅgha council and the government to support his rulings simply highlighted the decline of his authority in recent years. The situation also raised questions about the overall impotence of the saṅgha administration, a topic that I will address in the Conclusion.

Dhammakāya Buddhism and Charges of Materialism

How do we make sense of this controversy, which captivated Thai audiences for over a year with stories of luxurious robes, monastic embezzlement, and heretical ideas concerning nirvāṇa? To begin, we must sift through the vast array of allegations against the Temple and identify the two primary fields of criticism: the charges of monastic materialism and of the intentional doctrinal distortion of the dhamma. These fields encompass the vast majority of issues raised during the Dhammakāya controversy, and they remain issues of the utmost concern to the Thai saṅgha. Issues of monastic excess and heresy have confronted Buddhist communities from the earliest days of the tradition, but the ways in which the debates are constructed within communities and their implications for Buddhist practice, doctrine, and authority in these communities are fundamentally connected to specific cultural and historical contingencies.

The first criticism, which focused on the allegations of monastic excess, was built upon existing perceptions of the Temple as ultra-modern, wealthy, and cosmopolitan. For over a decade critics and scholars alike have described the Temple as materialistic in its general orientation. Several key factors buttress this characterization. As we saw in Chapter 2, the Temple tends to attract educated persons from the middle and upper economic classes. The collective wealth of the Temple's lay base facilitates the collection of millions of baht each month in donations. As a result of these monetary resources, the Temple is in a position to devote substantial amounts of money on Temple projects ranging from new buildings to educational scholarships and international exchange programs. Like all temples in Thailand, the Dhammakāya Temple must participate in fund-raising activities, and the larger the project, the larger the donation drive. In 1992, for instance, the *Bangkok Post* reported that the Temple raised 400 million baht during the Kathin ceremony.[29] Temple officials deemphasized the large sums of money by stating that, "such a big temple like Wat [Dhammakāya] needs such funds to keep its activities going."[30] One prominent Thai scholar identifies the Temple's ability to raise billions of baht in donations as an index of its success in promoting its message and drawing adherents, but he warns that this ability may also lead to possible conflicts and corruption in the future.[31] While some critics today focus on the Temple's income as a sign of the corruption of Buddhist ideals, others criticize the means by which these donations are procured, that is, through the Temple's aggressive fund-raising techniques, especially its "direct-sale" methods.

The condemnation of the Temple's wealth rests on a distinction between otherworldly spiritual values, ideals, and goals and those of this world. Individuals who draw this distinction invariably view the accumulation of monastic wealth as corrupt or decadent in contrast to their otherworldly view of ideal religiosity. Such an appraisal is a religiously informed critique. It is based upon a particular reading of one's tradition. It is not, as some scholars have argued, an a-priori distinction, but rather a power-laden discourse that seeks to establish boundaries between the "authentic" and the "corrupt." When viewed within a historical context, we can trace instances of both widespread support and condemnation of monastic wealth. In fact, as we saw in Chapter 1, Theravāda history has "periods of monastic accumulation supported by justification of monastic wealth and periods of monastic reform accompanied by the condemnation of monastic wealth."[32]

In the context of contemporary Thailand, many critics promoted a modernist version of Buddhism that emphasized simplicity and moderation. They equated the material wealth of the Dhammakāya Temple with decadence and the corruption of the Buddha's teachings. Ravee Phawilai, director of Chulalongkorn University's Dharma Satharn Centre, for instance, has accused the Temple of "commercializing Buddhism to seek money and power," and using "unusual" solicitation techniques that might lead Buddhists "into committing unorthodox acts."[33] A reporter echoed these criticisms: "The temple preaches that the more you donate, the more 'merits' you receive, but critics note that what's missing is the essence of true Buddhism which does not recognize worldly materials as a channel to eventual enlightenment."[34] Buddhist scholar Sathianpong Wannapruek described the Temple as an "anathema to mainstream Buddhism," and its "teachings were dangerous and an ugly direct sale that plays on human greed in order to contribute to the false belief that merit can be bought."[35] And the outspoken social critic Sulak Sivaraksa claimed that, "the temple teaches its followers greed, wealth, and delusion, an extreme far cry from Buddhist principles."[36] For some of these critics, the Temple's latest construction projects represented overt examples of monastic excess, a tendency within Thai Buddhism to view the "biggest as the best." Yet, temples throughout Thailand boast the possession of large temple edifices and images. Wat Phai Rong Wua in Suphan Buri, for example, is known for having the largest reclining Buddha, the largest *bot* (ordination hall), and the largest bell in the world.[37] Nakhon Pathom is home to the tallest Buddhist structure in the world, the Phra Pathom Chedi, which stands at an impressive 127 meters. In Bangkok, Wat Thammamongkhon has a fourteen-ton solid jade Buddha sculpture; Wat Traimit houses a five-and-a-half-ton solid gold Buddha image, and

Wat Indrawihan has a thirty-two-meter standing Buddha image that towers over the northern part of Bangkok's old city. Pilgrims and tourists alike visit these wonders of the Buddhist world and marvel at the devotion that produced these splendid creations. Criticizing this tendency for constructing impressive structures and images of the Buddhism, Dr. Napaporn Havanont argues that "[n]o matter whether the phenomenon of lavish construction projects undertaken by Buddhist temples is viewed through the eyes of an architect, an economist, or a good Buddhist, it reveals itself a practice that should be discontinued."[38] Dr. Havanont's vision of Buddhism, therefore, clearly rejects the long history of wealth and splendor associated with some of the largest temples in Asia. For other critics of the "bigger is better" mentality, it is not the size of the project that is so objectionable as much as the means by which the funds are raised in order to subsidize the construction of these projects. Suthon Sukphisit suggests that some temples advocate a policy of encouraging their monks to offer auspicious items and magical services in exchange for monetary donations. The funds derived from this "false advertising" are used to construct lavish buildings on temple grounds. "The more splendid the buildings that appear, the more visitors trust in the power of the temple's occult objects and practices. And therefore, the more money that is spent on fancy construction, the more money comes pouring into the temple."[39] As we saw in the previous chapter, many critics employed this line of criticism in their condemnation of the Dhammakāya Temple's technologies of proselytization, especially its marketing of the miracle in the sky and of the asset-sucking Phra Mahasiriratthat amulets.

This array of criticisms in popular arenas of discourse and media led many Thais to conclude that the Dhammakāya Temple contributes to and profits from the commercialization of Buddhism (*Phuttha phanit*). During the controversy, many people with whom I spoke described the Temple's activities as *thurakit* (business), not *satsana* (religion). They cited stories printed in the various newspapers or discussed on television that "proved" the Temple was interested only in money, not religion. Stories involving the purchase of honorary sashes,[40] installment plans for large donations, the permanent millionaires' club, and the infamous "asset sucking amulets" became topics of debate. Many of these reports emphasized the analogy between Dhammakāya activities and the business world, such as direct sale marketing techniques and reward systems for reaching fund-raising targets. One report in the Business and Finance section of *The Nation*, for instance, did a profile of Manit Ratanasuwan, a marketing expert and cofounder of MGA, the distributing arm of Grammy Entertainment, who helped the Temple create a multifaceted marketing campaign for the Mahathammakai Chedi. The report described his campaign in these terms:

> With decades of experience in the private sector, Manit approached
> the Dhammakāya project somewhat like a commercial enterprise

and boldly used advanced marketing techniques to woo the monastery followers. . . . His targets were mostly well-educated, well-to-do worshippers sharing a common belief in the project. Manit sent out a powerful message to the target groups from teenagers to adults or anyone who wanted to make merit by contributing to the shrine's construction. The shrine was described as a "miraculous" edifice for Buddhists that will help them achieve a better life.[41]

From this perspective, the business of Dhammakāya Buddhism was deliberately manipulative.

The characterization of Dhammakāya fund-raising as manipulative and the characterization of the Temple as excessive and decadent culminated in the allegations of embezzlement leveled against Phra Dhammachayo and in the calls for his disrobing.[42] During an investigation into the assets of the Temple, it was revealed that he owned 1,900 rai (approximately 700 acres) of land, most of which was titled to him under his lay name, Chaibul Sutthipol.[43] Some critics questioned the integrity of the abbot by contrasting his personal wealth to the religious ideals of modesty and simplicity.

> Buddhist monks are supposed to be devoid of the desire for valuables or assets, but the massive landholdings of the controversial abbot of Dhammakaya Temple, Phra Dhammachayo, have more than raised the eyebrows of other practitioners of the Lord Buddha's teachings. Over his years in the saffron robe, Dhammachayo has steadily amassed vast tracts of land and become a landlord to be reckoned with.[44]

Critics also questioned how this land was obtained. It was clear that the some of the land tracts were donations, but others appeared to be purchases made by the Temple. This revelation fueled further speculation over the true intentions of the donors: Did donors intend to give the land to Phra Dhammachayo as his personal property or were these donations intended as gifts to the Dhammakāya community as a whole?

The Supreme Patriarch answered this question by arguing that Phra Dhammachayo must transfer legal ownership of the land from himself to the Temple. When Phra Dhammachayo delayed the transfer of title deeds, the Supreme Patriarch wrote a letter to the Council indicating that Phra Dhammachayo should be defrocked for failing to transfer the land. As the grounds for his defrocking, the Supreme Patriarch cited the injunction against theft, one of the four *pārājika* offenses which carry the penalty of expulsion. In response, Dhammachayo appeared to be conciliatory in that he agreed to the Supreme Patriarch's request; but obstacles arose, such as the need to confer with donors regarding their wishes, which delayed the transfer. Needless to say, Dhammakāya critics interpreted this as a sign of the abbot's reluctance to relinquish his personal claims to the land. The Temple countered this criticism by raising questions over the authenticity of the Supreme Patriarch's letter and with questions concerning the legal rights of monks to own land under the Thai constitution. One pro-Dhammakāya report in the *Ban-Muang* newspaper noted that most monks in Thailand receive donations throughout the year for various activities. According to this commentator, if Dhammachayo was guilty of theft for receiving donations, then so too were most monks in Thailand.[45] This Dhammakāya supporter was drawing attention to the fact that most monks in Thailand possess personal property in one form or another, whether the source is a stipend from the government, donations made by faithful laypersons, or simply familial property.

The Dhammakāya Temple's Response to Charges of Materialism

Temple representatives responded to the characterization of the Temple as materialistic in a book entitled *Choluk Wat Phra Thammakai*, which the Dhammakāya Foundation published at the beginning of the controversy.[46] The book sought to educate the public at large about Dhammakāya teachings and practices and to redress criticisms made against the Temple, particularly the charges of materialism. The authors of *Choluk* suggested that many people mistakenly confused the possession of luxury objects with materialism or materialistic motives. Problems arise not from the possession of material wealth but rather from craving the acquisition of goods, from craving the acquisition of goods— whether these goods are grand and expensive or small and trivial. Later, in the same article, the authors agreed that many of their lay practitioners are not opposed to material wealth. They argued that the embracing of material wealth should not be viewed as "materialistic" since Dhammakāya practitioners use material wealth to foster the Buddhist community—through activities, educational facilities, and religious monuments that will inspire faith (*sattha*). As for the claims that Dhammakāya monks live luxurious lives, the *Choluk* authors formally declared that Dhammakāya monks possess only the minimum of personal belongings. The material wealth of the Temple is the collective property of the Dhammakāya community, and not that of individual monks.

In response to questions concerning the Temple's motivations for building large monuments, the authors argued that such buildings have kept Buddhism strong over its 2500-year history. They cited the well-known canonical story of Anatabindika (Anāthapiṇḍika, Pāli), whose impressive wealth facilitated the building of Wat Phrachetuwan Mahawihan (Jetavana, Pāli), at which the Buddha spent over twenty *phansa* (rainy seasons). The authors suggested that many practitioners were able to gather at that temple to hear the teachings of the Buddha because of Anatabindika's enormous generosity. In a similar vein, generous donations by Dhammkāya practitioners have enabled the Temple to expand its facilities, and thereby accommodate more practitioners. Using this reasoning, the authors insisted that all new buildings are constructed not only for the benefit of the Temple but, more importantly, for the benefit of Buddhism. The donations gathered for these projects are the products of Buddhist generosity, and as such, they served to highlight the strength of Buddhist piety in Thailand. The authors adamantly opposed the characterization of Temple practitioners as materialistic; they are, in their view, exemplary donors who are willing to relinquish vast amounts of wealth for the benefit of the Dhammakāya tradition.

The authors also responded to the criticism that these donations would be better spent on building schools or hospitals rather than on gratuitously large religious structures. Investments in education and medical services are necessary and commendable according to the authors, but religious structures, such as the Mahathammakai Chedi, serve to cultivate the ethical virtue of generosity by providing practitioners with an object for giving. Without the chedi project, many Buddhists might have spent their money on drinking, smoking, and other forms of entertainment. Ethically minded practitioners, in contrast, recognized the need to patronize temples for the betterment of themselves and society. To the criticism that the Temple should not have sought substantial donations for the building of large temple structures during a period of economic decline, the authors of *Choluk Wat Phra Thammakai* responded in several ways. First, they stated that they built the Dhammakāya Sala (pavilion) and started the chedi during a period of great economic prosperity. Second, they compared the building of the chedi in the current economic crisis to the building of Wat Phra Kaew and the Grand Palace by King Rama I following years of war with Burma. Third, they highlighted the fact that people continue to purchase alcohol, cigarettes and pay for films like *Titanic* (which grossed more than one million baht in Thailand) in the midst of the economic crisis.

The response of the Temple to criticisms of materialism, as articulated in *Choluk Wat Phra Thammakai*, was multidimensional. On the one hand, the authors countered claims of materialism by emphasizing the virtuous motives behind giving and receiving donations. The wealth of the Temple was merely a sign of the enormous generosity of its practitioners according to the authors; it was not an index of craving, greed, or attachment. On the other hand, the authors effectively used the stories of exemplary donors from the past to show how their actions are consistent with Theravāda and Thai Buddhist history. As we saw in the previous chapter, the Temple explicitly referenced the rich history of exemplary donors in their marketing of individual Phra Dhammākaya images.

The Debate over Doctrine: Nirvāṇa is *attā*

Stories concerning the Dhammakāya Temple's purported materialism dominated the headlines in 1998 and 1999, but it was not the critique of choice for all. During the first few months of the controversy, I found that most monks were reluctant to talk about the controversy surrounding the Dhammakāya Temple, let alone address questions about "selling merit" and the assets of individual monks. After the live taping of a popular religious television program, for instance, I questioned several monks about the teachings and practices of the Dhammakāya Temple. Most were reluctant to speak directly about the Temple with me, even though the program had explicitly covered issues pertaining to the Dhammakāya Temple. One monk told me that because he had never visited the Temple, he could not comment on it. Another monk answered circuitously, first comparing the goals of Dhammakāya meditation with samatha (absorption/concentration) meditation, and then describing the limitations of concentration meditation in comparison to vipassanā (insight). A week later I attended a field trip with a group of monks from MahaChulalongkorn University and found that they were also reluctant to speak directly about the allegations against the Dhammakāya Temple. It is possible that some of these monks were genuinely not interested in the topic of the Dhammakāya Temple or had little to no information about the controversy. The reluctance of a majority of monks, however, reflected normative views on proper monastic behavior as based on both the *Vinaya* and Thai tradition. The manner in which a monk engages with others is influenced by several factors, including the religious status of the other person, his or her gender, and the topic of discourse. If the subject of discussion is the character, practice, or teachings of another monk, then the disciplinary admonitions prohibiting slander (one of the ten *Musāvādavagga*) and frivolous speech may influence the way in which some monks choose to speak about Phra Dhammachayo and other Dhammakāya monks. This is not to say that their behavior is determined by monastic regulations, but rather that appraisals of proper or appropriate behavior are often constructed in reference to canonical ideas of ideal or practically efficacious conduct. Furthermore, it is quite reasonable to assume that many of these monks were reluctant to participate in discussions that might lead to the airing of the saṅgha's dirty laundry to me, a woman and a foreigner, lest it reflect on others by association and the state of Buddhism in Thailand more generally.

As the controversy gained momentum over several months, however, one topic of criticism emerged that enabled monks to speak more freely about the controversy. While many monks were reticent to comment on sensational stories involving the abbot, such as his U.S. immigration status or his purported appetite for gourmet meals, they did engage in discussions about the Temple's controversial interpretation of nirvāṇa. Since this topic falls within the parameters of normative monastic discourse, the Temple's claim that "*nip-phan pen atta*" (nirvāṇa is self) became a focal point for discussing whether the Temple truly distorts the Buddha's teachings. In the press, the Temple's interpretation of nirvāṇa was mentioned regularly in articles concerning the controversy. One newspaper report declared that "(t)he Temple has taught, either explicitly or implicitly, that nirvana is a state of existence and the Dhammakāya meditation is a way to meet the Lord Buddha in heaven."[47] Later reports released transcripts from a recorded sermon on nirvāṇa by Dhammachayo. In this sermon, Dhammachayo states that Dhammakāya is the manifestation of the Lord Buddha in *ayatana nipphan*, an existence beyond physical corporeality that can be accessed through meditation. He tells his followers that they can gain a glimpse of nirvāṇa if they merge their minds with the dhammakāya, since the true path to nirvāṇa is through the realization of the dhammakāya.[48]

The strongest critique of this teaching came from the venerable Phra Prayudh Payutto, one of Thailand's leading academic monks and voices of Theravāda orthodoxy, who published a book on the controversy entitled *Korani Thammakai* (The Dhammakāya Incident).[49] The book quickly went to the top of the bestseller list in Thailand in the spring of 1999. In it, Phra Payutto clarified what he saw as "misconceptions" about dhamma-vinaya—most notably, ideas about nirvāṇa. Several sections of the book focused specifically on the topic of nirvāṇa; one addressed the description of nirvāṇa as *attā*, whereas another questioned the Temple's use of the phrase "*ayatana nipphan.*" He argued that the Dhammakāya interpretation of nirvāṇa as attā or as *ayatana* was not substantiated by any teaching in the Pāli canon. He classified the description of nirvāṇa as a permanent heaven as more similar to Mahāyāna conceptions of nirvāṇa because Theravāda Buddhism teaches that nirvāṇa is not a place but rather a state free from the three fetters of greed, hatred, and delusion. In his opinion, the Dhammakāya Temple was marketing Mahāyāna Buddhism in the form of Theravāda for the Temple's own financial benefit. Phra Payutto criticized this blurring of divisions between the traditions and argued that, "Theravāda Buddhism in Thailand cannot survive" if its "doctrines and disciplines are tampered with, or rendered incredible."[50]

Phra Payutto's discussion of contentious issues concerning the Dhammakāya Temple legitimized the place of these discussions in monastic circles. Other monks proffered opinions on the controversy, and some, such as the media-savvy Phra Phayom Kalyano, relayed these opinions to a more than eager press, but few (if any) could offer an opinion that carried the same weight of authority as Phra Payutto. As one reporter stated, the learned Phra Payutto "commands high public respect and his verdict is usually considered the last word in religious controversies."[51] This was evident in 1988 when Phra Payutto published *Korani Santi Asok*, which detailed how Phra Phothirak, the founder of Santi Asok, had deviated from the teachings and discipline of orthodox

Theravāda.[52] Before the publication of Phra Payutto's book, an ecclesiastical committee had spent years investigating the charges against Santi Asok without reaching a resolution. Shortly after the publication of Phra Payutto's opinion, however, the saṅgha committee ruled that the Phra Phothirak had violated the *Vinaya* and the Saṅgha act of 1962, and must therefore be defrocked. Phra Payutto's definitive conclusions helped to overcome internal divisions within the saṅgha over Santi Asok and gave legitimacy to the council's decision to disrobe Phra Phothirak.

As with the debates over the Dhammakāya Temple's materialism, questions about the Temple's teachings on nirvāṇa had circulated in academic discourses prior to the controversy of 1998–1999. In 1987, for instance, Prawase Wasi had argued that the nirvāṇa attained through Dhammakāya meditation is not the same as the nirvāṇa the Buddha described as that which is accessed through wisdom (*paññā*).[53] Similarly, Santianphong Wannapok criticized the Temple's equation of the dhammakāya with "hypnosis" rather than with the wisdom attained through following the *ariyamagga* (the noble path).[54] International scholars also drew attention to the Temple's unique interpretations of dhammakāya, and the similarities to certain strands of Mahāyāna philosophy.[55] In terms of the public sphere, however, there was little or no discussion of the nuances of Dhammakāya philosophy and soteriology. But during the Dhammakāya controversy of 1998 and 1999, questions over the character of nirvāṇa, the differences between samatha and vipassanā meditation, and the ontological status of the self emerged as popular topics in the news.

These public debates raised additional questions about the role of orthodoxy in Thai Buddhism. Buddhist scholars often emphasize the importance of orthopraxy in constructions of Buddhist identity over and against orthodoxy. A. Thomas Kirsch, for instance, compares the emphasis on doctrine and belief in Christianity to the emphasis on monastic discipline in Theravāda Buddhism.[56] Similarly, Paul Williams states that "(i)n theory a monastery could happily contain monks holding quite different doctrines as long as they *behaved* in the same way—crucially, so long as they adhered to the same monastic code."[57] It is true that Buddhists often define the differences between Buddhist communities in terms of discipline rather than in terms of doctrine, and many Thais describe the difference between the two dominant monastic lineages in Thailand, the Mahanikāi and Thammayutnikai, in terms of practice; the latter are considered to follow a stricter interpretation of the monastic code. Having said this, we should not ignore the role of an accepted normative doctrinal tradition within past Buddhist societies, and it most certainly should not be ignored in the modern era. Buddhists debate issues of dhamma, just as they debate issues of *Vinaya*, and these debates can lead to power-laden distinctions between those who allegedly adhere to the dhamma and those who distort it. These distinctions are power-laden because they are grounded in a statement of authority from a person or group of persons who establish normative doctrine. In the modern period, debates over orthodoxy have taken on even more importance as modernization has led to a renewed focus on textual orthodoxy in Modernist or Protestant forms of Buddhism.[58]

In the case of the Dhammakāya controversy, Phra Payutto's rejection of the Temple's interpretation of nirvāṇa as atta established a normative Thai Theravāda Buddhist discourse concerning the status of nirvāṇa. This is not to say that normative discourses on nirvāṇa emerged only in late twentieth-century Thailand but rather that Phra Payutto's reading of the Buddhist tradition became an authoritative construction of normative Buddhism in Thailand at a particular point in history.[59] Contrary to the great tradition theory, normative traditions are continually constructed, debated, and contested. The important question is not, What is the normative tradition? But rather, How and under what circumstances is the normative tradition established and by whom? In *Korani Thammakai*, Phra Payutto appealed to the canonical tradition in his rejection of the Temple's interpretation of nirvāṇa. As stated previously, he argued that there are numerous references to nirvāṇa as anatta in the Pāli tipiṭaka, but no reference to nirvāṇa as atta or as ayatana as articulated by the Temple. In addition, he critiqued the Temple's reference to early Western Orientalist scholarship in its interpretation of nirvāṇa as atta. For example, Phra Somchai Thanawuttho, a Dhammakāya monk, referenced the pro-Self interpretations of nirvāṇa put forward by Caroline Rhys Davids, I. B. Horner, and Christmas Humphries in his Dhammakāya publication, *Nipphan pen Atta ru Anatta*.[60] Needless to say, Phra Payutto dismissed these Orientalist interpretations of nirvāṇa as erroneous. In a similar vein, Phra MahaBoonthuang criticized the Temple's reliance on Mahāyāna interpretations of nirvāṇa. In a rather scathing attack on the Temple's teachings, Phra MahaBoonthuang hypothesized that Phra Somchai, a Thai Theravāda monk, had been influenced by Mahāyāna philosophy while studying for his M.A. in Buddhist Studies at a university in Tokyo.[61] According to Phra MahaBoonthuang, Phra Somchai's heretical interpretation of *"nipphan pen atta"* is not only erroneous, it would destroy Buddhism. Using highly inflammatory language, he compared Phra Somchai to a termite eating a collection of Buddhist texts as well as to rust as it erodes and weakens iron.

Debates over the correct interpretation of nirvāṇa are not merely objective discussions between equals, but rather, power-laden debates between different authorizing entities. In Western scholarship on Buddhism, there has been a tendency to over-rationalize the tradition, to emphasize how Buddhism requires each person to discover the truth for himself instead of relying on blind faith and tradition. This discourse is certainly present within the tradition, as evidenced in the oft-quoted *Kālāma-sutta*,[62] but so too are discourses on the importance of authority and an established tradition of orthodoxy and orthopraxy. Canonical literature, for example, has the sanction of *Buddha-vacana* (the word of the Buddha), referring either to its status as an actual utterance of the Buddha or to a statement consistent with the Buddha's teachings. Also, the canonical literature presents us with the four great authorities (*mahāpadesa*) for judging whether a particular teaching is orthodox: one heard it from (1) the Buddha himself, (2) a community of elder monks (*theras*), (3) a group of learned monks; or (4) one learned monk.[63] In practical contexts, however, who is authorized as a "learned monk" can be a subject of contentious debate.

In the Dhammakāya controversy, the question of authority related not only to whose voice represented authentic Buddhism—Phra Dhammachayo's or Phra Payutto's—but also over the authoritative tradition with which the Temple identified. The issue of identity is crucial to the Temple if it is to continue to garner support from Theravāda Buddhists in Thailand and maintain convivial ties with the ruling saṅgha establishment. While Dhammakāya practitioners adamantly defended the Temple's allegiances to the Theravāda tradition, critics noted how the Temple's interpretations of the dhammakāya resembled Mahāyāna ontology—especially concerning ideas such as the *dharma-kāya*, the *tathagātagarbha*, and Buddha-nature. Sanitsuda Ekachai, a well-known Bangkok Post editorialist and commentator on religion in Thailand, for example, similarly wrote that Temple practitioners were free to "believe the teachings of Phra Dhammachayo even though these have been found by the Sangha and Buddhist scholars to be distortions of Buddhist tenets," and the "abbot can set up his own cult, found a new sect or establish his own church, and the authorities will not be able to stand in his way," but he "cannot do any of these things and profess to follow Theravada Buddhism, the country's principal denomination which adheres to the teachings of the Buddha as contained in the Tipitaka, the Holy Buddhist Scriptures."[64] Many Thai scholars echoed these sentiments in the public and the press.

The Public Nature of Controversy

Modern religious controversies demonstrate the public character of religion in the contemporary world because the most contentious debates play out in the public sphere, often superseding the internal debates of the interested parties. The global media provide a conduit for this new type of publicity. Satellite television, the Internet, and podcasts disseminate information about particular controversies and they relay differing (although rarely balanced) perspectives on the subjects of debate. The media coverage of the Terri Schiavo case in the United States in 2005, for instance, globalized the debate over euthanasia. What would have been a local case confined to family members and legal experts fifty years ago, became a discursive site for people all over the world to discuss issues relating to the nature of life and the rights of death. The global nature of this controversy became apparent to me as I watched local and satellite news programs on the Terri Schiavo case in Japan and Thailand and attempted to answer questions about the relationship between religion and the law in America to groups of curious Buddhist monks.

We cannot assume that all religious controversies or scandals occupy the same discursive space within contemporary public spheres. In Thailand, religious controversies are frequently covered in the press (as are political scandals involving allegations of corruption and cronyism), but obviously some stories have more mass appeal and hence more staying power than others do. The Dhammakāya controversy was literally on the front page of newspapers every day for over one year. Since that time, other scandals have come and gone; some have lasted for only a few days whereas others have lasted for weeks or months. A scandal involving an abbot caught impersonating a military colonel during a sexual escapade, for instance, endured in the news for only a month. The press reported his detection and arrest on October 26, 2000, and by November 22, they were reporting on his six-month jail sentence. While this scandal piqued the interest of some ardent news watchers, it came and went without further general discussion or debate, probably because it concerned an errant individual rather than an issue of Theravāda religiosity.

The Dhammakāya controversy had, however, a captive Thai audience for over a year and even emerged on the global scene in August 1999 when Phra Dhammachayo was arrested on charges of embezzlement. One reason for the controversy's "popularity" was that it hit a collective public cord—it spoke of modern wealth in the midst of immense economic turmoil. Another reason was that the subject matter spurred a variety of topics that engaged a diverse Thai audience. A single newspaper article contained commentary on interpretations or misinterpretations of nirvāṇa (which we might normally term 'elitist' or doctrinal discourses) alongside sensational descriptions of the abbot's purported eccentricities and latest fund-raising projects. This broad discursive space facilitated the public nature of the controversy. In fact, the controversy's extensive audience is what first made me view this controversy as distinct from the ordinary sex and money scandals involving monks that fill the popular news dailies. Whether I was in a taxi, at a friend's house, or at the market, people were engaged in discussions about the Dhammakāya Temple. Upon telling new acquaintances that I was studying contemporary Buddhism in Thailand, they would frequently ask whether I knew about the Dhammakāya controversy. Such exchanges were not limited to Thailand. I had similar experiences while living in Chicago. On one occasion, a Thai travel agent pulled out a copy of *The Nation* weekly magazine with a picture of Phra Dhammachayo on the front and asked if I was familiar with the Temple and the controversy surrounding it.[65] I had said nothing about my interest in the controversy to prompt this line of discussion; I had mentioned only that I was interested in contemporary Thai Buddhism. The Dhammakāya controversy had become intimately linked to general discussions of Thai Buddhism, even in places as far away as Lincoln Village in Chicago.

From one perspective, the two main areas of debate—the Temple's purported materialism and its dissemination of controversial teachings—occupied different discursive spaces. Santikaro Bhikkhu, an American monk living in Thailand, argued that the area of debate involved "allegations of illegal acts and socially reprehensible behavior" whereas the second area of debate involved "strange interpretations of Buddha-Dhamma."[66] One might also argue that debates concerning materialism and commercialism have a more populist ring than the questions concerning orthodox interpretations of nirvāṇa. Topics concerning the Temple's overt wealth, its distribution of amulets that claim to "suck assets," and its advertising of a "miracle in the sky" provided grist for the gossip mill, and supplied the media with unlimited accounts of monastic excess and supernatural power. The second area of debate, in contrast, pertained to topics that are typically discussed within elite circles among scholar monks and laypersons who are well versed in dhamma-vinaya and Buddhist history. When monks were quoted in the press or on television, they focused on controversial Dhammakāya teachings rather than the issues of corruption and commercialization (although Phra Phayom Kalyano and Phra MahaBoonthueng are among some notable exceptions to this generalization).

While different discursive spaces can be identified—legal versus religious or elite versus popular—their boundaries are fluid. Discussions about the commercialization of Buddhism or the nature of nirvāṇa are neither confined to particular groups nor are they mutually exclusive. The Dhammakāya controversy highlights this expanded public forum. Debates over the teaching that nirvāṇa is a physical place, for instance, emerged out of observations about the Temple's ability to collect unprecedented amounts of donations: Critics questioned whether the Temple's teachings on nirvāṇa encouraged devotees to donate more money in the hope of buying a better next life. One editorial cartoon in *Krungthep Thurakit* (November 30, 1998) exemplified this merging of discourses. It satirized the Dhammakāya Temple's purported claim that the more money you donate to it, the more merit you will receive in this and future lives. The cartoon identified the various ways one can "reach" nirvāṇa: A rope, a ladder, an escalator, and an elevator reached into the clouds at the top of the page. Each mode of transportation corresponded to a specific donation: 10,000 baht for the rope, 100,000 baht for the ladder, 1,000,000 baht for the escalator, and more than one million baht for the elevator. A monk was sitting underneath the elevator with a megaphone in his hand, yelling, "lift service here . . . can accept installments." This cartoon explicitly raised questions about the practice of religious giving (*dāna*) and the intentions (*cetanā*) of the Temple and its donors. It implied that the Temple actively seeks wealth by marketing its path to heaven (*sawan*, Thai) as the fastest and that Dhammakāya devotees are willing to pay large amounts of money in the hope of procuring merit in this and future lives. The cartoon further illustrates not only the linkage of debates over commercialism and orthodoxy, but also the mechanisms of these debates and their potential audience. Since cartoons are consumed by a diverse public, they blur the simple dichotomies between "elite" and "popular" discourses.[67]

In contemporary society, communication media play a key role in advancing religious controversies and framing the issues for debate. The extensive coverage of the Dhammakāya controversy, as one instance, provided a means for the production and consumption of debates over donations, building projects, meditation methods, and theories of nirvāṇa. This role was not new for the Thai national media. Over the previous two decades, broadcast and print media within Thailand have created a space in the national culture for stories about contentious religious issues. Charles Keyes argues that the "widespread attention in newspapers and magazines given to four recent cases of monks in Thailand [Phra Nikorn, Phra Yantra, Phra Phothirak, and Phra Prachak] ... are indicative of a pervasive debate taking place about the salience of Buddhist charisma, barami, in modern Thailand."[68] Phra Nikorn, who was accused of sexual relations with a female follower, confronted his accuser on a news-radio program, while Phra Yantra who was also accused of sexual impropriety engaged in a debate over Buddhist piety with Phra Phayom, a spectacle that was serialized in all of the national newspapers. In contrast to these sensational stories of sexual misconduct, the stories of Phra Phothirak and Phra Prachak raised questions in the national media about the nature and power of the ecclesiastical authority in contemporary Thailand. What happens when a monk openly criticizes the national saṅgha, and what are the consequences of refusing to acknowledge the authority of the saṅgha establishment? In the cases of Phra Phothirak and Phra Prachak, the answers to these questions were the forced defrocking of "errant" monks.

The global media not only relay the drama of modern religious controversies; they are conduits for multiple perspectives on contentious issues. As with the examples above, Dhammakāya practitioners used the national media to serve their own purposes. At the height of the controversy, for example, television channels 5 and 11 televised a mass ceremony at the Temple, which drew over 100,000 people. This enabled the Temple to demonstrate its continued popularity and, hence, the strength of its power base. The Temple also instructed its followers to write letters to local newspapers describing their positive experiences at the Temple. One newspaper reported the receipt of over one hundred letters supporting Dhammakāya in one day. In one of these letters, a committed practitioner stated, "I want to live in an ideal world and the

Dhammakāya Temple is the place, because it is where everyone respects, forgives and is polite to one another. Everyone smiles and helps each other. It is where people uphold the five precepts and morality."[69] Even though temple supporters sent letters to the mainstream media, they remained suspicious of the mainstream media's presentation of the "facts." At the Temple, practitioners were urged to read *Phim Thai*, a pro-Dhammakāya newspaper, since it covered "the real news," in contrast to the "bad news."[70]

The Dhammakāya Temple's classification of newspapers as "good" and "bad" (in a manner similar to the Christian Right's embracing of Rupert Murdoch's Fox News over other mainstream television news programs) draws attention to the fact that the media are not simply relaying objective facts. They frame the debates in terms of which topics they choose to cover, the manner in which they cover them, and the voices they authorize to speak. In the case of the Dhammakāya controversy, the headlines alone revealed the dominant perspective of the media: "Temple attacked for putting merit on sale" (*The Nation*, November 29, 1998); "Thammakai sucks another 30 million" (*Daily News*, February 9, 1999), and "Dhammachayo–Thammakai has 50,000 million" (*Daily News*, February 23, 1999). The various Thai media chose their "informants" from a broad base of individuals who tended to reinforce a critical appraisal of the Temple, including former and present government officials (especially within the Departments of Education and Religious Affairs), high-ranking monks in the Saṅgha Council, media-savvy monks such as Phra Phayom Kalyano and Phra MahaBoonthuang, former monks of the Dhammakāya Temple, renowned social critics and academics, as well as disgruntled former practitioners. Despite the fact that official Dhammakāya spokespersons and unofficial supporters were occasionally quoted in the press, their voices tended be confined to the space of simply rebutting specific criticisms or providing fodder for the media frenzy.

Conclusion and Epilogue to the Controversy

This chapter has examined the Dhammakāya controversy as an instance in history when conflicting views of the relationship of wealth and piety came to the forefront of discourses on religion in the contemporary world. The controversy assumed center stage in public discourse because of the larger socioeconomic context of the Asian economic crisis. This climate linked debates over monastic wealth to general questions about the character of Thai Buddhism and the authority of the saṅgha establishment. Was Thailand's economic prosperity leading to the ruination of Buddhist practice? Did Thailand really need another multibillion baht chedi or should such funds be funneled in other more "productive" directions? Does the Temple teach heretical views on nirvāṇa in order to lure people into donating more money? And if so, what should the saṅgha establishment do to rectify it? All of these questions came into public view at the end of the twentieth century because of a new religious climate fostered by the Asian economic crisis. The intensity and longevity of the Dhammakāya controversy indicated the level to which issues of monastic excess, materialism, and religious manipulation mattered to the Thai public at that moment in history.

But moments in history are transitory and, even though the Dhammakāya controversy dominated the headlines for over a year in Thailand, it eventually died out as time passed and new events occurred. The arrest of Phra Dhammachayo on August 26, 1999, was both the fevered zenith of the controversy as well as the beginning of its exit from the public forum. As the months passed after his arrest (and immediate release), fewer and fewer stories occurred in the Thai media regarding the Temple until there were no new stories at all in the press. By December of 1999, the media was consumed with positive stories about the new millennium. In subsequent years, stories of the rise of the Thai Rak Thai (TRT) party and the 2004 Boxing Day Tsumani would dominate the headlines. The Dhammakāya controversy would not occupy that place again in the headlines until August of 2006. As observers of the Thai judicial system will know, its legal process can move at an inordinately slow pace in Thailand. This was true for the case against Phra Dhammachayo and Thavorn Phromthavorn, the two individuals named in the embezzlement case. It was not until August 22, 2006, that the case was finally resolved. On that date all charges were dropped against the two defendants, as the court noted the defendants' return of 959.3 million baht in assets to the Temple. According to the Bangkok Post, "[the] prosecution stated that the suit stood to create a bigger rift between the clergy and laymen had it been pursued. It felt that it would be best to withdraw the case for the sake of unity in society."[71] In her op-ed comments on the dismissal of charges, Sanitsuda Ekachai argued that the dismissal of charges represents the influence of the Dhammakāya Temple on powerful politicians in the country, who wanted to ensure that the charges were dropped before they lost power.[72] Sanitsuda's allusion to a crumbling government proved prophetic when the government collapsed one month later.

The collapse of the Thaksin government in 2006, on the heels of corruption allegations and the increase in violence in the South, has led to a fresh crop of debates over the signification of prosperity within the kingdom, and has brought the Dhammakāya Temple once again back into the headlines. Phra Mettanando, the Oxford-educated former superstar monk of the Dhammakāya Temple, wrote an opinion piece in *The Nation* entitled, "TRT and the Dhammakāya Temple—Perfect Match," which was published eight days after the coup d'état on September 27, 2006. In the essay, Phra Mettanando compared Thaksin's Thai Rak Thai (TRT) party to the Dhammakāya Temple,

arguing that they share "the same philosophies of management and administration . . . both use the media relentlessly for self-promotion . . . [both] are
huge organizations—two of the largest and most powerful in the country. Their
leaders are known to be shrewd investors, bold enough to take on new risks—
both are equally fond of the latest technologies, capitalism and modernism in
general." Phra Mettanando argued that the comparison of the TRT party and
the Dhammmakāya Temple extended beyond ideological similarities; he con-
tended that the two have been intimately linked since 2000 when Phra Dhammachayo began to openly support candidates in the TRT party.

> The Thai Rak Thai-Phra Dhammakaya Temple relationship proved
> mutually beneficial. It allowed the Thai Rak Thai Party to promote
> itself with greater efficiency. Phra Dhammakaya Temple also be-
> gan broadcasts on Dow Tham [satellite] . . . Never before in its his-
> tory was the temple able to expand its powers so quickly. The
> temple was able to significantly build up its local, national and in-
> ternational networks after Thai Rak Thai came into power. At the
> end of August of this year, all legal cases against Phra Dhamma-
> jayo were released from the judicial process . . . It must be remem-
> bered that the overarching threat to Thailand is no longer just
> Thaksinomics, but the real menace is the Dhammakaya-Thai Rak
> Thai consortium.[73]

Phra Mettanando's critical assessment of the relationship between TRT and
the Dhammakāya Temple reflects the depth to which issues of wealth play in
discourses about society, politics, and economics in Thailand and across the
globe today.

Chapter 5

Consumerism and Commercialization of Buddhism

The linkage of wealth with piety is not a new phenomenon within the Buddhist tradition, but the contemporary world offers new modes for its expression and new fuel for its critique. Today, the assessment of wealth in contemporary Buddhism is embedded within complex social matrices where wealth is connected to the driving forces of globalization and consumer capitalism. Contemporary Buddhists who correlate wealth with religious piety employ the traditional idea that wealth is a sign of merit and infuse it with contemporary sensibilities, aesthetics, and identities, many of which are mediated through the lens of global capitalism. In this postmodern cultural context, the Dhammakāya Temple correlates golden amulets, Swiss-made saffron robes, and successful business careers with notions of superior piety.

Conversely, some Buddhists today argue that contemporary relations between religion and global capitalism undermine authentic forms of religiosity and foster socioeconomic trends that are antithetical to the core values of the tradition. In response to the unequal distribution of wealth in contemporary Sri Lanka, for instance, A. T. Ariyaratne, the founder the Sarvodaya Shramadana movement, advocates an approach to development that creates a "no poverty–no affluence" society, which he presents as the middle path of development. Ariyaratne envisions a society of simplicity and sustainability rather than a society ruled by consumerism.[1] In Thailand, Phra Somsak Duangsisen argues that a sustainable society, where Thai villagers would "practice the *middle way* of living and right livelihood," would prevent young women from turning to prostitution in order to support their families or to improve their status through the acquisition of material possessions.[2] In the same spirit, Preecha Changkhwanyuen, a faculty member in the Department of Philosophy at Chulalongkorn University, argues that consumerism, with its equation of happiness with consumption, is antithetical to Buddhism since consumerism depletes natural resources, exploits laborers, widens the gap between the rich and the poor, and leads to the destruction of the human mind.[3]

These commentators are not alone in their portrayal of Buddhism as the antidote to rampant, out-of-control consumerism. Many sympathetic Western Buddhist converts view Buddhism through this lens as well. In the nineteenth century, Orientalists portrayed Buddhism as an atheistic and rational soteriology, which was set in contradistinction to the faith-based (and hence "irrational") theism of Christianity. Today, neo-Orientalists contrast Eastern Buddhism, with its focus on simplicity and moderation, with Western materialism, capitalism, and consumption. As a result, many argue that Buddhism and money simply do not mix. When money becomes associated with Buddhism, it taints the religion. Take, for instance, one American Buddhist business owner's *problem* with making money:

> Linsi Deyo believes she is doing some good with Carolina Morning Designs [a *zafu* pillow company], helping to encourage people everywhere to meditate, to look into their lives more closely and make better choices ... But she isn't sure how much longer the *zafu* company will continue to exist ... "Patrick and I don't know if we are going to go on with this," she says. "There is this desire, you know, to feel comfortable. We don't make enough money to do the things we need to do. So that sort of fits with the question, Can I let myself make money? ... It's sort of ironic that I have all of these issues with money, and here I am operating a meditation-related business. A lot of Buddhists have tremendous issues around money, and a lot of people who sell my cushions, if they are related to Buddhist centers, they themselves don't want to make any money off the cushions—it's like tainted money."[4]

This quote captures the popular theme in contemporary American Buddhist discourses that authentic Buddhism rejects wealth. The Buddhists described by Linsi Deyo view profit as "tainted money" rather than as righteously earned income.[5] As argued in Chapter 1, there are discourses on the righteous accumulation and use of wealth within canonical literature, but many contemporary Buddhists choose to emphasize the tradition's criticisms of the abuses of wealth because these discourses fit within their portrait of Buddhism as anti-materialistic.

The discursive contrast between a spiritual East and a capitalist West is a new version of reverse Orientalism,[6] popularized in the nineteenth and early twentieth centuries by Asian modernists such as Swami Vivekananda in India (1863–1902) and Anagarika Dharmapala (1864–1933). They used this dichotomy to elevate Asian national pride in the face of Western colonialism and Christian proselytization. The following quote from Anagarika Dharmapala exemplifies this dichotomy.

The British have built roads, extended railways, and generally in-
troduced the blessings of their materialistic civilization into the
land. . . . Practices which were an abomination to the ancient noble
Sinhalese have today become tolerated under the influence of Se-
mitic sociology. The Buddhists complain that opium, alcohol, ar-
rack, bhang, ganja, and other poisons are distributed in the villages
by men holding licences, without regard to the degenerating effects they produce in the human organism. In the days of the Sinhalese kings and under the Buddhist rule no liquor was sold, no
animals were slaughtered; land was not sold.[7]

This reverse Orientalism equated the West with material progress (roads,
buildings, and technology) and the East with spiritual, philosophical, and ethical superiority. This contrast continues today in popular discourse as evidenced
in the 1991 documentary *India: Empire of the Spirit*, in which the narrator,
historian Michael Wood, uses Mark Twain's famous description of India as an
"Empire of the Spirit" in order to draw a sharp contrast between the material
West and the deeply spiritual East.

Today, neo-Orientalist discourses redefine the material West as the
capitalist West. In this framework, Eastern religions appear as the alternative
to a consumption-oriented society. Neo-Orientalists focus on the themes of
simplicity and renunciation within Asian religions and devalue or ignore the
various positive assessments of wealth and this-worldly benefits within these
traditions. From this perspective, mega-temples such as the Dhammakāya
Temple or Foguang Shan, with their golden Buddha images and satellite television stations, appear as horrific distortions of authentic Buddhism. In a critique of the commodification of the concept of spirituality in the modern West,
for instance, Jeremy Carrette and Richard King argue that the Asian traditions
of Hindu yoga, Buddhism, and Daoism (Taoism) are increasingly being com-
modified in the West despite having philosophies that are inherently antithetical to consumer culture:

The renunciatory spiritualities of Asia, such as Hindu yoga, the
various Buddhist Traditions and early Taoist philosophy, far from
providing sustenance for a philosophy of accommodation to contemporary consumerism and atomistic individualism, furnish us
instead with ancient 'inner technologies' and philosophies for overcoming the destructive cycle of cravings that we valorize today as
'consumerism.'[8]

Carrette and King acknowledge that Asian religions encompass an incredibly
diverse set of practices and doctrines, but they remain critical of what they view

as the use of the renunciatory spiritualities of Asia for corporate gain. They present two examples of contemporary Asian "philosophers" who have promoted the idea that there is no dissonance between religion and material success: Deepak Chopra, the best-selling author of "mind-body" connection books, and the infamous Bhagwan Shree Rajneesh, the neo-Hindu/Buddhist guru who championed the phrase, "Jesus Saves, Moses Invests, and Bhagwan Spends."[9]

The discursive contrast between a spiritual East and a capitalistic West is also one component of a broader Asian critique of the global hegemonic forces of Westernization. As elsewhere in the world, Thai social critics note how the processes of globalization have destabilized and reconstructed local identities. Kasian Tejapira argues that contemporary global consumption unanchors Thai identity and creates a form of cultural schizophrenia.[10] Other critics of Western cultural and economic hegemony focus less on the problem of identity and more on the material and psychological effects of global capitalism. One recent critique highlights how the dominant International Monetary Fund (IMF) discourse—which links a "romantic tale of progressive capital with the romantic story of modernization and exhorts 'underdeveloped' subjects to move towards a liberatory and prosperous future"—fails to acknowledge the effects of IMF policy on factory workers in the "developing" countries of Thailand and Malaysia.[11] In such cases, critiques of development, capitalism, and globalization inevitably question the material impact of Western hegemony upon local cultures: Those processes that negatively affect local workers are identified not simply as "modern" or "capitalist," but more importantly, as Western in origin.

The Asian economic crisis of 1997 brought the issues of progress and development to the forefront of Thai public discourse. As the once thriving Thai economy stagnated, scholars, government officials, monks, and journalists alike were asking salient questions concerning global capitalism. What is the true nature of wealth in a modern capitalist society? What are the social and ecological costs of large-scale development? Who benefits and who loses because of modern economic "progress"? Such questions prompted reflection on the character and effects of global capitalism. For some commentators, this reflection entailed a linkage between the values of Western capitalism and the dissolution of Thai values. Pravit Rojanaphruk, a well-known Thai economist, raised questions about the nature and role of development within Thailand.[12] She described development as a "part of that Westernizing process of excluding differences by imposing sameness (a global consumer culture or monoculture) in terms of 'naming,' 'studying,' 'helping' and above all 'speaking' for others."[13] Thailand's upper middle classes have benefited from this Western-dominated model of development, but she asked, At what price?

> Besides wanting to dress like *farang*, we now wanted to industrialize lest we fall into poverty and backwardness; this despite the fact

that others had defined 'poverty' and 'backwardness' for us. We were measured by a Western standard, set by others. We felt that we were poor so we rushed into development. But the more we develop, the poorer we become—pristine forest and rivers have become rarities.

Fifty years ago, some religious modernists argued that Asian states should modernize by combining Western technologies of development with Asian values. This idealistic rendering of Asian development was probably never tenable, but following the Asian economic crisis it became clear to many social commentators that either "Asian values" was a mask for cronyism and corruption or that Western modernization was having a negative impact on "Asian values." In the latter instance, commentators highlighted Western consumerism and the commercialization of traditional forms of religion.

Debates over the character and effects of global capitalism, therefore, became linked more specifically to discourses on the effects of global capitalism on Buddhism as well as to discourses on how Buddhism could serve as an important corrective to the destructive forces in contemporary society. Some Thais even viewed the Asian economic crisis as a boon for the resurgence of authentic Buddhism:

> "This crisis is great," insists Abbot [Phra Phayom Kalyano], as he adjusts his saffron robe in the torpid afternoon heat at a temple near the Thai capital of Bangkok. "It is going to force people to go back to the traditional lifestyle. They had lost their way. . . . The current decline in morality is a side effect of industrialization," adds Khun Payong, a retired teacher who has set up 'morality camps' for young Thais. "We should go back to our old traditions and not depend so heavily on material things."[14]

Debates over the Dhammakāya Temple's purported commercialization of Buddhism and its prosperity-oriented teachings were embedded within this broader discussion of the state of Buddhism and society in an economically volatile contemporary Thailand.

This chapter examines postmodern debates concerning the effects of global capitalism upon Buddhist religiosity. The scope of these debates encompasses a critique of consumerism by some of the leading Buddhist voices of reform and a critique of the commercialization of Buddhism, particularly the sale of Buddhist-related objects for profit and the consumption of such items for personal satisfaction. This chapter also analyzes the public culture in which social critics, intellectuals, popular monks, and government officials identify the manifestations and implications of commercialization and consumerism and, in so doing, question the character and role of Buddhism in the global consumer culture of contemporary Thailand.

The Growth of a Consumer Culture in Thailand

The story of Thailand's transition from a traditional agricultural society to an export-oriented, industrialized modern society began with incremental development. In contrast to the so-called Asian Tigers (Korea, Taiwan, Hong Kong, and Singapore), whose economies had boomed through the production of export goods, Thailand appeared to many economic analysts as a country whose economic development was inhibited by political instability and its traditional dependence on agriculture and tourism.[15] In the 1980s, however, with the massive influx of Japanese capital into the region, Thailand's economic prospects improved, and an explosion of unexpected economic growth typified Thailand's development. In a relatively short span of time, the Thai economy transitioned from a predominantly agricultural-export economy to a manufacturing economy. With this economic transition, the demographics of Thailand changed— a mass influx of workers migrated to urban areas—and the average income doubled.[16] The economic boom of the 80s and 90s generated new wealth in Thailand's urban communities and benefited the groups commonly referred to as the "middle class," the "new rich," the "white-collar worker," and the "salaried class,"[17] who "spent this new wealth with glee."[18] What they bought were goods from around the world, goods that were linked to Thai images of modernity, prosperity, and cosmopolitanism.

Today, one cannot fail to notice the presence of this consumer-centric culture in Bangkok. In Siam Square, teens flock to Mahboonkrong, one of Bangkok's most prosperous shopping complexes, where customers buy the latest trends in cell phones, MP3 players, pagers, video games, and clothing. Just north of Mahboonkrong, on Petchaburi Road, amidst the bustling throngs of shoppers, people purchase computer hardware and bootlegged software in Pantip Plaza, a five-story complex in the heart of Pratunam. The newly constructed sky train transports potential shoppers from the heavily business-oriented streets of Sukhumvit and Silom all the way up to the famous Chatuchak weekend market. And while traditional markets virtually unchanged by technology continue to service shoppers, it is clear that the business districts of Siam Square, Pratunam, Silom, and Sukhumvit market their products to those consumers whose wealth enables them to purchase products with a higher retail cache than the more utilitarian products commonly found in the traditional markets.

In Thailand, the economic boom of the 1980s created a new type of consumer culture, a culture that was at once intimately linked to the larger global consumer culture of late capitalism. The role that this nascent, postmodern, western-styled consumer culture played in the construction of Thai lifestyles, values, and identities became an issue not only of Thai modernity but also globalization and Westernization.[19] The consumption of capitalism's products "entails learning a specific set of cultural symbols and values."[20] The global marketing of products such as clothing, cars, and food gave rise to and now sustains a global culture of consumption, a culture that equates the formation of identity with the procurement of specific kinds of goods, thus divorcing the formation of identity from culturally bounded influences.[21] Kasian Tejapira highlights this disconnect in his analysis of the effects of global consumer culture on Thai identity.[22] In one highly instructive example, he deconstructs a portrait of Thai identity as found within an advertisement for the Association of Siamese Architects in 1993. A beautiful Thai woman appears with a plethora of global consumer products: a Parisian hairstyle, Italian earrings, an American fragrance, an English business suit, a Swiss watch, and Japanese silk stockings. The caption in the corner of the advertisement reads: "Bok dai mai khun pen thai thi trong nai?" (Can you tell which part of you makes you Thai?). The bottom of the advertisement reads, "It's not strange if we are used to bread and coffee more than rice and curry. There's nothing wrong with the fact that we are dressed in Western style. It's not unusual that we drive Japanese cars. Because Thai-Thai feelings remain in our spirit."[23] Kasian notes how the contemporary presumption that Thai-ness and the consumption of non-Thai commodities can coexist without qualms of dissonance differs dramatically from the period in the 1970s when enthusiastic Thai nationalists boycotted Japanese goods.

While it is clear that the global consumer culture has influenced Thai patterns and ideologies of consumption, it is neither determinative nor monolithic. In a study of public culture in late modern India, Arjun Appadurai and Carol Breckenridge emphasize that "modernity is today a global experience" and that this experience "is as varied as magic, marriage, or madness."[24] The public culture that emerges out of this experience is not to be understood "as a type of cultural phenomenon but a *zone* of cultural debate."[25] Within this zone of debate, consumers are actively engaged in determining the patterns and processes of consumption. In the Thai cultural sphere, cosumers are active agents who choose from a variety of products; their choices are not monolithic. In an article on the patronage of *ram thai* (traditional Thai dance) by the Thai middle class, for instance, Paritta Koanantakool effectively problematizes simple descriptions of the Thai middle class as merely "consumers of Western-oriented goods." She illustrates how some members of this group embrace *ram thai* "as an assertion of the local while never relinquishing their self-consciousness of being 'modern' people."[26] In a similar vein she references a study by Nidhi Eosiwong, who argues that while the Thai middle class is associated with democratic, egalitarian, and progressive views, as a group members of the Thai middle class also adhere to a so-called traditional cultural worldview, especially with their ideas of karma and *barami* (charismatic power).[27]

The complexity and heterogeneity of the Thai middle class in late capitalism is also reflected in the realm of religion where varying religious perspectives appraise the state of Thai society and the role of global consumerism in it. Nowhere is this complexity and heterogeneity more apparent than at the Dhammakāya Temple. The Temple promotes a religious practice and identity that is consistent with select values of the dominant consumer culture, but in consort with its critics, it too warns against the wholesale unquestioning embrace of global consumerism. Dhammakāya practitioners may foster the traditional linkage between wealth and piety, but they condemn unabashed hedonism as seen in the Temple's ardent campaigns against smoking, drinking, and illicit drugs. Once again, the Temple's success is due, in large part, to its ability to ground Dhammakāya practice in the past while simultaneously promoting itself as relevant to the modern world. Its modern-ness, however, is not a wholesale adoption of every aspect of modernity but rather a selective adoption of those elements that appeal to a modern and ever-increasingly global audience.

The Religion of Consumerism and the Crisis of Values

The religious critique of global consumerism gained momentum in Thailand following the onslaught of the Asian economic crisis, but the critique had been gestating in Thai discourses for several decades, principally in the writings of socially engaged Buddhists who champion issues of social equality, economic justice, and environmental ethics.[28] Monks and lay critics alike have raised questions about the social implications of the kingdom's economic transformation from an agricultural-based economy to a global market economy, highlighting what they see as the detrimental social effects of the processes of modernization. Chief among their concerns are mass urbanization; the plight of the average rural farm family; the dramatic increase in violent crime, prostitution, drug consumption and trafficking; and the dissolution of religious values.

In the aftermath of the Asian economic crisis, the International Network of Engaged Buddhists, a group of socially engaged Buddhists from around the world, dedicated an entire year to the discussion of the intersections of religion and economics. These discussions culminated in the publication of a special edition of its journal, *Think Sangha Journal*, in 1998 with the title, *The Religion of the Market: A Buddhist Look at the Global Economy, Consumerism, Development and the Role of Spirituality in Society*. The lead article by Jonathon Watts suggested that the Asian economic crisis was due, in part, to a "crisis of values," which combined the worst aspects of western modernism (individualism, economic greed) with the worst aspects of indigenous Asian values (feudal patronage systems, social prestige over individual merit).[29]

> What is taking place today in Asia then is not its emergence into the ideal of the modern world, that is the free individual enjoying material prosperity amidst democratic government. Rather we are seeing a tragic warping of this vision: material prosperity exists for a small group of patron elite in government and business circles; feudal cronyism is disguised as representative democracy; and a mass of disempowered citizens are increasingly cut off from their historical and cultural identities by the "clear-cut" of economic "development" and consumerism.[30]

Watts' analysis echoes the sentiments of many Thai and international social commentators who linked the collapse of the Thai economy to a crisis of values that had been burgeoning in Thailand since its dramatic entrance into the modern global economy. Corruption and cronyism became dominant themes within these discourses on social, political, and economic crises. Stories focusing on corrupt politicians, bankers, educators, and monks made headlines during this time and highlighted what many critics described as an endemic problem in Thai society—the pervasive power of patronage and big money.[31]

The list of contributors to this special edition of the *Think Sangha Journal* included Western academics and practitioners as well as Buddhist monks from Thailand and Japan, demonstrating how religious discourses on global capitalism, consumerism, and Buddhist ethics are globally constructed and mediated. This is not simply to say that these discourses exist throughout the world, but more importantly, that Buddhists from a variety of backgrounds engage with each other in religious discussions of capitalism and consumerism. In the nineteenth and early twentieth centuries, European scholars and Buddhist elites were engaged in dialogue about the historical Buddha and the rational and ethical foundations of Buddhism. The Buddhism that emerged from this conceptualization of the tradition is what many scholars refer to as Buddhist modernism. Today, Buddhist practitioners from around the globe contribute to discussions concerning wealth, consumerism, capitalism, and development. In so doing, they create a Buddhist "ideoscape," a space in which contributors constitute "authentic" Buddhism and assess contemporary society and the "state" of Buddhism within it.[32]

While there are many convergences within discourses on global capitalism, consumerism, and Buddhist ethics, such as the belief that Buddhism offers alternative visions of well-being, not all participants in the discussion focus on the same parts of the debate or interpret key terms in the same way.[33] As an instance of this, David Loy, a Buddhist scholar and practitioner, uses key Buddhist ideas to critique not only global capitalism and consumerism, but also to reconstruct what he considers to be authentic Buddhism. As with many Western Buddhist converts, Loy views Buddhism as a tradition that is inherently anti-materialistic and critical of the accumulations of wealth. [34] In Loy's latest book, *Money, Sex, War, Karma: Notes for a Buddhist Revolution*, he constructs Buddhism as an antidote to the ills of global capitalism and consumerism; but in a manner similar to that of Stephen Batchelor in *Buddhism without Beliefs*, he argues that Buddhism must first be demythologized.[35] Loy argues that "[i]f the Dharma is to fulfill its liberative potential, it must make the transition from being an Asian tradition (more accurately, several Asian traditions) into a teaching that speaks more directly to the spiritual needs of modern people living in a globalizing world."[36] Implicit within this statement is his assertion that Buddhism in America must extract the Buddha's teachings from institutional (i.e., Asian) Buddhism. The reason, according to Loy, is that most Buddhists today focus on "spiritual materialism"—supporting the saṅgha and making merit rather than key ideas such as *anattā* (not-self) and the three poisons (greed, hatred, and delusion).[37]

In Thailand, the progressive monks and social critics who participate in the debate on consumerism and global capitalism similarly use key Buddhist ideas as a tool for critiquing current social, political, and economic conditions, and they also tend to offer commentary on the state of Buddhism in Thailand today. But unlike Loy, these Buddhists do not call for the "de-Asianizing" of the tradition. On the contrary, they argue that global capitalism and consumerism have facilitated the erosion of Thai values, which are deeply embedded within authentic Buddhism. As a result, there is a tendency for these reformers to imagine a past in which peasant farmers and local monks lived in harmony with dhammic principles. In other words, these reformers are not merely engaged in discourses on the effects of globalism—they are simultaneously engaged in constructions of Thai-ness (*khwam pen Thai*) and Thai history (*phrawattisat Thai*). Thongchai Winichakul addresses the reformist assessment of Thai-ness in his highly informative examination of Thai nationalism:

> Another contending interpretation of Thainess which is more recent and still influential is an intellectual tendency that attracts many people by its conservative radicalism. Basically it attacks the failure of modern Thai society in the light of Buddhist Thai tradition, arguing that modernity, capitalism, and consumerism have uprooted Thai people from the fundamentals of Thai civilization— hence the degradation of modern culture and the deterioration of morality and Buddhism in Thai society as a whole. In turn, it calls for a return to Thainess, the roots or fundamental values of Thai

civilization, and the reassertion of Thai intellect, all of which are based on Buddhism.[38]

Over the past three decades, some of the leading voices in this critique have been those of Bhikkhu Buddhadāsa (Phra Phutthathat) and his students Phra Kalyano and Santikaro Bhikkhu, Phra Payutto, Sulak Sivaraksa, Samana Phothirak (formerly Phra Phothirak), Suwanna Sattha-Anand, and Phra Phaisan Wisalo. Some of these figures have faced intense criticism within Thailand—including rumors of communist sympathies (Bhikkhu Buddhadāsa) and charges of *lèse-majesté* (Sulak Sivaraksa)—and have been forced to disrobe for boasting about false spiritual attainments (Samana Phothirak).

Bhikkhu Buddhadāsa

Bhikkhu Buddhadāsa, who has been described as "the most influential contemporary Buddhist philosopher monk in Thailand,"[39] and as "Thailand's greatest contemporary spiritual leader,"[40] spent many years of his life raising poignant questions about the state of Buddhism in Thailand and the effects of economic development on Thai society. Bhikkhu Buddhadāsa's reinterpretation of dhammic practice emphasized the import of understanding key Buddhist ideas such as *aniccā* (impermanence), *dukkha* (un-satisfactoriness), *anattā* (not-Self) and *nibbāna* over the so-called popular practices of merit making and magical ritualism.[41] Because Buddhadāsa's version of dhammic practice was not consistent with the dominant expression of the tradition within Thailand, he gradually disassociated himself from the saṅgha establishment and founded Wat Suan Mokkh (The Garden of Liberation), which was dedicated to the study and practice of dhamma as outlined by Buddhadāsa.

Buddhadāsa's interpretation of core Buddhist teachings and his critique of contemporary Thai Buddhist practice informed his discussion of social and political issues, especially his assessment of modern development. His teachings, for instance, provided a substantive alternative to the dominant model of development that is based, according to Buddhadāsa, on materialism and on the glorification of the personal, independent ego. He highlighted the manner in which this paradigm of social growth came to foster a form of material progress that has led to the destruction of Buddhist communities and the decay of Buddhist ideals and values. His alternative model of development, labeled "dhammic socialism," resembled the ideology of Buddhist socialism espoused by other Buddhist reformers in the two decades following the end of World War II, which marked the end of the colonial period and the emergence of new Asian nation-states. As stated in Chapter 1, these views led some of his critics to denounce him as a communist sympathizer.

In his article "Exchanging Dhamma while Fighting," Buddhadāsa described material progress without spiritual progress as a path that "will lead to hell or transform the world into hell."[42] He argued that material progress alone makes people more selfish, degrades ethics, creates a state of excessiveness and inflation, and makes the world more materialistic. These effects in turn lead to the degeneration of religious values and ideals, promote an imbalance between the mind and body, and increase competition and conflict between people. Materialism, according to Bhikkhu Buddhadāsa, is an epidemic disease that is gradually wearing away the real wisdom of the dhamma and its application to society. Phra Kalyano and Santikaro Bhikkhu, two of Buddhadāsas most outspoken students, continue to challenge society and the saṅgha to reject materialism in favor of a dhamma-based society. As an example, Phra Kalyano hosts a flea market at his temple, Wat Suan Kaew, where people can donate their possessions for a good cause, and people in need can purchase them at a relatively low price.

Phra Payutto

As noted in the previous chapter, Phra Payutto (Phra Dhammapitaka) is arguably the most well-known and respected living Buddhist scholar in Thailand today. The popularity of his critiques of the Santi Asok movement and the Dhammakāya Temple demonstrates his authoritative status. He is a prolific writer on issues of dhamma—his *Buddhadhamma* is found in the curriculum at Mahachulalongkorn Buddhist University—and he is a leading commentator on issues concerning the relationship between Buddhism and society. In the introduction to a collection of essays compiled in honor of Phra Payutto's sixtieth birthday, Bruce Evans writes, "The strength of his writing lies not in the new information it may provide, but in its application of intelligent thought to what has already been laid down. It is Venerable Prayudh's astute awareness of the state of people in the present time, a result of his keen interest in other fields of knowledge, that has guided his approach to presenting the Buddha's teaching."[43] His astute awareness of contemporary topics prompted Phra Payutto to critique modern development and capitalism from a Buddhist perspective. In his *Buddhist Economics: A Middle Way for the Market Place*, he urges individuals to incorporate Buddhist ethics into the conception and practice of economics—which, up to this point, had been articulated primarily through the lens of Western discourse and practice.

> Western academic disciplines and conceptual structures have reached a point which many feel to be a dead end, or if not, at least

a turning point demanding new paradigms of thought and methodology. This has led many economists to rethink their isolated, specialized approach. The serious environmental repercussions of rampant consumerism have compelled economists to develop more ecological awareness. Some even propose that new students of economics incorporate basic ecology into their curriculum.[44]

The primary problem with Western conceptions of economics, according to Phra Payutto, lies in its propensity to separate economics from other spheres of activity. He argues that one of the central tenets of Buddhism is the interconnectedness of life, a doctrine that facilitates recognition of the relational effects of all thoughts and actions. Buddhist economics has this doctrine at its base: "While modern economics confines its regard to events within its specialized sphere, Buddhist economics would investigate how a given economic activity affects the three interconnected spheres of human existence: the individual, society and the nature of the environment."[45] In the case of economics, therefore, we must move beyond a focus on the satisfaction of consumer demand and move towards a more comprehensive analysis of the conditions and effects of economic activities.

Phra Payutto uses his theory of Buddhist economics to address the problem of consumerism in Thailand. He states that the current trend is towards the consumption of "flashy" products that serve to enforce "vain and fickle" values. Advertising feeds on popular values, "on common aspirations, prejudices and desires in order to produce advertisements that are appealing." The result of such practices is an increase in materialism and selfish indulgence that leads to the destruction of public morality and the creation of a society full of "hungry ghosts, striving to feed an everlasting craving."[46] He describes the hungry-ghost syndrome of contemporary society as one epitomized by waste and extravagance.

> Things are used for a short while and then replaced, even though they are still in good condition. Advertising also caters to peoples' tendency to flaunt their possessions as a way of gaining social status. When snob-appeal is the main criterion, people buy unnecessarily expensive products without considering the quality. In extreme cases, people are so driven by the need to appear stylish that they cannot wait to save the money for the latest gadget or fashion—they simply use their credit cards. Spending in excess of earnings can become a vicious cycle. A newer model or fashion is advertised and people plunge themselves deeper and deeper into debt trying to keep up. In this way, unethical advertising can lead people to financial ruin.[47]

Phra Payutto argues that Buddhist ethics, in contrast to this portrait of unlimited consumerism, stresses moderation, not overconsumption. Well-being, not maximum satisfaction, should be the focus.

Sulak Sivaraksa

Sulak Sivaraksa, a lay social critic and founder of numerous NGOs, is another leading voice in the critique of consumerism and Thai society. He openly admonishes the development forces within the world that value profit over social justice and encourage development over the interests of natural resources.

> The capitalistic system aims for profit, not for the general welfare of the pubic. Capitalists may indulge in some forms of philanthropy, as long as a majority of the people remain under their control. But since profit is their goal, they must take every advantage they can, beginning with taking advantage of the workers and finally taking advantage of the consumers.[48]

While Sulak's general message resonates with those of Buddhadāsa and Phra Payutto, his critique differs in style and focus, which is perhaps due to the fact that he is not bound to the same rules of decorum that typically govern the behavior of monks. He directly attacks those forces in Thai society that breed consumerism, namely, what he perceives as a corrupt polity and saṅgha establishment. He argues that Thailand's pervasive social, economic, and political problems derive from the marriage of an uncritical appropriation of Western values and progress models by political elites with the failure of religious elites to effectively inform the decisions of policy makers. These overt criticisms led him to be charged in 1984 and 1994 with violating Thailand's strict lèse-majesté laws.

In contrast to the portrayal of Theravāda Buddhism as asocial or otherworldly, Sulak argues that Buddhist practice is comprised of two steps, both of which are inherently social. First, the individual must focus on inner contemplation. This endeavor reveals to the practitioner that all forms of life are interconnected. Any focus on individual gratification is therefore illusionary. Second, the individual must use this knowledge to transform society to reflect Buddhist ideals and therefore seek to promote social justice: the maintenance of human rights, equitable economic development plans, and the preservation of the environment.

> Buddhism is not concerned just with private destiny, but with the lives and consciousness of all beings. This inevitably entails a

> concern with social and political matters, and these receive a large
> share of attention in the Pali canon.... I agree with Trevor Ling
> when he says that Buddhism can be regarded as a prescription for
> both the restructuring of human consciousness and restructuring
> of society.[49]

Sulak uses this interpretation of Buddhism to criticize an array of develop-
ments in modern Thailand that he views as antithetical to Buddhism. He criticizes the Thai populace for abandoning Buddhism in favor of the religion of
consumerism, a religion which focuses on self-gratification rather than on
community development and social justice. According to Sulak, the religion of
consumerism developed through the Thai government's misguided attempts at
modernization that placed undue emphasis on the economic progress of the
elite. He describes the government's theory of progress as "the think-big strategy of development," a strategy which favors big business, the wealthy elite,
and the image of the government.[50] He argues that the government's failure to
contain the religion of consumerism directly relates to the government's uncritical co-option of Western political, economic, and social models and contemporary Western values.

Samana Phothirak and Santi Asok

Sulak is not the only social critic to implicate the political and religious establishments in the promotion of consumerism and the unreflective co-option
of Western values. For the past three decades, Samana Phothirak (formerly
known as Phra Phothirak),[51] the founder of the Santi Asok movement, has
made headlines for promoting a strict form of Buddhist practice that de-
nounces those aspects of Thai Buddhism that he perceives as ritualistic and
commercial.[52] Samana Phothirak's condemnation of these aspects of Thai Buddhism has provided a subtext for his promotion of Santi Asok, his counter-
consumerist religious movement. In an interview with Prakobpong Panapool
during the Dhammakāya controversy, Phothirak stated, "[The] Dhammakaya
Temple is a showcase of Buddhism trapped in the capitalist system while Santi
Asoke always adheres to the principle of modesty."[53] He compared Santi Asok
strict practices of eating only one vegetarian meal a day and handling no money
to the luxurious lifestyles of the monks at the Dhammakāya Temple. In the
same article, Thirajitto, chief administrator of Santi Asok, criticized the Dhammakāya Temple's use of "direct-sale" methods in their campaign to raise donations for the Mahathammakai Chedi. He argued that merit making should
not be a commercial endeavor but rather one based on the purity of the donor's
intention.

In February of 2001, I attended a taping of the popular *Searching for the Essence of Buddhism* television program at Santi Asok in Bangkok. On this occasion, Sulak and Phothirak both addressed the implications of capitalism for Thai society. When fielding a question over the merits of socialism over capitalism, both Sulak and Phra Phothirak argued that socialism is more consistent with the ideals of the Buddhist middle path. Sulak argued that the community of the saṅgha represents the ideal of cooperation over competition, while Phothirak described Buddhism as a religion that helps one to reduce the ego. When asked by another audience member, "How should we combat the problems of capitalism?" both Sulak and Phothirak linked capitalism to the generation of the three defilements of greed, hatred, and delusion. Sulak championed Bhikkhu Buddhadāsa's message of dhammic socialism with its emphases on social and environmental benefits as a solution to capitalism's focus on material profit, and in a similar vein, Phothirak suggested that one way to combat the onslaught of capitalism is for the Thai populace to elect officials who lives are informed by dhamma practice, not personal interest.

Suwanna Satha-Anand and Phra Phaisan Wisalo

Dr. Suwanna Satha-Anand, professor of Buddhist philosophy at Chulalongkorn University, and Phra Phaisan Wisalo, abbot of Wat Pha Sukato in Chaiyaphom province and prolific author of books on Buddhism and society, offer a striking critique of wealth in contemporary Thai society in the book, *Ngoen kap Sasana* (Money and Religion),[54] which was written during the beginning of the Asian economic crisis. In their respective sections, they collectively question the equation of wealth with piety in Buddhism, and they argue that religion should serve to challenge contemporary consumption rather than to endorse it.

Dr. Suwanna begins by examining the value attributed to money and how religions can offer alternate sources of value. She first argues that money is a human creation that has been used by societies not only as a medium of exchange of goods and services but also to measure social status, to measure the severity of a crime (the amount of particular fine), to purchase brides, and even procure human organs. In so doing, money, through complex institutional quantification of values into prices and costs, neutralizes all values and facilitates consumption. Dr. Suwanna argues that standard economic theory assumes that humans are born to consume, while religions can serve to challenge this premise.[55]

She then examines discussions and critiques of wealth in Christianity, Buddhism, and Islam. In the case of Christianity, she cites a number of biblical references that support a reading of the New Testament as a critique of wealth:

Jesus' teaching that one cannot serve both God and Mammon at the same time (Matthew 6:24); Jesus' condemnation of commercial practices at the temple in Jerusalem (Mark 11:15–19); his suggestion that a rich young man give to the poor in order to enter the kingdom of God (Matthew 19:16–30); his critique of greed (Luke 12: 12–21); the teaching that the amount of a donation is not equivalent to its religious benefit (Mark 12: 41–44); and Jesus' sermon on the Mount, in which he famously stated, "Blessed are the poor in spirit, for theirs is the kingdom of heaven" (Matthew 5:1–11).[56] Dr. Suwanna next turns her attention to Buddhism, in which she outlines the Buddha's teachings about money to monastic and lay audiences. Regarding monks, she states that the Buddha unequivocally banned monks from economic activity, as seen in the rule against the handling of money. Monks were not to value possessions, as evidenced in the early practice of collecting clothes from the dead to be used as monastic robes. Laypersons may obviously use money, but there are three principal teachings regarding its use: (1) the admonition in the *pañca sīla* (five precepts) against theft; (2) the importance of right livelihood (not selling weapons, animals, or alcohol) in the eight-fold path; and (3) the Buddha's teachings on earning money honestly and using it to support one's family, society, and monks. The noblest forms of wealth (*ariya sap*) are the virtues and wisdom of a person, not his material possessions.[57] Lastly, Dr. Suwanna makes a few references to Islam, in which she states that Islam admonishes against taking advantage of people, as evidenced in the law against usury, and the ideal of distributing wealth throughout society through its collection of *zakat*.[58] From her analysis of the critique of wealth in Christianity, Buddhism, and Islam, Suwanna makes several suggestions: (1) religious institutions must decide, if, when, and to what extent they want to be influenced by religion; (2) people must understand that the worship of money is equal to the worship of the self, which contradicts the doctrines of all three traditions; (3) religions could clearly articulate that religious wisdom is not constituted by the simple satisfaction of desires—that idea presents a reductionist attitude toward the value of human life; (4) religious persons could promote their traditions through a careful personal reading of the texts and a reflected commitment to practice; (5) religions should enter into interreligious dialogue; (6) people could reference religion in their everyday lives, and (7) Thais, in particular, could view the economic crisis as an opportunity to return to the ideals of religion—people today are too rich, too fatigued, too bored, and too consumeristic, and as a result, they are spiritually impoverished. Suwanna ends her piece with a call for the regeneration of Buddhism.[59]

Following Suwanna's comprehensive essay on religion and money, Phra Phaisan Wisalo offers a specific appraisal of Buddhism in Thai society and an assessment of the Asian economic crisis. He writes that the economic crisis is the result of greed, the delusion that money can buy happiness, and the fact that the Thai economy is based on money not on its natural resources. In the past, according to Phra Phaisan, Thais used a system of barter; today, people consume, use credit, and produce inferior products that cannot be exported. In the past, borrowing was viewed as a sign of laziness, whereas today borrowing is valued as a means for receiving good credit, which only leads to more borrowing. To remedy this situation, Phra Phaisan offers several solutions: (1) depend less on money as a source of happiness; (2) spend less time trying to earn money that is subsequently used to consume material goods; (3) return to an economic system of exchanging goods for products and labor; and (4) develop a sustainable economy that is not based on credit. In other words, people need to realize that "rice is more important than a Rolex." Not only does Phra Phaisan criticize the "religion of consumerism" in Thailand, he is one of the most vocal opponents of the commercialization of Thai Buddhism.[60]

The Commercialization of Buddhism

In the last section, I offered a broad sampling of some of the discourses on global capitalism, consumerism, and development and its effects on Thai society. Now, I address another set of discourses relating to the commercialization of Buddhism—the sale of Buddhist-related objects for profit and the consumption of such items for personal satisfaction. The exchange of these items brings into sharp relief the relationship between the daily life of Buddhist practice and modern consumerism. Many of the reformers mentioned in the previous section condemn what they view as the commercialization of Buddhism for profit.

The sale or exchange of religious items is not a practice unique to late modern capitalist societies, but the nature of the exchange today is influenced by the culture of consumerism that exists in the contemporary world. Religious items enter the marketplace and compete with other religious and non-religious items for customers: Kabbalah Water versus Dasani, a *Left Behind* novel versus Stephen King's latest thriller, or a Third Day album versus an album by Britney, Rhianna, or Fergie. These religious items are products that must be marketed, sold, and consumed. Mara Einstein argues that religious media such as the film *The Passion of the Christ* are commodities:

> The Passion of the Christ showed in the most blatant of ways that religion is a product, no different from any other commodity sold in the consumer marketplace . . . And while initially the objective was to sell a film, we can see from the sustaining campaigns and comments made by the director that the ultimate objective was to promote religion itself.

Many forms of religion are being advertised and promoted in a way never seen before. Churches advertise on billboards and in print media. Books sell us all types of religious and spiritual wisdom. Television has become overrun with religious content with no fewer than eight channels presenting sermons and faith-based programming 24 hours a day, not to mention religious content in broadcast prime time and as regular content for nightly newsmagazines.[61]

Einstein attributes this religious consumption in America to the diminished authority of traditional religious institutions. The result is an ever-increasingly personalized and autonomous religion.

In the American context, sociologists of religion have identified the increasingly eclectic character of religiosity as one sign of the effects of consumer culture on religion. Peter Berger, for instance, argues that religion in America often resembles a shopping market, whereby individuals selectively choose aspects of religious traditions that suit their individual tastes.[62] The result of such a competitive and individualistic religious environment is the diversification of religious practice and identity. This environment has also led to the restructuring of religiosity based on a "wide range of people's causes, interests, and curiosities (for example, people interested in 'eco-spirituality,' 'Motorcyclists for Jesus,' 'channeling sessions')."[63]

These trends have led to a serious assessment of how traditional religions can maintain their uniqueness and identity in the midst of such diversification. One response has been the co-option of this marketplace as a venue for the expression and spread of religiosity. R. Laurence Moore characterizes this shift as a sign of the commodification of religion in nineteenth-century America, as churches grew through a participation in the market and as religious authorities established themselves in commercial culture.[64] He argues convincingly that this process of commodification has not merely been the effect of the consumer culture on religion. This process also demonstrates how religion has influenced "the taste of people who were learning to purchase 'culture' as a means of self-improvement and relaxation."[65] Raymond Benton similarly argues that a consumer society is one that spends money during leisure time and one that equates ownership with happiness. "Individual lifestyles and identity become linked to consumption activities; 'consumerism' is then based on accepting consumption as the way to self-development, self-realization, and self-fulfillment."[66]

Phra Phaisan Wisalo argues that this type of consumer-based society has had a significant impact on Buddhist practice in Thailand: "Consumerism rests on the principle that happiness and success come about through consuming or purchasing things, not through creating or realizing it by oneself. This belief causes people to see religion as merely another aspect of consuming, rather than something which should be applied and practiced."[67] O'Connor describes this transformation in Thailand as a shift in the relation of wealth to patronage: "Where old money approached wat as patrons wanting honour, this new wealth comes to religion as consumers expecting results."[68] Phra Paisan Wisalo similarly argues that the distinction between Buddhism and consumerism is becoming increasingly vague because religious practice is now being defined as the purchase of auspicious objects. "One's faith (saddha) is no longer measured by how one applies it, how one lives life, but by how many holy or sacred articles one possesses."[69] Thailand's monasteries have been transformed into trading centers, providing glossy photographs of famous monks, amulets, yantra cloths, protective lockets for rearview mirrors, figurines, and signs with magic phrases to an eager clientele. He notes how some of these commodities are instant successes.

> In one instance, people developed a belief about the special powers of a certain kind of bamboo from one village in Thailand. More than 20 different kinds of sacred objects made from this bamboo were available within a few days of the "discovery" of its potency. Soon, hundreds of thousands of baht (Thai currency—40 baht/$1) were being generated each day in more than 200 shops that mushroomed in the once sleepy, peaceful little village."[70]

According to Phra Phaisan, these commercialized Buddhist products appeal to those individuals who are interested in an "instant coffee kind of religion where the results are quick and immediate." With such religious practices, commitment to long-term practice, to a particular temple or teacher, becomes obsolete and is replaced with a spiritual market that is driven by the latest and greatest religious products.

Phra Phaisan Wisalo and other critics of the commercialization of Thai Buddhism note how the temple has become a site of commercial activities. Lottery tickets are a common sight outside of temple entrances, where temple visitors are able to purchase tickets after procuring suggestions for numbers from auspicious signs at the temple. Those who visit Wat Mahabut in Bangkok, for instance, can obtain lottery numbers from a myriad of sources—"a rooster's legs and toes, the trees, an abandoned boat, and the age of a maintenance worker have been used by the enthusiasts to bet on lotteries—and many of them have claimed to have won."[71] Along with the colorful display of lottery tickets, the outer edges of Thai temples typically offer a diverse array of goods, ranging from conspicuously religious objects such as amulets and images of the Buddha and famous Thai monks to noodle shops, medicine shops, and stalls selling such mundane consumer products as beauty accessories, handbags and watches, and mass market books. Other temples, such as Wat Rajanadda in

Storefront of an Image Shop in Bangkok. (Photograph by Rachelle M. Scott.)

Bangkok, are known for their wide selection of Buddhist items. At the temple's market one can peruse row upon row of Buddha images of all sizes—Buddha images for temples, homes, or cars, and amulets of the Buddha and famous Thai monks. While there are no vendors inside Wat Mahatat in Bangkok, there are numerous vendors offering their goods for sale in businesses near Wat Mahatat and on the footpath adjacent to it.

Amulet Vendor, Bangkok. (Photograph by Rachelle M. Scott.)

Of the many items sold at temples, the "sale" of amulets has been the focal point of the most heated discussions over the commercialization of Buddhism. Critics of the Dhammakāya Temple focused on the Temple's distribution
of the Mahasiriratthat amulets as a clear sign of its commercialized practices.
But this criticism is not only reserved for the Dhammakāya Temple. The critique of the amulet industry extends to the distribution of amulets at other
temples, to the "sale" of amulets at commercial stalls in places like Pantip Plaza,
the computer mega-center in Pratunam, and to popular magazines, such as
Phutthakhun and *Pawarat*, that relay stories about potent amulets and the people who possess them. Sanitsuda Ekachai, a prominent editorial writer for the
Bangkok Post, argues that the popularity of amulets derives from the intermin-
gling of the "spirit of capitalism" of contemporary Thailand with traditional
beliefs concerning supernatural powers. She describes how amulets made of
fossilized mammoth ivory are advertised in local newspapers.

> In an open marketing blitz, the jewelry company importing the
> fossilised ivory to produce the charms recently placed a half-page
> advertisement in the newspapers. The ad features a huge hairy
> mammoth with a pair of majestic tusks.
>
> In one corner is a replica of an ivory coin bearing the image of
> King Chulalongkorn, who posthumously has become the god of

wealth for today's Thai entrepreneurs. On the back of the coin is a "yantra," an ancient symbol believed to ward off danger. In another corner is a photograph of Luang Por Uttama, a well-known elderly monk, who has sanctified the coins with magical powers. The background colour is glowing saffron, the same as the monks' sacred robes. Strengthen charisma and power, proclaims the banner.[72]

Sanitsuda suggests that the marketing of these amulets plays on the association of antiquity with sanctity, as well as Thai notions of the grandeur of elephants and the value of ivory. She also notes how these amulets offer a "hodge-podge of magic, like the 7–Eleven one-stop-shop around the corner," which is unlike the more specialized amulets of the past. Moreover, these amulets are now produced and distributed through amulet businesses, not simply through independent temples. She describes these practices as examples of occultism, as practices that seek help from supernatural powers in order to perpetuate greed.

Critical discourses on the production and distribution of amulets are often stirred by successes in the amulet industry. Prior to debates over the Dhammakāya Temple's distribution of the infamous asset-sucking Phra Mahasiriratthat amulets, Luang Pho Khun's wide range of "prosperity" amulets commonly graced the covers of Thai newspapers and magazines. Luang Pho Khun's fame derived, in part, from the narratives of prosperity and wealth associated with his amulets.[73] Peter Jackson argues that during the 1990s "the marketing of [Khun's] blessed amulets and other cultic products became a multimillion-baht industry." Some of the amulets distributed in the 1990s were intimately linked to the accumulation of wealth as indicated by their names: "Fortune, success, increase," "Multiplying fortune," "Rich for sure," "Multiplying wealth," and "Increasing wealth."[74] These amulets were named by the consuming public, however, and not by Luang Pho Khun. Jackson insists that the Luang [Pho Khun] phenomenon has been significantly influenced, if not determined, by media owners and newspaper editors eager to promote sales with stories of miracles and by entrepreneurs interested in profiting from commodifying [Khun's] supernatural charisma." The degree to which Luang Pho Khun distances himself from this phenomenon is relevant in that it testifies to the contestability of the cult of amulets in contemporary Thailand.[75]

Debates over the commercialization of Buddhism also extend to the political sphere.[76] In 1993, for instance, Samphan Thongsamak, the Education Minister, publicly stated that he was "concerned by the growing influence of 'commercial Buddhism' within Thailand." According to his reading of Buddhism, the "business of selling Buddhist amulets for worship is not in accordance with the teachings of the Lord Buddha."[77] At the same time, however, many politicians in the Department of Education and other departments publicly offer patronage to monks such as Luang Pho Khun, and receive amulets in return. The critique of the commercialization of Buddhism is therefore not a straightforward critique of a deviant practice. It is embedded within one vision of Buddhist religiosity and is by no means a hegemonic discourse in Thailand.

Conclusion

A century ago, Buddhist reformers in Thailand and elsewhere sought to diminish or eliminate elements of the tradition that they viewed as magical, irrational, and steeped in superstition. In that historical context, reformers presented a purified Buddhism as a highly rational religion consistent with modern Enlightenment thought. Today, reformers continue to criticize the magical elements in Buddhism, as seen in their fervent condemnation of the "cult of amulets." But rather than focusing on how these elements are inconsistent with modern rational thought, critics today focus on how these elements are indicative of the effects of consumerism and global capitalism on Buddhism.

Although the critique of money making by Buddhist temples is certainly not confined to the late twentieth century, postmodern critical discourses on consumerism and the commercialization of Buddhism do nevertheless focus on these trends within postmodern societies. Contemporary critics who denounce the commercial activities of temples, such as the distribution of widely advertised amulets, link the commercialization of religion to late capitalism, not to an inherent tendency within the tradition to value wealth. In so doing, these discourses enter into a larger public debate over religion and society in the late twentieth- and early twenty-first centuries. In the case of the Dhammakāya Temple, critics have used the controversy surrounding the Temple's marketing techniques as a means to critique the late capitalist consumer culture of contemporary Thailand. What is imperative for us to recognize is that these critiques of the effects of consumerism on religion and of the "commercialization of religion" are also embedded within critical assessments of contemporary society. The critics who condemn consumerism and the commercialization of religion have an agenda that extends beyond the simple analysis of religious change in the modern world. Their critiques of contemporary Buddhism are one component of a more comprehensive call for social, economic, and political reform.

Conclusion

At first glance, the middle-aged businessman driving a luxury car seems to have nothing in common with the young gas station worker. On the surface, there are the obvious disparities in age, lifestyle and income, yet both have a similar preoccupation with what the future holds in store . . . neither would leave home without donning their most treasured accessory—a Jatukam amulet the size of a small coffee cup. Jatukam is the most popular deity in Thailand today. His full name is Jatukam Ramathep and his image can be seen almost everywhere—on amulets, coins and statuettes, and even on incantation cloths.

> —Nithinand Yorsaengrat, "Talismanic Tales," *The Nation*, February 11, 2007.[1]

In 2007, the southern province of Nakorn Si Thammarat experienced an unusual financial boom. The dramatic increase in economic activity in the region was the result of the mass production and distribution of Jatukam Ramathep amulets that had become a new amulet craze throughout Thailand.[2] Police Major-General Phantarak Rajadej had created the first Jatukam Ramathep amulets over twenty years ago, but it was only upon his death at the age of 104 that the demand for the amulets would literally overcome the ancient southern temple of Wat Mahatat, the temple that originally blessed and distributed the amulets. Phantarak Rajadej was a well-respected police chief, but he was also a Thai historian, politician, and a man reputed to possess magical powers, a fact that may explain why over 200,000 people, including Crown Prince Vajiralongkorn, attended his funeral. The amulets depicting an image of Jatukam Ramathep, a guardian deity of an ancient Southern Thai kingdom, were distributed at the funeral. Soon thereafter, stories began to propagate about the magical abilities of the amulets, and crowds flocked to Wat Mahatat to receive the amulets and have them blessed by monks. The popularity of the Jatukam Ramathep amulets has led many other temples to produce them. In fact, a monumental advertisement for the amulet was displayed in Bangkok on the side of the Biyoke Tower, Thailand's tallest building, which incidentally, is quite close to the area where the Dhammakāya Temple advertised the Mahathammakai Chedi on a flashing billboard in 1998.

As with the popularity of other amulets, the cult of the Jatukam Ramathep amulets has served as an occasion for commentary on the place of amulets in Thai Buddhism and on the state of Buddhism itself. In one report, Sulak Sivaraksa stated, "They've lost their way. . . . Monks are supposed to renounce money. The teachings of the Buddha have been killed by the demonic religion of consumerism."[3] Phra Phayom Kalyano, the abbot of Wat Suan Kaew and student of Bhikkhu Buddhadāsa, similarly argues that "materialism and amulets have diverted people from the core of Buddha's teaching . . . This makes Buddha's teaching fade away."[4] To counter the craze for Jatukam amulets and to highlight its absurdity, Phra Phayom started to sell Chatu Kham (literally, Four Bites) cookies at Wat Suan Kaew.[5] These cookies resembled the Jatukam Ramathep amulets in shape, size, and design, and their name bore an obvious resemblance to that of the amulets.

> One side of the cookie has Chatu Kham imprinted on it and the Sanskrit letters "U - A - Ka - Sa" on the other side. The Sanskrit is from a Buddhist teaching that to be wealthy one must be industrious (uthansampatha); to save up what has honestly been earned (arakkhasampatha); surround oneself with good friends who do not lead one to vices (kalayanamitra) and have prudent spending habits (samachivata).

> Questioning the craze of the Jatukam talisman, and noting it was not exactly compatible with the essence of Buddhism, Phra Payom said his Chatu Kham cookies were a simple way to teach the Lord Buddha's teachings so that Thai people would be aware and refrain from getting "unreasonably attached" to material wealth. [6]

The Chatu Kham cookies became so popular that Phra Phayom decided to diversify his product line by distributing Jatukam T-shirts that encouraged people to be industrious and save money.[7] The money from the sale of these items, according to Phra Phayom, would go to the poor and temples in need.

The popularity of Jatukam Ramathep amulets as sources of power, protection, and good fortune on the one hand, and the criticism of their commercialization of Buddhism on the other, aptly demonstrate two radically different orientations towards Buddhism, global capitalism, and consumer society. Current debates concerning the Jatukam Ramathep phenomenon closely resemble those involving the Dhammakāya Temple ten years ago. Both cases highlight the presence of conflicting visions of Thai Buddhism in contemporary Thai society, but there is one notable difference between the two cases. The

Dhammakāya controversy emerged in the midst of the Asian economic crisis when the value of the baht decreased by fifty percent and thousands of people had lost their jobs. In contrast, the Jatukam Ramathep phenomenon, with its stories of prosperity and security, evolved during a period of intense political strife in the southern-most provinces of Thailand and a period of increased insecurity over the effectiveness and legitimacy of the Thaksin government. The first context led to a nationwide condemnation of the Dhammakāya Temple's wealth and marketing. The second context provided fertile ground for the emergence of a new cult of prosperity and security. Both cases demonstrate how Buddhist discourses on piety and wealth are historically contingent and linked to broader issues of religious identity and authority at specific moments in time.

This book advocates a method for viewing the relationship between wealth and piety not in terms of identifying the orthodox Buddhist appraisal of wealth and tracking consistencies and divergences, but rather in practical terms—focusing instead on how Buddhists at a particular moment in time assessed the relationship between wealth and piety. This approach entailed moving back and forth between two different, yet interrelated fields: the field of Theravāda Buddhism, with its varying assessments of the role of wealth; and the field of contemporary Thai Buddhism, in which disparate interpretations of the relationship between wealth and piety have profound implications for Buddhist identity, practice, and authority at the beginning of a new millennium. The immense popularity and intense notoriety of the Dhammakāya Temple—which exudes an aura of wealth, prosperity, and modernity—provided the principal lens for viewing contrasting conceptions of Buddhism in contemporary Thailand. Chapter 2 presented the Dhammakāya Temple's successful merging of piety and prosperity in the 1980s and 1990s as a striking example of the conflation of wealth and piety in the context of modern Thailand. During this economically prosperous period in Thailand's history, the Dhammakāya Temple grew to be one of the largest and wealthiest of temples in Thailand, drawing over 200,000 practitioners to its events. At the same time, we examined how this prosperous temple became embroiled in a national controversy in 1998 and 1999 over its teachings, practices, and marketing techniques. This was an instance in history when religious wealth stimulated debates over the correlation of wealth with piety, the commercialization of Buddhism, and the authority of religious elites.

While both the national and international press framed the controversy as the story of a big temple gone bad, using characterizations strikingly similar to those leveled against controversial churches and religious organizations in America,[8] none of these reports delved into the more poignant question of why the controversy became such an extensive public uproar in the late 1990s. The Dhammakāya Temple did not become rich overnight, nor was its building of the Mahathammakai Chedi its first large-scale project. Moreover, the Theravāda tradition has a long history of correlating piety with the creation and construction of monumental pieces of Buddhist art and architecture, as demonstrated in both its narratives and material culture. In 1998, however, the Dhammakāya Temple's correlations of wealth with piety and generous giving with Buddhist monuments became the focus of a year-long controversy within the public sphere. This was a period in Thai history when these aspects of Theravāda religiosity became suspect and broadly controversial. It is not to say that critics such as Prawase Wasi or Sulak Sivaraksa did not speak out against the perceived excesses of the Dhammakāya Temple prior to 1997; rather, the Asian economic crisis provided a cultural context conducive to public debates over the correlation of wealth with piety.

For Buddhist reformers, debates over the Dhammakāya Temple's wealth, marketing techniques, and interpretations of nirvāṇa highlighted the urgent need for religious reform within the kingdom. One of the principal targets of reform, as in the past, was the Thai saṅgha. Painting with broad brushes, critics characterized the Dhammakāya Temple as an exemplar of all that was wrong with the saṅgha in Thailand: monastic excess and the desire for prestige; the commercialization of Buddhism through the "selling" of personal Phra Dhammakāya images that promise material benefits; the distribution and marketing of amulets that miraculously garner assets to those who possess them; and the failure of the monastic power establishment to adequately redress such decadence.[9] For Buddhist reformers, this critical portrayal of the Temple highlighted the urgent need for a restructuring of the monastic system in Thailand, especially the centralization of authority within an outdated and impotent ecclesiastical institution. In a talk at Cornell University in 2000, Santikaro Bhikkhu, an American monk and student of the late Bhikkhu Buddhadāsa, succinctly articulated this call for reform. He stated that the Dhammakāya controversy "has ripped the bandages and scabs off the festering wounds in the Institutional Thai Sangha."[10] For Santikaro Bhikkhu and other liberal-democratic-oriented Buddhist reformers, these wounds included the divide between Mahanikai and Thammayutnikai monks, the ineffective and outdated bureaucratic structure of the religious administration, the increasing social irrelevance and isolation of the religious establishment, and the low standards for monastic training in Thailand. Because many of these reformers pointed to the forces of modernization both within and outside of the saṅgha as the cause for the current religious "crisis," their calls for reform tended to take aim at the effects of saṅgha modernization, especially the centralization of power in the Supreme Patriarch and the Supreme Saṅgha Council as instituted in the Saṅgha Act of 1962.[11]

Criticism of the current governing Saṅgha Act tends to increase as monastic scandals and controversies occupy center stage within the media. Following a slew of sexual scandals in the mid-1990s, for instance, an amendment to the Saṅgha Act was proposed in 1996 that sought to revise the role of the Supreme Patriarch (making the role more symbolic), to increase the number of governing committees, and to empower authorities to censure errant monks more quickly and effectively.[12] The Supreme Saṅgha Council itself co-opted the language of reform in 2001 when it backed a bill that would have created an Office of National Buddhism under the prime minister and a new organization, the Maha Kanissorn, to handle administrative duties.[13] Neither piece of legislation was passed as differing factions within the saṅgha critiqued the method and scope of reform encapsulated within the bills. But the call for reform continues.

While saṅgha reform occupies a principal place within reformist discourses, the call for religious reform in contemporary Thailand encompasses more than just monastic instruction and adherence to the *Vinaya*. Today, reformers in Thailand target Thai Buddhism itself as they lament a "crisis in Buddhism" (*wikrit phutsatsana*). Just as new notions of Thai identity, Thai culture, and the Thai nation arose in the modern period, so too Thai Buddhism became a category for fostering national consciousness and pride in the first part of the twentieth century. Buddhism constituted one of the pillars of modern Thai civic religion along with *chat* (the nation) and *mahakesat* (the king or monarchy). King Wachirawut (Rama VI, r. 1910–1925) viewed Buddhism as the foundation of moral order in society and of effective government.[14] Thai Buddhism, therefore, became not only a source of Thai national pride and of Thai national consciousness but also a barometer for assessing the state of Thai society itself. Today, Buddhist reformers such as Sulak Sivaraksa, Phra Phaisan Wisalo, and Phra Payutto point to the "crisis in Buddhism" as a sign of a larger crisis in contemporary Thai society.[15]

As we assess these calls for reform and the place of the Dhammakāya controversy within them, scholars of religion must be careful not to co-opt reformist discourses within our own assessments of contemporary Thai Buddhism.[16] As Anne Blackburn convincingly argues in her examination of reformist discourses in eighteenth-century Sri Lanka, contemporary historians of Buddhism have often co-opted the Buddhist trope of decline and reform in their analyses of Buddhist societies, failing to recognize the power and function of these tropes within reformist discourse.[17] In the case of Sri Lanka, Blackburn criticizes the argument made by some contemporary Theravāda historians, such as Richard Gombrich and Michael Carrithers, that Theravāda Buddhism has required cycles of "degeneration and reform" for its stability.

> A close look at indigenous histories produced by Lankan Buddhists
> connected with the Siyam Nikāya during the period of the order's
> formation clearly shows that modern historians of "traditional"

Buddhism have erred in their understanding of these indigenous narratives, and that the decline-and-revival (that is, degeneration-and-reform) perspective that dominates eighteenth-century Buddhist historiography is not evidence of essential continuity within the Lankan Theravāda. Rather, this decline-and-revival perspective signals a moment of profound change in Lankan Buddhism. In this moment, monastic and lay elites linked to the Siyam Nikāya altered the terms in which desirable and authoritative Buddhist monasticism was understood.[18]

We must be equally careful to historicize discourses on the "crisis in Buddhism" in our analyses of contemporary Buddhism. Today, Buddhist reformers in Thailand are lamenting what they perceive as a crisis in Buddhism—from the sexual scandals of prominent monks to the commercialization of Buddhism.[19] This critical assessment of the state of Buddhism is couched within a particular reading of the tradition at a particular moment in time. To proclaim that the sangha is in a state of crisis is to contribute to the debate, not to foster understanding of the historical, political, or religious importance of such statements within specific religious communities.[20]

When we view Thai Buddhism as a site for critical thinking and debate rather than as an expression of either authenticity or deviance, then we open our analysis to disparate voices within the tradition.[21] This perspective enables us not only to acknowledge the diversity that exists within Thai Buddhism and religion, but also allows us to examine how disparate voices vie with each other for the power to define authentic Buddhist doctrine and practice. As Tessa Bartholomeusz has effectively demonstrated with regard to competing discourses of violence and pacifism in Sri Lanka,[22] I contend that one of the most relevant discussions in Thailand and around the world today concerns the relationship between Buddhism and notions of prosperity and simplicity. Some Buddhist groups such as the Dhammakāya Temple, Soka Gakkai, and Foguang Shan maintain the traditional linkages between wealth and piety but package these linkages in ways that reflect the social values of postmodern societies. Other Buddhists view these contemporary expressions of Buddhist piety as deviant and corrupt, and therefore inherently un-Buddhist. Many of these Buddhists champion the themes of simplicity and moderation in their constructions of authentic Buddhism, and offer this Buddhism as an antidote to the rampant consumerism that is engulfing societies today.

In analyzing specific debates over the relationship between wealth and piety, our task should not be to render judgment on whether a specific religious group corrupts the tradition for material profit. Our task should be a critical examination of the ways in which such debates reflect differing conceptions of religiosity and identity at a new moment in history. Today, as religious groups operate in radically new sociocultural contexts, debates over wealth and piety are proving to be a powerful lens for viewing religion in the contemporary world. It is also the case that current debates over wealth and piety provide an entrée into broader cultural debates over the benefits and limitations of globalization. There is no doubt that religion will figure into the reimaginings of prosperity in the future as communities wrestle with the realities of climate change, limited energy resources, global trade, mass migration, the ramifications of war, and radically new distributions of wealth.

Notes

Introduction

1. The Thai word *chedi* refers to both a *cetiya* (*caitya*, Sanskrit) and a *thūpa* (*stūpa*, Sanskrit). See Kevin Trainor, *Relics, Ritual, and Representation in Buddhism: Rematerializing the Sri Lankan Theravāda Tradition* (Cambridge: Cambridge University Press, 1997). As Trainor argues, the terms cetiya and stūpa are used interchangeably in contemporary scholarship and in Pāli post-canonical literature. However, the terms have different connotations in some early texts: cetiya was distinguished in some texts as either as a site of a sacred grove or tree or as a memorial without relics.

2. *Mahathammakai Chedi: Mahachedi Phua Santiphap Lok* (Pathum Thani: Dhammakāya Foundation, 2000). I translated the word sattha (*saddhā*, Pāli, *śraddhā*, Sanskrit) as faith since this is a translation frequently used in Temple publications. Buddhist scholars, however, commonly prefer to translate the Pāli *saddhā* as "confidence" or "trust" since these terms are more religiously neutral than "faith," which is inherently linked to Protestant definitions of religion.

3. Chedis containing the Buddha's physical relics are classified as *dhātu-cetiya*, whereas chedis for his personal belongings are *pāribhoga-cetiya*, for his teachings *dhamma-cetiya*, and for Buddha images *uddesika-cetiya*. For analyses of relic veneration, see Kevin Trainor, *Relics, Ritual, and Representation in Buddhism: Rematerializing the Sri Lankan Theravāda Tradition* (Cambridge: Cambridge University Press, 1997); Gregory Schopen, *Bones, Stones, and Buddhist Monks: Collected Papers on the Archaeology, Epigraphy, and Texts of Monastic Buddhism in India* (Honolulu: University of Hawaii Press, 1997); John Strong, *Relics of the Buddha* (Princeton: Princeton University Press, 2004); and David Germano and Kevin Trainor, eds., *Embodying the Dharma* (Albany: State University of New York Press, 2004).

4. For a discussion of the significance of stūpa-building in the *Mahāvaṃsa* and early Indian Buddhism generally, see Gregory Schopen, "The Stūpa Cult and the Extant Pāli *Vinaya*," in Gregory Schopen, *Bones, Stones, and Buddhist Monks: Collected Papers on the Archaeology, Epigraphy, and Texts of Monastic Buddhism in India* (Honolulu: University of Hawaii Press, 1997).

5. *Mahāparinibbāna Sutta* (Dīgha Nikāya 16). This translation is from Maurice Walshe, *The Long Discourses of the Buddha: A Translation of the Dīgha Nikāya* (Boston: Wisdom Publications, 1995), 264.

6. See the full-page advertisement in the *Bangkok Post*, October 5, 1998.

7. "Sun 'Halo' Heats up Temple Critics," *The Nation*, November 28, 1998.

8. Duncan McCargo, "Populism and Reformism in Contemporary Thailand," *South East Asian Research* 9:1 (March 2001): 99.

9. See Stanley J. Tambiah, *Buddhism Betrayed?: Religion, Politics, and Violence in Sri Lanka* (Chicago: University of Chicago Press, 1992); Paul Strange, "Religious Change in Contemporary Southeast Asia," *The Cambridge History of Southeast Asia, Volume Two, Part Two*, ed. Nicholas Tarling (Cambridge: Cambridge University Press, 2000), 201–256; Ananda Abeysekara, *Colors of the Robe: Religion, Identity, and Difference* (Columbia: University of South Carolina Press, 2002); Ian Harris, *Cambodian Buddhism: History and Practice* (Honolulu: University of Hawaii Press, 2005); and Anne Hansen, *How to Behave: Buddhism and Modernity in Colonial Cambodia, 1860–1930* (Honolulu: University of Hawaii Press, 2007).

10. Two analyses of this phenomenon are Kamala Tiyavanich, *Forest Recollections: Wandering Monks in Twentieth-Century Thailand* (Honolulu: University of Hawaii Press, 1997), and J. L. Taylor, *Forest Monks and the Nation-State: An Anthropological and Historical Study in Northeastern Thailand* (Singapore: Institute of Southeast Asian Studies, 1993).

11. See the collection of essays in Melvyn C. Goldstein and Matthew T. Kapstein, eds., *Buddhism in Contemporary Tibet: Religious Revival and Cultural Identity* (Berkeley: University of California Press, 1998).

12. Stephen G. Covell, "Buddhism in Japan: The Creation of Traditions," in *Buddhism in World Cultures: Comparative Perspectives*, ed. Stephen C. Berkwitz (Santa Barbara: ABC-CLIO, 2006), 219–243.

13. See Richard Hughes Seager, *Buddhism in America* (New York: Columbia University Press, 2000).

14. Jean Comaroff and John Comaroff, "Millenial Capitalism: First Thoughts on a Second Coming," *Millenial Capitalism and the Culture of Neoliberalism*, eds. Jean and John Comaroff (Durham and London: Duke University Press, 2001), 4.

15. Jackie Alnor, "Joel Osteen: The Prosperity Gospel's Coverboy," *The Christian Sentinel* (June 2003).

16. Joel Osteen, *Your Best Life Now: 7 Steps to Living at Your Full Potential* (New York: Warner Faith, 2004). Osteen's book reads like a Christian version of Stephen Covey's enormously popular self-improvement manual, *The Seven Habits of Highly Effective People: Powerful Lessons in Personal Change* (New York: Free Press, 1990).

17. See Richard H. Roberts, ed., *Religion and the Transformations of Capitalism: Comparative Approaches* (London and New York: Routledge, 1995).

18. David Loy, "The Religion of the Market," *Journal of the American Academy of Religion* 65:2 (1997): 275–290.

19. Frances Fitzgerald, "Reflections: Jim and Tammy," *New Yorker*, April 23, 1990, 45–87.

20. H. L. Seneviratne, *The Work of Kings: The New Buddhism of Sri Lanka* (Chicago: University of Chicago Press, 1999), 25–55.

21. J. L. Taylor, *Forest Monks and the Nation-State: An Anthropological and Historical Study in Northeastern Thailand* (Singapore: Institute of Southeast Asian Studies, 1993).

22. The portrayal of Theravāda as the most authentic form of Buddhism had an "elective affinity" with representations of the Theravāda tradition by Theravāda Buddhists themselves. Charles Hallisey, in his invaluable assessment of Theravāda studies, correctly

notes that Orientalists in Europe were in conversation with Theravāda Buddhists in South and Southeast Asia, some of whom similarly portrayed Theravāda as an inherently conservative, rational, and ethical religion. See Charles Hallisey, "Roads Taken and Not Taken in the Study of Theravāda Buddhism," in *Curators of the Buddha: The Study of Buddhism Under Colonialism*, ed. Donald S. Lopez, Jr. (Chicago and London: University of Chicago Press, 1995), 31–61.

23. Edward Said, *Orientalism* (New York: Pantheon Books, 1978) and for an in-depth discussion of the use of the term and its implications, see Richard King "Orientalism and the Study of Religions," in *The Routledge Companion to the Study of Religion*, ed. John R. Hinnells (London and New York: Routledge, 2005), 275–290.

24. Philip C. Almond, *The British Discovery of Buddhism* (Cambridge: Cambridge University Press, 1988).

25. Ibid., 5–6.

26. Richard S. Cohen, *Beyond Enlightenment: Buddhism, Religion, Modernity* (London and New York: Routledge, 2006), 3.

27. Quoted in Thomas Tweed, *The American Encounter With Buddhism, 1844–1912: Victorian Culture and the Limits of Dissent* (Chapel Hill: University of North Carolina Press, 2000), 103.

28. Gregory Schopen, *Bones, Stones, and Buddhist Monks: Collected Papers on the Archaeology, Epigraphy, and Texts of Monastic Buddhism in India* (Honolulu: University of Hawaii Press, 1997), 1–22.

29. T. W. Rhys Davids, *Buddhism: Being A Sketch of the Life and Teachings of Gautama, The Buddha*, Revised Edition (London: Society for Promoting Christian Knowledge, 1912), 188.

30. Tweed, *The American Encounter With Buddhism, 1844–1912: Victorian Culture and the Limits of Dissent* (Chapel Hill: University of North Carolina Press, 2000), 123.

31. See Charles Hallisey, "Roads Taken and Not Taken in the Study of Theravāda Buddhism," in *Curators of the Buddha: The Study of Buddhism Under Colonialism*, ed. Donald S. Lopez, Jr. (Chicago and London: University of Chicago Press, 1995), 31–61.

32. Monier Monier-Williams, *Buddhism: In Its Connexion with Brâhmanism and Hindûism, and in Its Contrast with Christianity* (London: John Murray, 1889). For a discussion of Monier-Williams's construction of Buddhism within the history of Buddhism as a "World Religion," see Tomozo Masuzawa, *The Invention of World Religions* (Chicago and London: University of Chicago Press, 2005), 121–146.

33. T. W. Rhys Davids, *Buddhism: Being A Sketch of the Life and Teachings of Gautama, The Buddha*, Revised Edition (London: Society for Promoting Christian Knowledge, 1912).

34. Patrick Jory, "Thai and Western Buddhist Scholarship in the Age of Colonialism: King Chulalongkorn Redefines the Jatakas," *The Journal of Asian Studies* 61:3 (August 2002): 891–918, and Kamala Tiyavanich, *The Buddha in the Jungle* (Seattle: University of Washington Press, 2004), 309.

35. Winston L. King, *Theravāda Meditation: The Buddhist Transformation of Yoga*, first Indian edition, (Delhi: Motilal Banarsidass Publishers, 1992), 28.

36. T. W. Rhys Davids, *Buddhism: Being A Sketch of the Life and Teachings of Gautama.*

37. Max Weber, *The Religion of India: The Sociology of Hinduism and Buddhism*, trans. H. H. Gerth and D. Martindale (New York: The Free Press, 1958).

38. Ibid., 215.

39. Gananath Obeyesekere, "The Great Tradition and the Little in the Perspective of Sinhalese Buddhism," *Journal of Asian Studies* 23: 2 (February 1963): 139–153.

40. For a fascinating deconstruction of the idea of "World Religions" see Tomozo Masuzawa, *The Invention of World Religions* (Chicago and London: University of Chicago Press, 2005).

41. Gananath Obeyesekere, "The Great Tradition and the Little in the Perspective of Sinhalese Buddhism," *Journal of Asian Studies* 23: 2 (February 1963): 151.

42. Melford E. Spiro, *Buddhism and Society: a Great Tradition and Its Burmese Vicissitudes* (Berkeley: University of California Press, 1982).

43. David Chidester makes a similar argument regarding the concept of religion in David Chidester, "The Church of Baseball, the Fetish of Coca-Cola, and the Potlatch of Rock 'n' Roll: Theoretical Models for the Study of Religion in American Popular Culture," *Journal of the American Academy of Religion*, 64:4 (Winter, 1996): 743–765.

44. Stephen Covell notes that the critique of monastic wealth commonly facilitated the seizure of property by the state in both China and Japan. Stephen G. Covell, *Japanese Temple Buddhism: Worldliness in a Religion of Renunciation* (Honolulu: University of Hawaii Press, 2005), 141. Also see Jacques Gernet, *Buddhism in Chinese Society: An Economic History from the Fifth to the Tenth Centuries*, trans. Franciscus Verellen, Studies in Asian Culture (New York: Columbia University Press, 1995).

45. Thomas Tweed argues that during the counter-culture movement of 1950s to 1970s, many Americans were "[l]ess confident about American 'civilization,' capitalist 'advance,' and technological 'progress,' some welcomed—to use Jack Kerouac's term—the 'lunacy' of Zen masters and, even, the passivity of Buddhism." Thomas Tweed, *The American Encounter With Buddhism, 1844–1912: Victorian Culture and the Limits of Dissent* (Chapel Hill: University of North Carolina Press, 2000), 160.

46. Charles Hallisey argues that most studies of Buddhist ethics have focused their agendas on "identifying the method by which Buddhists have decided whether a particular action or character trait is a good one"—on establishing the criteria for assessing Buddhist ethics on a theoretical as well as practical level. This task is ill-founded, according to Hallisey, because it presupposes a single moral theory that "defines the fundamental principles of Buddhist morality and establishes the authority of those principles," and history shows us that Theravāda Buddhists have employed a variety of moral theories in their constructions of Buddhist ethics. Instead, Hallisey suggests that we "revision" the study of Buddhist ethics by pursuing it historically: "When we wish to make generalizations about the Theravāda, we must acknowledge, even if we cannot take into account, the full range of evidence available to us and not limit ourselves only to the Pāli canon," and by considering the "full scope of the ethical heritage of the Theravāda" in our studies. This approach enables us to see how "some texts or traditions (such as the commentarial tradition of the *Mangalasutta*) approach ethics in a manner that might be called ethical particularism." In his reading of the *Mangalasutta*, for instance, he argues that this *sutta* appears to be a "list of thirty-eight prima facie duties" and does not, in fact, provide a "portrait of an ideal moral agent"; rather, the sutta only informs us that "all sorts of things matter." Based on this reading of the sutta, Hallisey concludes that Buddhists might recognize instances of auspiciousness, but they may not agree on the criteria for judging whether a particular act is auspicious or not. Charles Hallisey

"Ethical Particularism in Theravada Buddhism," *The Journal of Buddhist Ethics* 3 (1996): 32–43.

47. Tessa J. Bartholomeusz, *In Defense of Dharma: Just-War Ideology in Buddhist Sri Lanka* (London and New York: RoutledgeCurzon, 2002).

48. Ibid., 10.

49. Talal Asad, "The Idea of an Anthropology of Islam," Occasional Paper Series, (Washington, D.C.: Georgetown University Center for Contemporary Arab Studies, March 1986).

50. Lise McKean, *Divine Enterprise: Gurus and the Hindu Nationalist Movement* (Chicago: University of Chicago Press, 1996).

51. Ibid., 10.

52. Ibid., 17.

53. Phra Phaisan Wisalo, "Spiritual Materialism and the Sacraments of Consumerism: A View from Thailand," in "The Religion of the Market: A Buddhist Look at the Global Economy, Consumerism, Development and the Role of Spirituality in Society," *Think Sangha Journal* 1:1 (1998): 34–39.

54. See David Scott, *Formations of Ritual: Colonial and Anthropological Discourses on the Sinhala Yaktovil* (Minneapolis: University of Minnesota Press, 1994); and Ananda Abeysekara, *Colors of the Robe: Religion, Identity, and Difference* (Columbia: University of South Carolina Press, 2002).

55. Talal Asad, "The Idea of an Anthropology of Islam," Occasional Paper Series (Washington, DC: Georgetown University Center for Contemporary Arab Studies, March 1986).

56. Ibid., 15–16.

57. Ananda Abeyesekara offers a fascinating and compelling analysis of these processes in Sri Lanka. See *Colors of the Robe: Religion, Identity, and Difference* (Columbia: University of South Carolina Press, 2002).

58. Thomas A. Tweed, *Crossing and Dwelling: a Theory of Religion* (Cambridge: Harvard University Press, 2006).

59. My theoretical orientation is indebted to David Scott, in *Formations of Ritual*, and Ananda Abeyesekara, in *Colors of the Robe*, who place these types of questions at the forefront of their analyses of Buddhism in Sri Lanka.

Chapter 1   Buddhism, Renunciation, and Prosperity

1. For more information on nineteenth-century constructions of Buddhism, see Philip Almond, *The British Discovery of Buddhism* (Cambridge: Cambridge University Press, 1988) and Donald Lopez, *Curators of the Buddha: The Study of Buddhism under Colonialism* (Chicago: University of Chicago Press, 1995).

2. For general overviews, see Stanley J. Tambiah, "Buddhism and This-Worldly Activity," *Modern Asian Studies* 7:1 (1973), 1–20; and Melford Spiro, "Buddhism and Economic Action in Burma," *American Anthropologist* 68:5 (October 1966), 1163–1173.

3. Charles Hallisey, "Roads and Taken and Not Taken in the Study of Theravada Buddhism," *Curators of the Buddha: The Study of Buddhism under Colonialism*, ed. Donald

Lopez (Chicago: University of Chicago Press, 1995), 31–61; Gregory Schopen, *Bones, Stones, and Buddhist Monks: Collected Papers on the Archaeology, Epigraphy, and Texts of Monastic Buddhism in India* (Honolulu: University of Hawaii Press, 1997); and Winston Davis, *Japanese Religion and Society: Paradigms of Structure and Change* (Albany: State University of New York Press, 1992).

4. Stanley J. Tambiah, *World Conqueror and World Renouncer: A Study of Buddhism and Polity in Thailand against a Historical Background*, Cambridge Studies in Social Anthropology 15 (Cambridge University Press, 1976).

5. Christopher S. Queen and Sallie B. King, eds., *Engaged Buddhism: Buddhist Liberation Movements in Asia* (Albany: State University of New York Press, 1996).

6. Donald Swearer, "The Worldliness of Buddhism," *The Wilson Quarterly* 21:2 (Spring 1997), 81–93.

7. Gregory Schopen, "Archaeology and Protestant Presuppositions in the study of Indian Buddhism," *Bones, Stones, and Buddhist Monks: Collected Papers on the Archaeology, Epigraphy, and Texts of Monastic Buddhism in India* (Honolulu: University of Hawaii Press, 1997), 1–22.

8. Ibid., 14.

9. Ian Reader and George J. Tanabe, Jr., *Practically Religious: Worldly Benefits and the Common Religion of Japan* (Honolulu: University of Hawaii Press, 1998).

10. Vesākhā Pūja day commemorates the birth, enlightenment, and *parinibbāna* of the Buddha. It is customary for monks to offer sermons about the life of the Buddha on this occasion.

11. Greg Bailey and Ian Mabbett, *The Sociology of Early Buddhism* (Cambridge: Cambridge University Press, 2003), 9.

12. Some scholars use the Buddhist terms *lokiya* and *lokuttara* to correspond to the English this-worldly and otherworldly, but they are not equivalents. *Lokiya* and *lokuttara* are better translated as mundane and transmundane since these translations capture the dichotomy between the ordinary and the extraordinary (which may or may correspond to our common understandings of worldly and otherworldly). For an extensive discussion of this issue, see John Ross Carter, *On Understanding Buddhists: Essays on the Theravāda Tradition of Sri Lanka* (Albany: State University of New York Press, 1993).

13. Michael Carrithers, *The Forest Monks of Sri Lanka: An Anthropological and Historical Study* (New Delhi: Oxford University Press, 1983).

14. Steven Collins, "On the Very Idea of the Pali Canon," *Journal of the Pali Text Society* 15 (1990), 89–126.

15. *Majjhima Nikāya* 36, trans. by Thanissaro Bhikkhu, www.accesstoinsight.org (accessed on January 15, 2005).

16. *Bhaddiyakaligodha-sutta.Udāna.*2.10, *Khuddaka Nikāya.*

17. *Therīgāthā* II.2.

18. Gregory Schopen questions the translation of *jātarū-parajata* as "gold and silver" in his analysis of the Sanskrit *Mūlasarvāstivādin Vināya*. Gregory Schopen, *Buddhist Monks and Business Matters: Still More Papers on Monastic Buddhism in India* (Honolulu: University of Hawaii Press, 2004), 13–14.

19. Richard Gombrich, *Theravada Buddhism: A Social History from Ancient Benares to Modern Colombo* (London and New York: Routledge and Kegan Paul, 1988), 88–89.

20. R. A. L. H. Gunawardana, *Robe and Plough: Monasticism and Economic Interest in Early Medieval Sri Lanka*, Association for Asian Studies Monographs and Papers 35 (Tucson: University of Arizona Press, 1979).

21. Gregory Schopen, *Buddhist Monks and Business Matters: Still More Papers on Monastic Buddhism in India* (Honolulu: University of Hawaii Press, 2004).

22. Ibid., 5.

23. John Kieschnick, *The Impact of Buddhism on Chinese Material Culture* (Princeton: Princeton University Press, 2003), 12.

24. Sri Dao Ruang, *Matsii* (Bangkok: Love and Live Press, 1990). For an English translation, see *The Lioness in Bloom*, ed. and trans. Susan Fulop Kepner (Berkeley: University of California Press, 1996), 95–103.

25. Charles Keyes, *Thailand: Buddhist Kingdom as Modern Nation-State* (Boulder: Westview Press, 1987)

26. Steven Collins argues that most scholarly interpretations of this *jātaka* tend to "ignore any possibility of complexity in the relation of text to context, reading the Vessantara story wholly in a reductive, documentary mode." Assumptions about the role of generosity within Theravāda Buddhism or about the solitary nature of the path lead to a straightforward unproblematic reading of the *jātaka* as simply a story about the bodhisatta's path. Collins suggests, however, that we should read this *jātaka* as a story that confronts, "in a quite extraordinarily direct and open-ended way, the real human difficulties attendant on the minority option of asceticism as well as the offensiveness—in Gellner's Kierkegaardian sense—of Buddhist ideology." Steven Collins, *Nirvana and other Buddhist Felicities* (Cambridge: Cambridge University Press, 1998), 45.

27. For more information on Thai Buddhist nuns, see Chatsumarn Kabilsingh, *Thai Women in Buddhism* (Berkeley: Parallax Press, 1991) and Sid Brown, *Even Against the Wind: The Journey of One Buddhist Nun* (Albany: State University of New York press, 2001).

28. Frank E. Reynolds, "Ethics and Wealth in Theravāda Buddhism: A Study in Comparative Religious Ethics," in *Ethics, Wealth, and Salvation: A Study in Buddhist Social Ethics*, ed. Russell F. Sizemore and Donald K. Swearer (Columbia: South Carolina Press, 1990), 62.

29. Gregory Schopen, "Archaeology and Protestant Presuppositions in the study of Indian Buddhism," *Bones, Stones, and Buddhist Monks: Collected Papers on the Archaeology, Epigraphy, and Texts of Monastic Buddhism in India* (Honolulu: University of Hawaii Press, 1997), 1–22.

30. Charles Hallisey and Anne Hansen, "Narrative, Sub-ethics, and the Moral Life: Some Evidence from Theravāda Buddhism," *Journal of Religious Ethics* 24:2 (Fall 1996): 305–327.

31. The sutta, moreover, tells how Prince Vipassi (the first in this lineage of Buddhas) was destined to be an *arahat*, a fully-enlightened Buddha or a *cakkavatti*, a wheel-turning and righteous monarch of law who maintains the security of his realm and who possesses the seven treasures. This story is, of course, identical to that of Prince Siddhattha whose thirty-two marks of a great man similarly signify his merit and future destiny.

32. Justin McDaniel, "The Curricular Canon in Northern Thailand and Laos," *MANUSYA: Journal of Humanities*, Special Issue 4 (2002): 20–59.

33. Ibid., 34.

34. *Aṅguttara Nikāya* IV.62.

35. Donald K. Swearer, Sommai Premchit, and Phaithoon Dokbuakaew, *Sacred Mountains of Northern Thailand and Their Legends* (Chiang Mai: Silkworm Books, 2004), 40–41.

36. Bonnie Pacala Brereton, *Thai Tellings of Phra Malai: Texts and Rituals Concerning a Popular Buddhist Saint* (Arizona State University: Program for Southeast Asian Studies, 1995), 111.

37. *Aputtaka-sutta Saṁyutta Nikāya* III.19.

38. *Aṅguttara Nikaya* V. 41. The *Ādiya-sutta* also lists the five benefits that can be obtained from the possession of wealth: (1) the ability to support and give happiness to one's family and servants, (2) to provide happiness for one's friends and associates, (3) to have the resources to combat natural, social, and economic disasters, (4) the ability to perform oblations to one's relatives, guests, the dead, kings, and gods, and (5) to have the resources with which to support priests and contemplatives who are worthy of gifts.

39. N. A. Jayawickrama, trans., *The Sheaf of Garlands of the Epochs of the Conqueror: Being a Translation of Jinakālamālīpakaraṇaṁ of Rananapañña Thera of Thailand* (London: Pali Text Society, 1978), 81.

40. Donald K. Swearer and Sommai Premchit, *The Legend of Queen Cāma: Bodhiraṁsi's Cāmadevīvaṁsa, a Translation and Commentary* (Albany: State University of New York Press, 1998), 98–99.

41. The main purpose of this sutta, however, is not necessarily the presentation of a Buddhist origin story; the main goal appears to be to the undercutting of brahmanical authority by supplanting the brahmanical origin story, which privileges brahmins with one that emphasizes the importance of righteous rulers. Moreover, with its emphasis on greed, it is making an ethical argument, over and against the cosmological argument of the bramins.

42. Frank Reynolds and Mani Reynolds, translators, *Three Worlds According to King Ruang: A Thai Buddhist Cosmology* (Berkeley: University of California Press, 1982), 71–72.

43. Phra Rājavaramuni, "Foundations of Buddhist Social Ethics," in *Ethics, Wealth, and Salvation: A Study in Buddhist Social Ethics*, eds. Russell F. Sizemore and Donald K. Swearer (Columbia: South Carolina Press, 1990), 41. At the time that this piece was written, Phra Payutto had the title Phra Rājavaramuni; he is now known as Phra Dhammapitaka.

44. See Richard Gombrich, *Theravada Buddhism: A Social History from Ancient Benares to Modern Colombo* (London and New York: Routledge and Kegan Paul Ltd, 1988); and Michael Carrithers, *The Forest Monks of Sri Lanka: An Anthropological and Historical Study* (Oxford: Oxford University Press, 1983).

45. Craig Reynolds, "The Buddhist Monkhood in Nineteenth Century Thailand" (PhD diss., Cornell University, 1972), 38.

46. In the *Visuddhimagga*, Buddhaghosa describes the path to purity as the purification of ethics (*sīla*), of concentration (*samādhi*), and wisdom (*paññā*).

47. Steven Kemper, "Wealth and Reformation in Sinhalese Buddhist Monasticism," in *Ethics, Wealth, and Salvation: A Study in Buddhist Social Ethics*, ed. Russell F. Sizemore and Donald K. Swearer (Columbia: South Carolina Press, 1990), 153.

48. Ibid., 154.

49. Ibid., 157.

50. Craig Reynolds, "The Buddhist Monkhood in Nineteenth Century Thailand," 39–40.

51. Ibid.

52. Klaus Wenk, *The Restoration of Thailand Under Rama I 1782–1809*, trans. Greeley Stahl, The Association of Asian Studies 24 (Tucson: University of Arizona Press, 1968).

53. Craig Reynolds, "The Buddhist Monkhood in Nineteenth Century Thailand," 39–40.

54. Steven Kemper, "Wealth and Reformation in Sinhalese Buddhist Monasticism," 155.

55. *Cūlavaṃsa* 54, 20, 22, 24. Quoted in R. A. L. H. Gunawardana, *Robe and Plough: Monasticism and Economic Interest in Early Medieval Sri Lanka*, The Association for Asian Studies: Monographs and Papers 35 (Tucson: University of Arizona Press, 1979).

56. Quoted in H.R.H. Prince Wan Waithayakon Krommun Naradhip Bongsprabandh, "The Boon of Buddhism to Thailand," *Visakha Puja* (1961).

57. Frank E. Reynolds, "Ethics and Wealth in Theravāda Buddhism: A Study in Comparative Religious Ethics," in *Ethics, Wealth, and Salvation: A Study in Buddhist Social Ethics*, eds. Russell F. Sizemore and Donald K. Swearer (Columbia: South Carolina Press, 1990), 70.

58. Nowhere is this more contentious than in Sri Lanka, where debates over the politicization of the saṅgha are embedded in anti-colonial and anti-missionary rhetoric and in a social context fraught with ethnic violence and conflicting nationalisms. The fact that S.J. Tambiah's book, *Buddhism Betrayed?: Religion, Politics, and Violence in Sri Lanka*, was banned in Sri Lanka for its questioning of the synergy between Buddhism's nonviolent philosophy and the justification of violence by monks and laypersons in the name of Buddhist nationalism indicates that the issue of the politicization of the saṅgha is one with far-reaching implications. How one describes the role of the saṅgha in social affairs, therefore, is not simply a matter of accurate scholarship—it is a matter of politics and power.

59. For an overview of the variability of "Buddhist economic ethics," see Charles Keyes, "Buddhist Economics and Buddhist Fundamentalism in Burma and Thailand," *Fundamentalisms and the State: Remaking Politics, Economics, and Militance*, ed. Martin Marty and Scott Appleby (Chicago: University of Chicago Press, 1993), 367–409.

60. Robert E. Elson, "International Commerce, the State and Society: Economic and Social Change," *Cambridge History of Southeast Asia, Volume Two, Part One: From c. 1800–1930s* (Cambridge: Cambridge University Press, 1992).

61. See E. Sarkisyanz, "Buddhist Backgrounds of the Burmese Revolution," in *Religion and Legitimation of Power in Thailand, Laos, Burma*, ed. Bardwell L. Smith (Chambersburg: Anima Books, 1978), 92.

62. For a description of the Saya San rebellion, see Robert L. Solomon, "Saya San and the Burmese Rebellion," *Modern Asian Studies* 3:3 (1969): 209–223.

63. Charles Keyes, "Buddhist Economics and Buddhist Fundamentalism in Burma and Thailand," p. 377.

64. Maureen Aung-Twin and Thant Myint-U translate "pyidawtha" as "Happy Land" whereas Charles Keyes (referenced above) follows the common translation of the term as "welfare state." In a footnote, Keyes notes that the term may be better understood as referring to "co-operation between people and government for the happiness of the country."

Maureen Aung-Thwin and Thant Myint-U, "The Burmese Ways to Socialism," *Third World Quarterly* 13:1, Rethinking Socialism (1992), 69.

65. E. Sarkisyanz, "Buddhist Backgrounds of Burmese Socialism," *Religion and Legitimation of Power in Thailand, Laos, and Burma*, ed. Bardwell Smith (Chambersburg, PA: Anima Books, 1978), 93–94.

66. Keyes, "Buddhist Economics and Buddhist Fundamentalism," 389.

67. Charles Keyes, "Buddhism and National Integration in Thailand," *Journal of Asian Studies* 30:3 (May 1971): 551–567.

68. Ibid., 569–566.

69. Paisal Sricharatchanya and Ian Buruma, "Praise the Buddha, and Pass the Baht," *Far Eastern Economic Review* (June 18, 1987): 53–55.

70. Ibid., 54.

71. See Peter Jackson, *Buddhism, Legitimation, and Conflict: The Political Functions of Urban Thai Buddhism* (Singapore: Institute of Southeast Asian Studies, 1989), 100.

72. Donald Swearer, *Me and Mine: Selected Essays of Bhikkhu Buddhadāsa*, ed. Donald K. Swearer (Albany: State University of New York Press, 1989), 12.

73. Peter Jackson, *Buddhadāsa: Theravada Buddhism and Modernist Reform in Thailand*, second edition (Chiang Mai: Silkworm Books, 1987) 257–258.

74. See Charles Keyes, "Buddhist Economics and Buddhist Fundamentalism."

75. Swearer, "Fundamentalistic Movements in Theravada Buddhism," *Fundamentalisms Observed*, ed. by Martin E. Marty and R. Scott Appleby, Chicago: University of Chicago Press, 1991: 668.

76. Sanitsuda Ekachai, "Phothirak May Have the Last Laugh," *Bangkok Post*, March 26, 1997.

77. J. L. Taylor, "New Buddhist Movements in Thailand: An 'Individualistic Revolution,' Reform and Political Dissonance," *Journal of Southeast Asian Studies* 21:1 (1990): 149.

78. For a discussion of how some environmentalist monks are fighting deforestation through the practice of ordaining trees, see Susan M. Darlington, "The Ordination of a Tree: The Buddhist Ecology Movement in Thailand," *Ethnology* 37:1 (Winter 1998): 1–15.

79. Jim Taylor, "Thamma-chat: Activist Monks and Competing Discourses of Nature and Nation in Northeastern Thailand," in *Seeing Forests for Trees: Environment and Environmentalism in Thailand*, ed. Philip Hirsch (Chaing Mai: Silkworm Books, 1997).

80. Peter Jackson, "The Enchanting Spirit of Thai Capitalism: The Cult of Luang Phor Khun and the Post-Modernization of Thai Buddhism," *Southeast Asia Research* 7:1 (1999): 5–60.

81. Paul Heelas, "Prosperity and the New Age Movement: The Efficacy of Spiritual Economics," *New Religious Movements: Challenge and Response*, eds. Bryan Wilson and Jamie Coswell (London: Routledge, 1999).

82. For more information on the Erawan Shrine, see Trilok Chandra Majupuria, *Erawan Shrine and Brahma Worship in Thailand*, Bangkok: Tecpress Serive, 1993.

83. See Stanley J. Tambiah, *The Buddhist Saints of the Forest and the Cult of Amulets* (Cambridge: Cambridge University Press, 1984) and B. J. Terwiel, *Monks and Magic: An Analysis of Religious Ceremonies in Central Thailand* (London: Curzon Press, 1979).

84. Jackson, "The Enchanting Spirit of Thai Capitalism," 6.

85. Ibid.

86. Ibid., 14–16.

87. *The Nation*, September 21, 1995.

88. Jackson, "The Enchanting Spirit of Thai Capitalism," 19.

89. The Thai word to sell, *khai*, is not used to refer to the transaction of procuring amulets from a vendor. Rather, Thais say that they rent (*chao*) amulets and talismans as to not presume ownership of their power.

90. Jackson, "The Enchanting Spirit of Thai Capitalism," 29.

Chapter 2   Modernity, Prosperity, and the Dhammakāya Temple

1. See H. L. Seneviratne, *The Work of Kings: The New Buddhism in Sri Lanka* (Chicago and London: University of Chicago Press, 1999).

2. Ananda Maitreya is known worldwide both for his extensive publications as well as his appearance in the now classic documentary, *The Footprint of the Buddha*, from the Long Search Series. For a description of his life and contributions to modern Buddhism, see Richard Gombrich and Gananath Obeyesekere, *Buddhism Transformed: Religious Change in Sri Lanka* (Princeton: Princeton University Press, 1988).

3. Bruce Matthews, "Buddhism and the Nation in Myanmar," in *Buddhism and Politics in Twentieth-century Asia*, ed. Ian Harris (London: Continuum, 1999), 35.

4. "Thai Culture Ministry Mulling Monk Zones in Mall," *The Nation*, November 26, 2005.

5. Mari Yamaguchi, "Japanese Monks Stage Fashion Show," Associated Press, December 15, 2007. (WorldWide Religious News Web site: www.wwrn.org/sparse.php?idd=27219).

6. Daniel A. Metraux, "The Soka Gakkai: Buddhism and the Creation of a Harmonious and Peaceful Society," in *Engaged Buddhism: Buddhist Liberation Movements in Asia*, eds. Christopher S. Queen and Sallie B. King (Albany: State University of New York Press, 1996): 365–400.

7. During this early period, the title of the organization was Soka Kyoiku Gakkai (the Value-Creation Education Society). When the founders adopted a more overtly religious identity, they dropped the word kyoiku from the name.

8. Daniel A. Metraux, "The Soka Gakkai: Buddhism and the Creation of a Harmonious and Peaceful Society," 371.

9. George Chryssides, *Exploring New Religions* (London and New York: Cassell, 1999).

10. David Barrett describes Soka Gakkai as "materialistic Buddhism," which is directed "at the middle classes, at professional people who either have or would like to have power, position and wealth." *Sects, 'Cults' and Alternative Religions: A World Survey and Sourcebook* (London: Blandford, 1996), 157.

11. Barrett, *Sects, 'Cults' and Alternative Religions*, 158.

12. This is the description of Soka Gakkai International on its Web site, www.sgi .org (accessed on January 10, 2008).

13. Stuart Chandler, "Spreading Buddha's Light: The Internationalization of Foguang Shan," in *Buddhist Missionaries in the Era of Globalization*, ed. Linda Learman (Honolulu: University of Hawaii Press, 2005).

14. The term "Humanistic Buddhism" (*renjian fojiao*) is used by a number of contemporary Buddhists in Taiwan to refer to a more this-worldly oriented Buddhism. Chandler notes that the Master Taixu (1889–1947) was the first to use the concept, but he favored the term *rensheng fojiao* (living Buddhism) in order to contrast his form of Buddhism with the normative practice that focused too much attention on funerary rites. His disciple, Venerable Yinshun (born 1906), preferred the term "renjian" (in the human domain, in the midst of the people) to emphasize the activism of the movement. Stuart Chandler, *Establishing a Pure Land on Earth: The Foguang Buddhist Perspective on Modernization and Globalization* (Honolulu: University of Hawaii Press, 2004), 43.

15. Chandler, *Establishing a Pure Land on Earth*, 50–63.

16. Ibid., 71.

17. Ibid.

18. Ibid., 95

19. Ibid., 104.

20. Ibid., 101.

21. Stuart Chandler argues that the "mainland complex" derives from four factors: "an underlying ambivalence about the tremendous American presence; discomfort with Taiwan's uncertain political status and future; recognition of the island's peripheral historical ties to China proper; and a sense of ever-increasing dissonance with contemporary mainland culture." Stuart Chandler, "Spreading Buddha's Light," 169.

22. Peter A. Jackson, *Buddhism, Legitimation, and Conflict: The Political Functions of Urban Thai Buddhism* (Singapore: Institute of Southeast Asian Studies, 1989).

23. Donald Swearer, "Fundamentalistic Movements in Theravada Buddhism," in *Fundamentalisms Observed* (Chicago: University of Chicago Press, 1991): 628–690.

24. Suwanna Satha-Anand, "Religious Movements in Contemporary Thailand: Buddhist Struggles for Relevance," *Asian Survey* 30:4. (April 1990): 395–408.

25. J. L. Taylor, "New Buddhist Movements in Thailand: An Individualistic Revolution, Reform and Political Dissonance," *Journal of Southeast Asian Studies* 21:1. (March 1990): 135–154.

26. See Suwanna Satha-Anand, "Religious Movements in Contemporary Thailand: Buddhist Struggles for Relevance;" Apinya Fuengfusakul, "Empire of Crystal and Utopian Commune: Two Types of Contemporary Theravada Reform in Thailand," *Sojourn* 8:1. (February 1993), 153–183; Donald Swearer, "Fundamentalistic Movements in Theravada Buddhism;" J. L. Taylor, "New Buddhist Movements in Thailand"; and Edwin Zehner, "Reform Symbolism of a Thai Middle-Class Sect: The Growth and Appeal of the Thammakai Movement," *Journal of Southeast Asian Studies* 21:2. (September 1990): 402–426.

27. Edwin Zehner, "Reform Symbolism of a Thai Middle-Class Sect: The Growth and Appeal of the Thammakai Movement," 404.

28. Peter Jackson, *Buddhism, Legitimation, and Conflict: The Political Functions of Urban Thai Buddhism* (Singapore: Institute of Southeast Asian Studies, 1989), 16.

29. I address the description of the Dhammakāya Temple as a "new religious movement" more extensively in my article, "A New Religious Sect?: The Dhammakāya Temple and the Politics of Difference," *Religion* 36:4. (December 2006): 215–230. Since writing that article, a new book on the Dhammakāya Temple and Santi Asok was published that places both religious organizations within the paradigm of "new religious movements." See Rory

Mackenzie, *New Buddhist Movements in Thailand: Towards and Understanding of Wat Phra Dhammakāya and Santi Asoke* (London and New York: Routledge, 2007).

30. James Beckford describes new religious movements as reactive movements, which typically differentiate themselves from what they identify as their mainstream counterparts. Beckford argues that new religious movements attract public attention through ideas or practices that are more specialized or esoteric than their institutionalized counterparts. Also, new religious movements are generally less hierarchical, as seen in the active participation of laypeople in the core practices of the tradition; these movements are proactive as well as reactive in that they tend to focus on translating spirituality into every day practice, and in so doing, renegotiate the boundaries between spirituality and materiality. James Beckford, "Introduction," in *New Religious Movements and Rapid Social Change*, ed. James Beckford (Paris and London: United Nations Educational, Scientific and Cultural Organization and Sage, 1986), xiii–xv.

31. I address the history of the word nikai (nikāya, Pāli) in Rachelle M. Scott, "A New Buddhist Sect?: The Dhammakāya Temple and the Politics of Religious Difference," *Religion* 36 (2006): 215-230.

32. See George Chryssides, *Exploring New Religions*, (London: Cassell Academic, 2000).

33. Jamie Hubbard makes a similar point regarding new religious movements (NRMs) in Japan. He argues that previous studies of NRMs have ignored the doctrinal basis of many of them, an omission that leads scholars to trivialize the doctrinal sophistication of NRMs and to emphasize the ways in which they deviate from the normative tradition. Jamie Hubbard, "Embarrassing Superstition, Doctrine, and New Religious Movements," *Journal of the American Academy of Religion* 66: 1. (Spring 1998): 59–92.

34. From a Dhammakāya pamphlet that was distributed at the main temple in Pathum Thani, Thailand. Pamphlets on Dhammakāya activities are routinely distributed at the Temple on Sundays.

35. This is not unlike Marty and Appleby's description of fundamentalistic movements as selectively modern and traditional in *Fundamentalisms Observed* (Chicago: University of Chicago Press, 1991). In fact, Donald Swearer's article in this volume classifies the Dhammakāya Temple as a a fundamentalistic-type movement. See Donald Swearer, "Fundamentalistic Movements in Theravada Buddhism," *Fundamentalisms Observed*, 628–690.

36. Edwin Zehner, "Reform Symbolism of a Thai Middle Class Sect," 402.

37. One example is the philosophy of Norman Vincent Peale whose *The Power of Positive Thinking* combined American individualism with a message of the immanence of the divine within our lives. Craig R. Prentiss argues that Peale combined his interest in psychotherapy with the theology of the New Thought Movement, which maintains a connection between the physical realm and the supernatural realm and emphasizes our ability to harness supernatural energies for our benefit. For Peale, these benefits included successful relationships with family and friends, improved health, and material prosperity. In essence, Peale linked religion to successful living, which according to Prentiss, "succeeded in bringing happiness and peace to millions of frazzled homemakers, stressed salespeople, and anxiety-ridden executives." See Craig R. Prentiss, "The Power of Positive Thinking," *Religion in the United States in Practice, Vol. 2*, ed. Colleen McDannell (Princeton: Princeton University Press, 2001).

38. Zehner, "Reform Symbolism of a Thai Middle Class Sect," 402.

39. Prawase Wasi criticizes the wearing of Dhammakāya uniforms as a form of Dhammakāya programming that seeks to create and maintain order and control within the masses. See Prawase Wasi, *Latthi Thammakai: Kap Botbat Khong Sanghkom Thai* (Bangkok: Samakhom Sitkao Mahachulalongkornratchawitthayalai, 1999).

40. See Benedict Anderson, "Studies of the Thai State: The State of Thai Studies," in *The Study of Thailand: Analyses of Knowledge, Approaches, and Prospects in Anthropology, Art History, Economics, History, and Political Science*, ed. Eliezer B. Ayal, Papers in International Studies, Southeast Asia series 54. (Athens: Ohio University Center for International Studies, 1978): 193–247.

41. See Suwanna Satha-Anand, "Religious Movements in Contemporary Thailand: Buddhist Struggles for Relevance"; Apinya Fuengfusakul, "Empire of Crystal and Utopian Commune: Two Types of Contemporary Theravada Reform in Thailand"; Donald Swearer, "Fundamentalistic Movements in Theravada Buddhism"; J. L. Taylor, "New Buddhist Movements in Thailand: An Individualistic Revolution, Reform and Political Dissonance"; and Edwin Zehner, "Reform Symbolism of a Thai Middle-Class Sect: The Growth and Appeal of the Thammakai Movement."

42. Richard A. O'Connor, "Interpreting Thai Religious Change: Temples, Sangha Reform and Social Change," *Journal of Southeast Asian Studies* 24: 2. (September 1993): 330–339.

43. It is worth noting that O'Connor mentions the Dhammakāya Temple in this article as an example of a new religious movement that caters to the "religious market" of contemporary Thai Buddhism, thereby reflecting an increased separation between local wats and their communities. While I agree that the Dhammakāya Temple employs consumer-oriented language in its promotion of the benefits of dhammakāya meditation, I also recognize that the Dhammakāya Temple seeks to create a distinct community that provides all of the services once common in wats throughout Thailand.

44. O'Connor, "Interpreting Thai Religious Change," 331.

45. A. Thomas Kirsch, "Modernizing Implications of Nineteenth Century Reforms in the Thai Sangha," *Religion and the Legitimation of Power in Thailand, Laos, and Burma*, ed. Bardwell L. Smith (Chambersburg, PA: Anima Books, 1978).

46. Ibid., 58–59.

47. Charles Keyes, "Buddhist Politics and their Revolutionary Origins in Thailand," *International Political Science Review* 10:2. (1989): 121–142.

48. J. L. Taylor, *Forest Monks and the Nation-State: An Anthropological and Historical Study in Northeastern Thailand* (Singapore: Institute of Southeast Asian Studies, 1993).

49. Stanley J. Tambiah, "Sangha and Polity in Modern Thailand," *Religion and Legitimation of Power in Thailand, Laos, and Burma*, ed. Bardwell Smith (Chambersburg, PA: Anima Books, 1978), 111–133.

50. Ibid., 118–119.

51. Ibid.

52. For an extensive description and analysis of these exams, see Yoneo Ishii, *Sangha, State, and Society: Thai Buddhism in History*, trans. Peter Hawkes (Honolulu: University of Hawaii Press, 1986), 81–99.

53. The author of this passage is unknown. It is found in a biography of Prince Wachirayan in the English translation of the *Nawakowat*. See *Navakovāda*, comp. Somdet Phra

Mahā Samana Chao Krom Phrayā Vajirañānavarorasa and trans. Bhikkhu Paññāvaddho (Bangkok: Mahāmakuta Buddhist University, 1993), iv.

54. Kamala Tiyavanich, *Forest Recollections: Wandering Monks in Twentieth-Century Thailand* (Honolulu: University of Hawaii Press, 1997).

55. Ibid., 23.

56. Ibid., 30. Patrick Jory also notes how King Chulalongkorn's publication of a collection of thirty jātakas in 1904 presented the jātakas as folktales (and perhaps not even Buddhist folktales) rather than as stories told by the Buddha about his past births. Patrick Jory, "Thai and Western Buddhist Scholarship in the Age of Colonialism: King Chulalongkorn Redefines the Jatakas," *The Journal of Asian Studies* 61:3. (2002): 891–918.

57. Kamala Tiyavanich, *Forest Recollections: Wandering Monks in Twentieth-Century Thailand*, 36.

58. Ibid., 42.

59. Paul T. Cohen, "Buddhism Unshackled: The Yuan 'Holy Man' Tradition and the Nation-State in the Tai World," *Journal of Southeast Asian Studies*, 32:2. (2001): 227–247.

60. Charles Keyes, "Buddhist Politics and Their Revolutionary Origins in Thailand," *International Political Science Review* 10:2. (1989): 129.

61. See J. L. Taylor "(Post)-Modernity, Remaking Tradition and the Hybridisation of Thai Buddhism," *Anthropological Forum* 9:2. (1999): 163–187.

62. Stanley J. Tambiah, *The Buddhist Saints of the Forest and the Cult of Amulets*, Cambridge Studies in Social Anthropology 49. (Cambridge: Cambridge University Press, 1984), 3.

63. Ibid., 342.

64. Richard O'Connor, "Urbanism and Religion: Community, Hierarchy, and Sanctity in Urban Thai Buddhist Temples," (PhD diss., Cornell University, 1978); Stanley J. Tambiah, *The Buddhist Saints of the Forest and the Cult of Amulets* (Cambridge: Cambridge University Press, 1984); and J. L. Taylor, *Forest Monks and the Nation-State: An Anthropological and Historical Study in Northeastern Thailand*, Social Issues in Southeast Asia (Singapore: Institute of Southeast Asian Studies, 1993).

65. Peter Jackson, "Royal Spirits, Chinese Gods, and Magic Monks: Thailand's Boom-time Religions of Prosperity," *Southeast Asian Research* 7:3. (1999): 245–320.

66. For an extensive analysis of spirit mediums in northern Thailand, see Rosalind Morris, *In the Place of Origins: Modernity and Its Mediums in Northern Thailand* (Durham and London: Duke University Press, 2000).

67. Pattana Kitiarsa, "Beyond Syncretism: Hybridization of Popular Religion in Contemporary Thailand," *Journal of Southeast Asian Studies* 36:3. (October 2005): 461–487.

68. Ibid., 482.

69. Ibid., 479–481.

70. Andrew Webb, "The Temple of Benz," *Bangkok TimeOut* (January 2001): 22–25.

71. Bond, "The Contemporary Lay Meditation Movement and Lay Gurus in Sri Lanka," *Religion* 33:1. (January 2003): 23–55.

72. Peter Jackson, *Buddhism, Legitimation, and Conflict: The Political Functions of Urban Thai Buddhism* (Singapore: Institute of Southeast Asian Studies, 1989), 206.

73. *The Life and Times of Luang Phaw Wat Paknam*, second edition (Pathum Thani: Dhammakaya Foundation, 1998), 19. In general, the births of remarkable Buddhists men and women, including Siddhattha Gotama, are generally marked by supernatural or unusual

occurrences, indicating the birth of a being with high spiritual perfections. This passage also alludes to the fact that his birth will lead to the salvation of many through the rediscovering of the dhammakāya meditation technique.

74. Ibid., 23.

75. Ibid., 33–37.

76. Ibid., 43.

77. Ibid., 47.

78. Ibid., 53.

79. Ibid., 55.

80. Ibid., 96.

81. Kamala Tiyavanich, *Forest Recollections*, 263.

82. *The Life and Times of Luang Phaw Wat Paknam*, 136.

83. The Temple now refers to Luang Po Sot as Luang Pu (Luang Phu), honorable "grandfather."

84. From the Dhammakāya Foundation website, www.dhammakaya.or.th/visitorzone/detail_page_03_en.php (accessed March 3, 2008).

85. See the Khun Yay story posted in both English and Thai on the Dhammakāya Foundation website www.dhammakaya.or.th/WhoWeAre/founder_kyay_story.php (accessed July of 2001).

86. The following is a version of Khun Yay's life story that was told to me on numerous occasions at the Dhammakāya Temple. For her complete biography, see *Second to None: The Biography of Khun Yay Maharatana Upasika Chandra Khon-nok-yoong*, Pathum Thani: Dhammakaya Foundation, 2005.

87. Quoted on the Dhammakāya Foundation website, www.dhammakaya.or.th/whoweare/founder_kyay_8.php (accessed July of 2001).

88. It is customary for friends and relatives to ask forgiveness from a person before death.

89. *Anuphap Haeng Bun* (the Miracle of Merit), December 3, 2000.

90. Ibid, pp. 5–6.

91. *The Khun Yay Story*, excerpts reprinted on the Dhammakāya Foundation website, www.dhammakaya.or.th (accessed October 10, 2002).

92. *The Khun Yay Story*, excerpts reprinted on the Dhammakāya Foundation website, www.dhammakaya.or.th/whoweare/founders.php (accessed on October 10, 2002).

93. The Dhammakāya Foundation webpage states that when "these important people pass away, the Buddhists believe that merit is the only means of bringing happiness to them. Thus, to share merits with the one who already passed away, Buddhists usually go to temple and listen to the chanting of Phra Abhidhamma." Merit transference is a popular Buddhist practice that is often done through temporary ordination or through the making of merit for a particular person.

94. For a discussion of the lives of Buddhist nuns in Thailand, see Chatsumarn Kabilsingh, *Thai Women in Buddhism* (Berkeley: Parallax Press, 1991) and Sidney Brown, *The Journey of One Buddhist Nun: Even Against the Wind* (Albany: State University of New York Press, 2001).

95. Phra Dhammachayo's biography, *Duang tawan haeng Santiphap* (*The Sun of Peace*), was published by the Dhammakāya Foundation in 2007 on the occasion of Makha Bucha day. Excerpts from his biography are available online at the Foundation's website: www.dhammakaya.or.th/whoweare/Sun_of_peace_Ven.Dhammajayo.php.

96. See Bond, "The Contemporary Lay Meditation Movement and Lay Gurus in Sri Lanka," *Religion* 33:1. (January 2003): 23–55.

97. Somjing Bunjarattanachot, quoted in Edwin Zehner, "Reform Symbolism of a Thai Middle Class Sect: The Growth and Appeal of the Thammakai Movement," *Journal of Southeast Asian Studies* 21, no. 2. (September 1990): 412.

98. Here the dhammakāya refers to the sum of the Buddha's spiritual perfections, in contrast to his *rupa-kāya* or physical form.

99. *The Life and Times of Luang Phaw Wat Paknam*, p. 68.

100. Somdet Phra MahaRajmangkalajahn, "Foreward," in *The Heart of Dhammakāya Meditation*, by Phra Ajahn MahaSermchai Jayamanggalo (Bangkok: Dhammakaya Buddhist Meditation Foundation, 1991).

101. Swearer, "Fundamentalistic Movements in Theravada Buddhism," 660.

102. See the Dhammakāya Foundation website, www.dhammakaya.or.th.

103. Dhammakāya apologists typically argue that the truth of the dhammakāya is only realized through personal experiential practice, not in the Buddhist texts. However, when pressed, apologists do cite scant references to the dhammakāya in the Pāli texts (especially the passage from the Saṃyutta nikāya 3, 120: "He who sees me, Oh Vakkali, sees the dhamma, and he who sees the dhamma, sees me.") and the wealth of literature on the three bodies of the Buddha in Mahayāna *sutras* (the *dharmakāya, saṃboghakāya*, and the *nirmāṇakāya*). As we shall see in Chapter 4, critics contend that the temple's interpretation of the dhammakāya as a personal, unchanging essence is more closely related to Mahayāna interpretations of the dhammakāya (the ultimate body of the Buddha—what a Buddha *really* is and hence, what we all are) than Theravāda. Frank Reynolds, however, has convincingly argued that *kāya* literature in Theravāda Buddhism is far more diverse than usually described. See Frank E. Reynolds, "The Several Bodies of Buddha: Reflections on a Neglected Aspect of Theravada Tradition," *History of Religions*, Vol. 16, No. 4, (May 1977): 374–389.

104. *The Life and Times of Luang Phaw Wat Paknam*, 45.

105. Phra Sermchai, *The Heart of Dhammakāya* (Bangkok: Dhammakaya Buddhist Meditation Foundation, 1991), 12. Dhammakāya meditation is taught at three principal locations in Thailand: Wat Paknam in Thonburi, Wat Phra Dhammakāya in Pathum Thani, and at the Dhammakāya Buddhist Meditation Institute in Ratchaburi. The latter two were founded by former pupils of Luang Pho Sot, but while all three share the same lineage and practice, there is relatively little interaction between them. Dissension among the disciples of Luang Pho Sot is often cited as the reason for this fissure. Phra Sermchai is the abbot of the Dhammakāya Buddhist Meditation Institute in Ratchaburi.

106. In fact, Phra Dhammachayo frequently makes this statement during the meditation sessions at the temple.

107. For a further discussion on positive descriptions of nirvāṇa see Steven Collins, *Nirvana and Other Buddhist Felicities: Utopias of the Pali Imaginaire* (Cambridge: Cambridge University Press, 1998).

108. Donald Swearer, "Fundamentalistic Movements in Theravada Buddhism," 660.

109. Ibid.

110. Winston King, *Theravāda Meditation: The Buddhist Transformation of Yoga*, second edition (Delhi: Motilal Banarsidass Publishers, 1992), 16

111. Sayadaw U Pandita, *In This Very Life* (Sri Lanka: Buddhist Publication Society, 1992), 183.

112. See Phra Maha Boonthuang, *Phra Thammakai kap Satthampathirup* (Dhammakāya with False Teachings) (no publisher listed, 1999). This book contains essays written by Phra MahaBoonthuang that were published in the news magazine, *Matichon*, in 1999.

113. *The Life and Times of Luang Phaw Wat Paknam*, p. 108.

114. Donald K. Swearer, "Fundamentalistic Movements in Theravada Buddhism." One could also argue that the temple presents only one description of *nibbāna* as authoritative—*nibbāna* as realization of the dhammakāya. For instance, Phra Dhammachayo recently gave a sermon where he stated that Buddhagosa's *Visuddhimagga* contains over forty paths to the realization of the dhammakāya. This is certainly a unique interpretation of Buddhaghosa's path to purity, and is perhaps an attempt by the abbot to place wicha thammakai in the lineage of Buddhaghosa's normative tradition.

115. See *Kanyanmit* magazines published by the Dhammakāya Foundation.

116. Phra Thattacheevo, *Blueprint for Global Being* (Pathum Thani: Dhammakāya Foundation, 2000), 62.

117. *Mongkhon Chiwit*, (Bangkok: Dhammakāya Foundation, 1982). Quoted in Donald Swearer, "Fundamentalistic Movements in Theravada Buddhism," 663.

118. The program began in 1972, and was initially a two-week Spring break retreat for college students. It has grown into a well attended two-month meditation retreat for young men between the ages of 16 and 35.

119. Pholwat Naklux, a college student at King Mongkut's Institute of Technology, quoted in *Dhammadāyāda: A New Hope for the Thai Nation* (Pathum Thani: Dhammakāya Foundation, n.d.).

120. *Dhammadāyāda: A New Hope for the Thai Nation* (Pathum Thani: Dhammakāya Foundation, n.d.).

121. This was highly criticized in the Thai Press in 1999. when these ordinations became public knowledge. Ordinations of women as novices or *bhikkhunī*s are not sanctioned by the Thai saṅgha due to the lack of a proper quorum of bhikkhunīs for the ceremony, and monks who have been involved in such activities have been severely censured by the *Mahatherasamakhom*. See Chatsumarn Kabilsingh, *Thai Women in Buddhism* (Berkeley: Parallax Press, 1991).

122. Zehner, "Reform Symbolism of a Thai Middle Class Sect," 410.

123. As Apinya notes in "Empire of the Crystal and Utopian Commune," 157–159, the lay personnel at Wat Dhammakāya are not the average *dek wat* (temple boy) nor are they like the traditional members of temple lay committees (*khana kammakan wat*) who serve the interests of the temple but who are not considered to be of a higher religious status than the average layperson. At Wat Dhammakāya, lay personnel are held to a higher standard, and are required to pass written exams on Buddhism, participate in a three-month training program, learn the skills of door-to-door marketing, adhere to the eight precepts, and possess a college certificate. They tend to be young men and women (ages 26 to 35), and all are single.

124. Apinya Fuengfusakul, "Empire of Crystal and Utopian Commune," 162–63.

125. From the Dhammakaya Foundation website at www.dhammakaya.or.th (accessed on June 15, 2001).

126. Swearer, "Fundamentalistic Movements in Theravada Buddhism," 657.

127. The galactic polity model allowed for substantial autonomy for local religious and political leaders. The Dhammakāya Temple's provincial centers, in contrast, are directly

linked to the main temple in Pathum Thani, and the activities at these centers are mandated by what leaders at the main temple deem legitimate and proper Buddhist practice.

Chapter 3   The Mahathammakai Chedi and Postmodern Merit Making

1. Ubosok-kaew is a Dhammakāya neologism—disciple (ubosok, Thai; uposatha, Pāli) of the crystal (kaew, Thai). Some Buddhist scholars rejected the Temple's characterization of the event as an ordination (buat, Thai) since the young men only undertook the eight precepts of pious laypersons, not the full ten precepts observed by novices. This was a popular topic of discussion on the radio and religious television programs during the week following the ceremony.

2. "Amulets Pledged to Woo Believers," *The Nation*, February 1, 1999.

3. See Phra Mahasupha Utto, *Wiphak: Wat Phra Thammakai* (Discussion: Wat Dhammakāya) (Bangkok: Amy Printing, 1999); Sathianpong Wannapok, *Botrian Chawphut chak Korani Thammakai* (Lesson for Buddhists to learn from the Dhammakāya Incident) (Bangkok: Sahathammik, 1999); Phra MahaBoonthuang, *Phra Thammakai kap Satthampathirup* (Dhammakāya with False Teachings) (no publisher listed, 1999); and Somkiet Meethum, *Chik Nakak Thammakai* (Tearing Dhammakāya's Mask) (Bangkok: Reunkeaw, 2000).

4. "Bun pen hatu haeng kwamsuk lae kwamsamret nai chiwit."

5. puññā, Pāli; pin, Sinhalese; kutho, Burmese; bun, Thai and Lao; bon, Khmer.

6. "Tam di dai di tam chua dai chua."

7. See Frank E. Reynolds and Mani B. Reynolds, eds., *Three Worlds According to King Ruang: A Thai Buddhist Cosmology*, Berkeley Buddhist Studies Series 4 (Berkeley: University of California Press, 1982).

8. Suwani Srisopha, *Chotmay Thueng Nanglek* (Pathum Thani: Dhammakāya Foundation, 1996).

9. For a review of classic anthropological descriptions of merit, see Jane Bunnag, *Buddhist Monk, Buddhist Layman* (Cambridge: Cambridge University Press, 1973); Jasper Ingersoll, "Merit and Identity in Village Thailand," in *Change and Persistence in Thai Society: Essays in Honor of Lauriston Sharp*, eds. G. W. Skinner and A. T. Kirsch (New York: Cornell University, 1975), 219–251; Charles Keyes, "Tug-of-war for Merit: Cremation of a Senior Monk," *Journal of the Siam Society* 63:1 (1975): 44–62; A. Thomas Kirsch, "Economy, Polity, and Religion in Thailand," in *Change and Persistence in Thai Society: Essays in Honor of Lauriston Sharp*, 172–196; Melford Spiro, *Buddhism and Society: A Great Tradition and Its Burmese Vicissitudes*, second edition (Berkeley: University of California Press, 1982); and Stanley J. Tambiah, "The Ideology of Merit and the Social Correlates of Buddhism in a Thai Village," in *Dialectic in Practical Religion*, ed. E. Leach (Cambridge: Cambridge University Press, 1968), 41–121.

10. See the *Cūḷakamma-vibhaṅga Sutta* (*Majjhima Nikāya* 135), *Mahākammavibhaṅga Sutta* (*Majjhima Nikāya* 136), and *Dhammapada* 354.

11. H. K. Kaufman, *Bangkhuad: A Community Study in Thailand*, Association for Asian Studies Monograph 10 (Locust Valley: J. J. Augustin, 1960).

12. Stanley J. Tambiah, *Buddhism and the Spirit Cults in Northeast Thailand*, Cambridge Studies in Social Anthropology 5 (Cambridge: Cambridge University Press, 1970).

13. See Charles Keyes, "Mother or Mistress but Never a Monk: Buddhist Notions of Female Gender in Rural Thailand," *American Ethnologist* 11:2 (1984): 223–41.

14. Donald Swearer, *The Buddhist World of Southeast Asia* (Albany: State University of New York Press, 1995), 19.

15. Nancy Auer Falk, "Exemplary Donors of the Pāli Tradition," in *Ethics, Wealth, and Salvation: A Study in Buddhist Social Ethics*, eds. Russell F. Sizemore and Donald K. Swearer (Columbia: University of South Carolina Press, 1990), 124–143.

16. Nancy Falk argues that Anānthapiṇḍika's story addresses several themes regarding the correlation of wealth and piety: the four types of lay bliss—gain, wealth, debtlessness, and blamelessness (A 4.62; GS 2, 77); how wealth should be pursued and used lawfully, shared with others, and enjoyed without attachment (A.10.91.23; GS 5, 123–124); how a wealthy person should seek happiness and security for himself, his family, and acquaintances, and make offerings to relatives, guests, ancestors, the king, and guardian spirits along with offerings to brahmans and *samaṇas* (A. 4.61.10–13; GS 2, 75–76). Nancy Auer Falk, "Exemplary Donors of the Pāli Tradition," 127–131.

17. See Frank E. Reynolds and Mani B. Reynolds, eds., *Three Worlds According to King Ruang: A Thai Buddhist Cosmology*, Berkeley Buddhist Studies Series 4 (Berkeley: University of California Press, 1982), 189–200.

18. Ibid., 200–205.

19. N. A. Jayawickrama, *The Sheaf of Garlands of the Epochs of the Conqueror: Being a Translation of Jinakālamālīpakaraṇaṁ of Rananapañña Thera of Thailand* (London: Pali Text Society, 1978), 80.

20. Donald K. Swearer and Sommai Premchit, *The Legend of Queen Cāma: Bodhiraṃsi's Cāmadevīvaṃsa, a Translation and Commentary* (Albany: State University of New York Press, 1998), 80.

21. Ibid., 5.

22. Donald K. Swearer, Sommai Premchit, and Phaithoon Dokbuakaew, *Sacred Mountains of Northern Thailand and Their Legends* (Chiang Mai: Silkworm Books, 2004), 24.

23. Griswold and Nagara state that the expression "phra jow" "can be singular or plural, and refer to monks, to objects associated with the Buddha such as relics, monuments, or images, or to the Buddha himself." In this inscription, however, they are inclined to think that "phra jow" refers to the Buddha, and by extension to the main image in the vihara. See A. B. Griswold and Prasert ṇa Nagara, "The Inscription of Vāt Khemā: Epigraphic and Historical Studies No. 15," *Journal of the Siam Society* 63:1 (1975): 127–142. The question of the presence/absence of the Buddha is an intriguing one. For an extensive discussion of this issue see Jacob N. Kinnard, *Imaging Wisdom: Seeing and Knowing in the Art of Indian Buddhism* (Surrey: Curzon Press, 1999).

24. A. B. Griswold and Prasert ṇa Nagara, "The Inscription of Vāt Khemā," 134.

25. Ibid., 134–136.

26. Ibid., 142.

27. Lucian M. Hanks, "Merit and Power in the Thai Social Order," *American Anthropologist* 64 (1962): 1247–1261; Charles Keyes, "Merit Transference in the Kammic Theory of Popular Theravada Buddhism," in *Karma: An Anthropological Inquiry*, eds. E. Valentine Daniel and Charles Keyes (Berkeley: University of California Press, 1983), 261–286; and Juliane Schober, "Religious Merit and Social Status among Burmese Buddhist Lay Associations,"

in *Merit and Blessing in Mainland Southeast Asia in Comparative Perspective*, ed. Cornelia Ann Kammerer and Nicola Tannenbaum, Yale Southeast Asian Studies Monograph 45 (New Haven: Yale University Press,1996), 197–211.

28. Lucian M. Hanks, "Merit and Power in the Thai Social Order," *American Anthropologist* 64 (1962): 1247–1261.

29. Ibid., 1248.

30. Juliane Schober refers to this as the social transivity of merit. See Juliane Schober, "Religious Merit and Social Status among Burmese Buddhist Lay Associations," 197–198.

31. Peter Brown, *Poverty and Leadership in the Later Roman Empire*, The Menahem Stern Jerusalem Lectures (Hanover: University Press of New England, 2001), 4 and 39.

32. Apinya Fuengfusakul, "Empire of the Crystal and Utopian Commune: Two Types of Contemporary Theravada Reform in Thailand," *Sojourn* 8:1 (February 1993): 153–183.

33. The style of the Dhammakāya amphitheatre reminds this author of the modern structure that surrounds the Kaaba in Mecca. Perhaps this is not a coincidence given the remarks of Phra Thattacheevo that the World Dhammakaya Center will be a "Mecca" for Buddhists from around the world.

34. *Mahāparinibbāna Sutta* (Dīgha Nikāya 16). This translation is from Maurice Walshe, *The Long Discourses of the Buddha: A Translation of the Dīgha Nikāya* (Boston: Wisdom Publications, 1995), 264.

35. Gregory Schopen, *Bones, Stones, and Buddhist Monks: Collected Papers on the Archaeology, Epigraphy, and Texts of Monastic Buddhism in India* (Honolulu: University of Hawaii Press, 1997).

36. Ibid., 93.

37. See, for instance, Richard Gombrich, *Theravāda Buddhism: A Social History from Ancient Benares to Modern Colombo* (London and New York: Routledge), 1988, 119–120.

38. For recent analyses of relic veneration, see Kevin Trainor, *Relics, Ritual, and Representation in Buddhism: Rematerializing the Sri Lankan Theravāda Tradition* (Cambridge: Cambridge University Press, 1997); John Strong, *Relics of the Buddha* (Princeton: Princeton University Press, 2004); and David Germano and Kevin Trainor, eds., *Embodying the Dharma* (New York: State University of New York Press, 2004).

39. See Donald Swearer, *Becoming the Buddha: The Ritual of Image Consecration in Thailand* (Princeton and Oxford: Princeton University Press, 2004), 35–39.

40. For more information on stūpa symbolism, see Adrian Snodgrass, *The Symbolism of the Stupa, Studies on Southeast Asia* (Ithaca: Cornell University Press, 1985), 353–359.

41. In Thai, there is no distinction between stūpa and caitya (chedi, Thai). André Bareau argues that the tradition initially made a distinction between a stūpa (thūpa, Pāli), which contains the physical relics of the Buddha, and a caitya (cetiya, Pāli), which marks events in his life such as the four principal places of pilgrimage. André Bareau, "La Parinirvāṇa dur Bouddha et la naisance de la religion bouddhique," *Bulletin de l'Ecole Française d'Extrême-Orient* 6 (1974): 275–299.

42. *Mahathammakai Chedi: Mahachedi phua samthiphap lok* (Pathum Thani: Dhammakaya Foundation, 2000), 27.

43. One Dhammakāya English language pamphlet on the chedi that I was given had the following description of the materials used for its construction: "Its 3,333 foundation piles are around 20 meters below the ground surface. Each of these piles has [a] stainless

steel cover which are 6.5 meters in length to protect them from the erosion caused by acid. Through intense research, the finest quality concrete was discovered and used throughout the construction. The Buddha images installed on the external and internal part of the Cetiya are made of silicon bronze with a special casting technology that incorporates three coats—one each of nickel, titanium, and gold respectively. The highest quality granite was used for covering the Sangha State which provides durability, consistent color throughout and quick transmission of heat. The granite was selected from the world's best granite mine."

44. See *Maha Thammakai Chedi: Mahachedi phua samthiphap lok*, 108–109.

45. *Kanyanmit*, (Pathum Thani: Dhammakaya Foundation, January 2000).

46. From a Dhammakāya pamphlet distributed at the temple in 1999.

47. Kanyanmit, (Pathum Thani: Dhammakaya Foundation, January 2000).

48. Gananath Obeyesekere, "Theodicy, Sin and Salvation in a Sociology of Buddhism," in *Dialectic in Practical Reason*, ed. E. R. Leach, Cambridge Papers in Social Anthropology (Cambridge: Cambridge University Press, 1968), 7–40.

49. Obeyesekere argues that karma is psychologically indeterminate, that while "the individual knows that the good which he does in his present lifetime will be rewarded in a future lifetime, he has no idea how his future will be related to his present existence." Obeyesekere, "Theodicy, Sin and Salvation in a Sociology of Buddhism," 21.

50. Craig J. Reynolds, "Power," in *Critical Terms for the Study of Buddhism*, ed. Donald S. Lopez, Jr. (Chicago and London: University of Chicago Press, 2005), 214.

51. M. L. Pattaratorn Chirapravati, *Votive Tablets in Thailand: Origins, Styles, and Uses* (Oxford, Singapore, New York: Oxford University Press, 1997), 6.

52. Ibid., 6–11.

53. Ibid., 67.

54. Stanley J. Tambiah, *The Buddhist Saints of the Forest and the Cult of Amulets: A Study in Charisma, Hagiography, Sectarianism, and Millennial Buddhism*, Cambridge Studies in Social Anthropology 49 (Cambridge: Cambridge University Press, 1984), 208–209.

55. B. J. Terwiel, *Monks and Magic: an Analysis of Religious Ceremonies in Central Thailand*, Third Edition (Bangkok: White Lotus, 1994), 64.

56. Ibid, 67.

57. Tambiah, *The Buddhist Saints of the Forest and the Cult of Amulets*, 342.

58. I have placed quotation marks around the word sale to indicate that Thais use the word chao (rent) to refer to the exchange of amulets, rather than the word sell, khai.

59. *Anuphap Phra Mahasiriratthat* 1 (Pathum Thani: Dhammakāya Foundation, 1998).

60. From an advertisement in *Anuphap Phra Mahasiriratthat* 30 (Pathum Thani: Dhammakāya Foundation, 1999).

61. In Pāli, this would be "samma arahant." It refers to a fully enlightened person. Typically, this would be reserved for praising the Buddha, as in the common chant of, Namo Tassa Bhagavato Arahato Samma Sambuddhassa, but Dhammakāya practitioners may use it as a means of recollecting the Buddha while simultaneously accessing and developing their own perfection.

62. *Anuphap Phra Mahsiriratthat* 1.

63. *Bangkok Post*, October 5, 1998.

64. Ibid.

65. This literally translates as, "conquer Māra," referring to the Buddha's defeat of Māra in the moments before his awakening.

66. *The Story of Gotama Buddha: The Nidāna-kathā of the Jātakaṭṭhakathā*, trans. N. A. Jayawickrama (Oxford: Pali Text Society, 1990).

67. Ibid., 92.

68. Ibid., 96.

69. Ibid., 119.

70. Donald K. Swearer, Sommai Premchit, and Phaithoon Dokbuakaew, *Sacred Mountains of Northern Thailand and Their Legends* (Chiang Mai: Silkworm Books, 2004).

71. Ibid., 48–49.

72. Ibid., 53.

73. Donald K. Swearer and Sommai Premchit, *The Legend of Queen Cāma: Bodhiraṃsi's Cāmadevīvaṃsa, a Translation and Commentary* (Albany: State University of New York Press, 1998), 39–40.

74. John Strong, *Relics of the Buddha*, 193.

75. Donald K. Swearer and Sommai Premchit, *The Legend of Queen Cāma: Bodhiraṃsi's Cāmadevīvaṃsa, a Translation and Commentary*, 41.

76. See Phra Mahasupha Utto, *Wiphak: Wat Phra Thammakai* (Bangkok: Amy Printing, 1999). In this book, Phra Mahasupha dedicates an entire chapter to miracles (Chapter 10), to materialism (Chapter 11), and to business activities (Chapter 13). In other parts of the book, he criticizes the Temple's meditation technique, its doctrine of "nipphan pen atta" (nirvāṇa is self), and its construction of the Mahathammakai Chedi. Also see Sathianpong Wannapok, *Botrian Chawphut chak Korani Thammakai* (Bangkok: Sahathammik, 1999).

77. Steven Kemper, "Wealth and Reformation in Sinhalese Buddhist Monasticism," in *Ethics Wealth and Salvation: A Study in Buddhist Social Ethics*, eds. Russell F. Sizemore and Donald K. Swearer (Columbia: University of South Carolina Press, 1990), 152–69.

78. Pierre Bourdieu, *Outline of a Theory of Practice*, trans. Richard Nice, Cambridge Studies in Social Anthropology 16 (Cambridge: Cambridge University Press, 1977), 17.

79. Katherine Bowie, "The Alchemy of Charity: Of Class and Buddhism in Northern Thailand," *American Anthropologist* 100, no. 2 (June 1998): 469–81.

80. Pierre Bourdieu's discussion of kinship highlights and supports this shift in orientation, and the implications of this theoretical move. He writes, "When the anthropologist treats native kinship terminology as a closed, coherent system of purely logical relationships, defined once and for all by the implicit axiomatics of a cultural tradition, he prohibits himself from apprehending the different practical functions of the kinship terms and relations which he unwittingly brackets." Rather than focusing on logical relationships (i.e., older brother signifies this, younger sister signifies that), Bourdieu suggests that we look at practical relationships—how agents make use of kinship terms. Pierre Bourdieu, *Outline of a Theory of Practice*, trans. Richard Nice, Cambridge Studies in Social Anthropology (Cambridge: Cambridge University Press, 1977), 37.

81. See Irene Stengs, "Millenial Transitions," *Millenial Capitalism and the Culture of Neoliberalism*, eds. Jean and John Comaroff (Durham and London: Duke University Press, 2001), 57.

Chapter 4 The Dhammakāya Controversy: Wealth, Piety, and Authority

  1. "Abbot Vows to Die in Saffron Robe: Dhammachayo Dares Authorities," *The Nation*, May 24, 1999.
  2. *The Nation Magazine*, March 11–17, 1999.
  3. *Matichon Sutsapda* (Weekly), May 4, 1999.
  4. *Matichon Sutsapda* (Weekly), May 11, 1999.
  5. Arjun Appadurai, "The production of locality," *Counterworks: Managing the Diversity of Knowledge*, ed. Richard Fardon (London and New York: Routledge Press, 1995), 206.
  6. "Temple Funds Go Begging in Age of Dud Cheques," *The Nation*, September 26, 1998.
  7. Ibid.
  8. "Poor Woman Claims Cold-hearted Monk Ruined Dad's Funeral," *Bangkok Post*, May 23, 1998.
  9. For an extensive analysis of the ways in which death is "marketed, visualized, and remembered" in contemporary Thailand, see Alan Klima, *The Funeral Casino: Meditation, Massacre, and Exchange with the Dead in Thailand* (Princeton and Oxford: Princeton University Press, 2002).
  10. "Poor Deserve Free Funeral," *Bangkok Post*, June 5, 1998.
  11. Williams suggests that this practice may reflect the adaptation of monastic rules to the emergent town-based mercantile economy of North India. Paul Williams, *Mahāyāna Buddhism: The Doctrinal Foundations* (London and New York: Routledge, 1989), 17.
  12. The other six crimes against the saṅgha include killing an *arahant*, molesting a bhikkhunī, "liv[ing] in communion by theft," joining another religion, committing a *pārājika* offense and leaving the saṅgha, and harming his teacher to the "point of shedding blood."
  13. Richard Gombrich, *Theravada Buddhism: A Social History from Ancient Benares to Modern Colombo* (London: Routledge and Kegan Paul, 1988), 111.
  14. As Williams notes, Chinese pilgrims in the sixth century portrayed Indian Buddhist communities as unified under one discipline despite doctrinal diversity. In Thailand, the label "Theravāda" historically refers to the use of the Pāli Vinaya as a standard for discipline. In practice, there were a myriad of "practical canons" with varying interpretations.
  15. For the modern interpretation of "*nikai*," see Rachelle M. Scott, "A New Buddhist Sect?: The Dhammakāya Temple and the Politics of Difference," *Religion* 36:4 (2006): 215–230.
  16. "Temple Evicted Villagers to Make Room for Gigantic Pagoda," *The Nation*, December 12, 1998.
  17. Ibid.
  18. "Sun Halo Heats up Temple Critics," *The Nation*, November 28, 1998.
  19. Bangkok Post, November 27, 1998.
  20. "Sun Halo Heats up Temple Critics," *The Nation*, November 28, 1998.
  21. "Temple has Exploited Community, Says Banished Disciple," *The Nation*, December 17, 1998.
  22. Ibid.
  23. "Former Dhammakaya Monk Threatened," *The Nation*, December 29, 1998.
  24. "Panel to Help Probe Temple," *Bangkok Post*, December 25, 1998.

25. Ibid.

26. "Adjustments Needed to End Religious Controversy," *The Nation*, January 30, 1999.

27. "Dhammakaya Beliefs Wrong, Says Monk," *The Nation*, February 15, 1999.

28. *Act on the Administration of the Buddhist Order of Sangha* (Bangkok: Mahamakuta University, 1989), 37.

29. "Temple Gets B400 Million from Faithful," *Bangkok Post*, November 2, 1992.

30. Ibid.

31. Prawase Wasi, *Suan Mokh, Thammakai, Santi Asok*, third edition (Bangkok: Mohchaoban Publishing, 1998), 55.

32. Frank Reynolds, "Ethics and Wealth in Theravada Buddhism: A Study in Comparative Ethics," in *Ethics, Wealth, and Salvation*, eds. Russell Sizemore and Donald Swearer (Columbia, SC: University of South Carolina Press, 1990), 70.

33. Sirikul Bunnag, "Famous Temple Faces Probe Over Teachings and Fund-Raising Methods," *Bangkok Post*, November 27, 1998.

34. "When Money Guarantees Nirvana," *The Nation*, December 1, 1998.

35. "Temple Attacked for Putting Merit on Sale," *The Nation*, November 29, 1998.

36. Ibid.

37. Suthon Sukphisit, "The Bigger the Better," *Bangkok Post*, August 20, 1998.

38. Ibid.

39. Ibid.

40. *Daily News*, February 5, 1999.

41. "Dhammakaya's Marketing Guru Shows His Merit Again," *The Nation*, January 15, 1999.

42. See "Dhammachayo–Thammakai has 50,000 Million," *Daily News*, February 23, 1999.

43. One rai is equivalent to two-fifths of an acre.

44. "Abbot's Lust for Land His Undoing," *The Nation*, May 1, 1999.

45. *Ban Muang*, May 30, 1999.

46. *Choluk Wat Phra Thammakai* (Pathum Thani: Dhammakāya Foundation, 1998).

47. *The Nation*, January 30, 1999.

48. *The Nation*, February 12, 1999. The phrase, ayatana nipphan, is a Dhammakāya neologism, which refers to a sphere of existence where the Buddha and arahants remain after their physical deaths (parinibbāna). According to Dhammakāya practice, one's ability to access ayatana nipphan fosters a special type of communion with the Buddha and all other fully-awakened beings who have died. The term, ayatana, is used in the Pāli canon to refer to the six internal and external sense-bases, but there are no direct references in the canon to "ayatana nibbāna" as the place of the Buddha's post-parinibbanic existence.

49. Phra Prayudh Payutto has received a number of ecclesiastical titles, including Phra Rajavaramuni and more recently, Phra Dhammapitaka. Phra Prayudh Payutto (Phra Dhammapitaka), *Korani Thammakai: Botrian Phua Suksa Phra Phutthasatsana Lae Sangsan Sangkhom Thai* (Bangkok: Kongthun Wutthitham Phua Kansuksa lae Patibattham, 1999).

50. "Phra Dhammapitika Accuses Temple of Doctrinal Distortion," *Bangkok Post*, February 19, 1999.

51. Ibid.

52. Phra Prayudh Payutto (Phra Rajavaramuni), *Korani Santi Asok* (Bangkok: Mulanithi Phutthatham, 1988).

53. Prawase Wasi, *Suan Mokh, Thammakai, Santi Asok*, third edition (Bangkok: Mo Chaoban Publishing House, 1998), 35–45. This book was originally published in 1987. He makes a similar argument in *Latthi Thammakai: Kap Botbat Khong Sanghkom Thai* (Bangkok: Samakhom Sitkao Mahachulalongkornratchawitthayalai, 1999).

54. Sathianphong Wannapok, *Suan Thaang Nipphaan* (Bangkok: Sormafai Publishers, 2530 (1987)), 21. Quoted in Peter Jackson, *Buddhism, Legitimation, and Conflict: The Political Functions of Urban Thai Buddhism* (Singapore: Institute of Southeast Asian Studies, 1989).

55. Edwin Zehner, "Reform Symbolism of a Thai Middle-Class Sect: The Growth and Appeal of the Thammakai Movement," *Journal of Southeast Asian Studies* 21:2 (1990): 402–426; and Juliana Schober, "The Theravāda Buddhist Engagement with Modernity," *Journal of Southeast Asian Studies* 26: 2 (September 1995): 307–325.

56. A. Thomas Kirsch, "Modernizing Implications of Nineteenth Century Reforms in the Thai Sangha," in *Religion and Legitimation of Power in Thailand, Laos, and Burma*, ed. Bardwell Smith (Chambersburg, PA: Anima Books, 1978).

57. Paul Williams, *Mahāyāna Buddhism: The Doctrinal Foundations* (London and New York: Routledge, 1989), 4.

58. See Richard Gombrich and Gananath Obeyesekere, *Buddhism Transformed: Religious Change in Sri Lanka* (Princeton: Princeton University Press, 1989).

59. *Korani Thammakai* quickly became the most popular source for information about the temple and the controversy. As such, it stood as a starting point for discussions on the Dhammakāya controversy while providing a framework for the articulation of these discussions. When I returned to Thailand in January of 2001, for instance, I noticed that excerpts from the book were being printed in the periodical published by Mahachulalongkorn Buddhist University. While other books have been published about the temple's teachings and practices, none have had the same impact as *Korani Thammakai*.

60. Phra Somchai Thanawuttho, *Nipphan pen Atta rue Anatta* (Nirvāṇa is Self or Not-self) (Pathum Thani: Dhammakāya Foundation, 1999).

61. Phra MahaBoonthuang, *Phra Thammakai kap Satthampathirup* (Dhammakāya with False Teachings) (no publisher listed, 1999), 12. These ideas were originally published in *Matichon*, January 13, 1999.

62. *Anguttara-nikāya* 3.65.

63. See Rupert Gethin, *The Foundations of Buddhism* (Oxford: Oxford University Press, 1998), 45–49; and George Bond, *The Word of the Buddha: the Tipitaka and its Interpretation in Theravāda Buddhism* (Columbo: Gunasena, 1982).

64. Sanitsuda Ekachai, "It's Exploitation That's Intolerable," *Bangkok Post*, September 3, 1999.

65. This incident happened in the spring of 2000, more than a year after the start of the controversy.

66. "Thai Sangha Crisis: The Wat Phra Dhammakaya Case," *Bangkok Post*, March 22, 2000.

67. This is evident on the popular television program, *Searching for the Essence of Buddhism*. When I attended tapings of the program at Wat Chonpratanrangsarit in Nonthaburi and at the Santi Asok center in Bangkok, I noticed that the hosts and the studio

audience posed questions that covered a range of issues including details of Buddhist history, proper conduct for bhikkhus, saṅgha reform, and religious authority, topics that we might typically identify as "elitist." The studio audience was clearly made up of individuals from a variety of different backgrounds, most of whom were lay practitioners from the respective temples. As for the television viewing audience, the program was broadcast on Channel 11, one of Thailand's regular non-cable stations that can reach the widest (and most diverse) viewing public. Discussions and debates over religious issues, therefore, enter this new public domain and transcend simple dichotomies between "elite" and "popular" discourses.

68. Charles Keyes, "Moral Authority of the Sangha and Modernity in Thailand," in *Socially Engaged Buddhism for the New Millennium* (Bangkok: The Sathirakoses-Nagapradipa Foundation, 1999), 123.

69. "Monks Urge Media Chiefs to Meditate," *The Nation*, January 5, 1999.

70. I heard this statement many times at the Temple during this period. In addition, the Dhammakāya Foundation uses the distinction between the "real news" and the "bad news" in a statement on the media that was printed on their website, www.dhammakaya.or .th. (accessed on July 15, 1999).

71. *Bangkok Post*, August 23, 2006.

72. Sanitsuda Ekachai, "Prosecutors let monk off the hook," *Bangkok Post*, August 24, 2006.

73. Phra Mettanando, "TRT and the Dhammakaya Temple—Perfect Match," *The Nation*, September 27, 2006.

Chapter 5   Consumerism and Commercialization of Buddhism

1. George Bond, *Buddhism at Work: Community Development, Social-Empowerment and the Sarvodaya Movement* (Bloomfield: Kumarian Press, 2004), 43.

2. Phra Somsak Duangsisen, "Consumerism, Prostitution, and Buddhist Ethics," *The Chulalongkorn Journal of Buddhist Studies* 2:1 (2003): 107–114.

3. Preecha Changkhwanyuen, "Buddhist Analysis of Capitalism," *The Chulalongkorn Journal of Buddhist Studies*, 3:2 (2004): 249–251.

4. Dinty W. Moore, *The Accidental Buddhist: Mindfulness, Enlightenment, and Sitting Still, American Style* (New York: Doubleday, 1997), 101. The author added the bracketed information for the purpose of clarification.

5. Wayne Dunn, a contributor to "Capitalism Magazine," also draws a sharp contrast between being Buddhist and making money in his critique of one hundred business executives who paid for personal audiences with the Dalai Lama. See Wayne Dunn, "Buddha Bad for Business," *Capitalism Magazine: In Defense of Individual Rights*, April 30, 2004.

6. For an analysis of reverse Orientalism within the Japanese context, see Bernard Faure, "The Kyoto School and Reverse Orientalism,' in *Japan in Traditional and Postmodern Perspectives*, eds. Charles Wei-hsun Fu and Steven Heine (Albany: SUNY Press, 1995); and Yuko Kikuchi, *Japanese Modernisation and Mingei Theory: Cultural Nationalism and Oriental Orientalism* (London and New York: Routledge, 2004).

7. Anagarika Dharmapala, *Return to Righteousness: A Collection of Speeches, Essays*

and Letters of Anagarika Dharmapala, ed. Ananda Guruge (Colombo: The Anagarika Dharmapala Birth Centenary Committee, 1965), 494.

8. Jeremy Carrette and Richard King, *Selling Spirituality: The Silent Takeover of Religion* (New York and London: Routledge, 2005), 120.

9. Ibid., 87–122.

10. Kasian Tejapira, "The Postmodernisation of Thainess," in *Cultural Crisis and Social Memory: Modernity and Identity in Thailand and Laos*, ed. Shigeharu Tanabe and Charles F. Keyes (Honolulu: University of Hawaii Press, 2002), 202–227.

11. Joseph Medley and Lorrayne Carol, "The hungry ghost: IMF policy, global capitalist transformation, and laboring bodies in Southeast Asia," in *Postcolonialism Meets Economics*, ed. Eiman O. Zein-Elabdin and S. Charusheela (London and New York: Routledge, 2004), 145–164.

12. "The Under and Over of Development," *The Nation*, March 9, 1999.

13. Ibid.

14. Yvan Cohen, "Some Thais see economic hardship as a boon to `traditional values'," *Christian Science Monitor*, July 24, 1998. Cohen transliterates Phra Phayom's name as Pra Payom Galyano. For the sake of clarity and consistency, I inserted Phra Phayom Kalyano.

15. Pasuk Phongpaichit and Chris Baker, *Thailand's Boom and Bust* (Chiang Mai: Silkworm Books, 1998).

16. Ibid., 4.

17. Paritta Chalermpow Koanantakool, "Thai Middle-Class Practice and Consumption of Traditional Dance: "Thai-ness" and High Art," in *Local Cultures and the "New Asia*,*"* ed. C. J. W.– L. Wee (Singapore: Institute of Southeast Asian Studies, 2002), 217–241. Koanantakool examines the construct of the middle class (kon chan klang) in Thai socioeconomic discourses, and its primary usage within academic and media circles. She notes how analyses of the Thai middle class tends to focus on the historical development of a middle-class mentality (starting with the emergence of a bourgeois mentality during the nineteenth and early twentieth centuries), the examination of the growth of an urban and educated population, the correlation of the middle class with political reformist movements, and a focus on the economic boom of the 1980s and 1990s which reinforced the rise of the "new rich" and consumerist ideals and lifestyles.

18. Phongpaichit and Baker, *Thailand's Boom and Bust*, 45.

19. The critique of Westernization goes hand in hand with similar discourses that critique the Western dominant narrative of consumer capitalism and its role within processes of globalization. The idea that the world is becoming increasingly homogenized as a result of the global production and consumption of market goods (goods that tend to be explicitly Western in origin such as Coca-cola, blue jeans, and Hollywood films replacing, co-opting, or displacing local products) tends to raise questions about the power dynamics implicit within the processes of globalization. See U. Hannerz, *Cultural Complexity: Studies in the Organization of Meaning* (New York: Columbia University Press, 1992).

20. Robert Bocock, *Consumption* (London and New York: Routledge, 1993).

21. For a fascinating discussion of the role of advertising in the formation of consumers in Sri Lanka, see Steven Kemper, *Buying and Believing: Sri Lankan Advertising and Consumers in a Transnational World* (Chicago and London: University of Chicago Press, 2001).

22. Kasian Tejapira, "The Postmodernisation of Thainess," in *Cultural Crisis and Social Memory: Modernity and Identity in Thailand and Laos*, eds. Shigeharu Tanabe and Charles F. Keyes (Honolulu: University of Hawaii Press), 202–227.

23. Ibid., 202–203.

24. Arjun Appadurai and Carol Breckenridge, "Public Modernity in India," in *Consuming Modernity: Public Culture in a South Asian World*, ed. Carol Breckenridge (Minneapolis: University of Minnesota Press, 1995), 1.

25. Ibid., 5.

26. Paritta Chalermpow Koanantakool, "Thai Middle-Class Practice and Consumption of Traditional Dance: 'Thai-ness' and High Art," 237.

27. See Nidhi Eosiwong, "Watthanatham Khong Chon Chan Klang Thai," *Journal of Thammasat University* 19:1 (1993).

28. For an overview of the various expressions of socially engaged Buddhism, see Christopher Queen and Sallie S. Queen, eds., *Engaged Buddhism: Buddhist Liberation Movements in Asia* (Albany: State University of New York Press, 1994); and Damian Keown, ed., *Contemporary Buddhist Ethics*, Curzon Critical Studies in Buddhism 17 (London: Routledge Curzon, 2004).

29. Jonathon Watts, "Is the Crisis Just Economic?" in *The Religion of the Market: A Buddhist Look at the Global Economy, Consumerism, Development and the Role of Spirituality in Society, Think Sangha Journal* 1:1 (Winter 1998), 4.

30. Ibid.

31. One such story involved the entrance examination system at Kesatsart University's demonstration school. After her child was denied admittance, Sumalee Limpaovart charged that the school did not base admittance on merit, but rather on "endowment payments" and the social standing of the family. In reference to this case, one editorial states, "The battle for civil society is a battle for fairness and a fulfilling life. For all its merits, the patronage system clearly has its liabilities, and Thailand as a country of "adaptability" must work at it, otherwise we will be eaten up by a cronyism which, at its worst, feeds on itself." See "Education Must Teach Virtue, not Cronyism," *The Nation*, March 2, 1999.

32. Arjun Appadurai coined the term ideoscape to refer to the flow of key ideas, terms, and images, such as freedom, welfare, and democracy, in the modern world. See Arjun Appadurai, *Modernity at Large: Cultural Dimensions of Globalization* (Minneapolis and London: University of Minnesota Press, 1996).

33. The fact that people read, hear, and interpret the components of a particular ideoscape differently is one of the key points in Appadurai's theory. He argues, for instance, that, "while an Indian audience may be attentive to the resonances of a political speech in terms of some keywords and phrases reminiscent of Hindi cinema, a Korean audience may respond to the subtle codings of Buddhist or neo-Confucian rhetoric encoded in a political document." Appadurai, *Modernity at Large*, 36–37.

34. David Loy, "The Religion of the Market," *The Religion of the Market: A Buddhist Look at the Global Economy, Consumerism, Development and the Role of Spirituality in Society, Think Sangha Journal* 1:1 (Winter 1998), 28. Previously published in *The Journal of the American Academy of Religion* 65:2 (summer 1997).

35. David R. Loy, *Money, Sex, War, Karma: Notes for a Buddhist Revolution* (Boston: Wisdom Publications, 2008); and Stephen Batchelor, *Buddhism without Beliefs: A Contemporary Guide to Awakening* (New York: Riverhead Books, 1997).

36. Ibid., 1.

37. Ibid., 5–6.

38. Thongchai Winichakul, *Siam Mapped: A History of the Geo-Body of a Nation* (Honolulu: University of Hawaii Press, 1994), 10.

39. Peter Jackson, *Buddhism, Legitimation, and Conflict*, 126.

40. Sanitsuda Ekachai, quoted in Peter Jackson, *Buddhism, Legitimation, and Conflict*, 126.

41. Donald K. Swearer, "Dhammic Socialism," in *Dhammic Socialism*, trans. and ed. Donald K. Swearer (Bangkok: Thai Inter-Religious Commission for Development, 1986), 23.

42. Bhikkhu Buddhadāsa, "Exchanging Dhamma While Fighting," in *Visakha Puja* (Bangkok: The Buddhist Association of Thailand, 1970).

43. Bruce Evans, "Contributions of Venerable Prayudh to Buddhism and Society," in *Socially Engaged Buddhism for the New Millennium* (Bangkok: Sathirakoses-Nagapradipa Foundation and Foundation for Children, 1999), 5–6.

44. Phra Payutto, *Buddhist Economics: A Middle Way for the Market Place* (Bangkok: Buddhadhamma Foundation, 1992).

45. Ibid., p.20.

46. Ibid., p.25.

47. Ibid., 26.

48. Sulak Sivaraksa, *A Buddhist Vision for Renewing Society* (Bangkok: Thai Inter-Religious Commission for Development, 1994), 63.

49. Sulak Sivaraksa, "Buddhism with a Small 'b'," *Seeds of Peace*, ed. Tom Ginsburg (Berkeley: Parallax Press, 1992), 65.

50. Sulak Sivaraksa, "The Religion of Consumerism," and "The Think-Big Strategy of Development," *Seeds of Peace*, ed. Tom Ginsburg (Berkeley: Parallax Press, 1992).

51. The word samana is Pāli for novice and refers to someone who observes the ten precepts. Since Phothirak was stripped of his monastic standing, he cannot use the honorific "Phra" before his name.

52. Phra Phothirak's assessment of contemporary Thai Buddhism played a crucial role in his eventual disrobing by the Supreme Sangha Council in 1989. As noted in Chapter 1, Phra Phothirak and all Santi Asok monks are no longer deemed ordained bhikkhus by the sangha establishment. While the official reason for their mandatory disrobing was Phra Photirak's alleged distortion of the dhamma, many commentators note that Phra Photirak's open and direct criticisms of so-called mainstream Buddhism was the primary reason for their ejection from the Mahanikai lineage.

53. Prakobpong Panapool, "Santi Asoke, Dhammakaya Show Contrast," *The Nation*, March 15, 1999.

54. Suwanna Satha Anand, *Ngoen Kap Satsana: Thepyut Haeng Yuk Samai* (Money and Religion: The Godly War of the Era) (Bangkok: Samnakphim Munnithi Komol Keemthong, 1999).

55. Suwanna Satha-Anand, *Ngoen kap Sasana*, 23-35.

56. Ibid., 42-54.

57. Ibid., 54-63.

58. Ibid., 63-68.

59. Ibid., 68-72.

60. (Phra) Phaisan Wisalo, "Mum Mong Choeng Phut To Yuk Setthakit Fong Sabu," *Ngoen Kap Satsana*, 73–145.

61. Mara Einstein, *Brands of Faith: Marketing Religion in a Commercial Age* (London and New York: Routledge, 2008).

62. Peter Berger, *The Sacred Canopy* (Garden City: Anchor Books, 1967).

63. Wade Clark Roof, *Spiritual Marketplace: Baby Boomers and the Remaking of American Religion* (Princeton: Princeton University Press, 1999), 91.

64. R. Laurence Moore, *Selling God: American Religion in the Marketplace of Culture* (Oxford: Oxford University Press, 1994), 5.

65. Ibid. One particularly salient late twentieth-century example of the effect of religion on consumer tastes is the multibillion dollar televangelism industry. Channels like the Trinity Broadcast Network compete with a wide range of broadcast and cable channels for viewers. The booming success of religious networks is evidence that its religious product is indeed one that many consumers are choosing. Of course, critics of the televangelism industry are quick to question the integrity of the programs and to highlight controversies, such the Jim Bakker scandal, as evidence of the corruption of religion by the consumer culture.

66. Raymond Benton, "Alternative Approaches to Consumer Behavior," quoted in Stephanie Gaza, "Overcoming the Grip of Consumerism," in *Socially Engaged Buddhism for the New Millennium* (Bangkok: Sathirakoses-Nagapradipa Foundation and Foundation for Children, 1999).

67. Phra Phaisan Wisalo, "Spiritual Materialism and the Sacraments of Consumerism: A View from Thailand," in *The Religion of the Market: A Buddhist Look at the Economy, Consumerism, Development and the Role of Spirituality in Society*, (Bangkok: International Network of Engaged Buddhists, 1998), 35.

68. O'Connor, "Interpreting Thai Religious Change: Temples, Sangha Reform and Social Change," *Journal of Southeast Asian Studies* 24:2 (1993): 336. (330–339)

69. Phra Phaisan Wisalo, "Spiritual Materialism and the Sacraments of Consumerism," 34.

70. Ibid.

71. Sukanya Sae-Lim, "Winning's Easy, Just Rub Any Old Tree," *The Nation*, September 16, 1999.

72. Sanitsuda Ekachai, "Sale of Amulets is Not So Charming," *Bangkok Post*, November 26, 1997.

73. Peter Jackson, "The Enchanting Sprit of Thai Capitalism," *Southeast Asia Research* 7:1 (1999): 5–60. Jackson transliterates Luang Pho Khun's name as Luang Phor Khoon. For the sake of clarity and consistency within this book, I have changed and bracketed the transliteration within the direct quote.

74. Ibid.

75. I recently heard a story that Luang Pho Khun told his supporters that he needed help just like everyone else following a road accident. In this statement, he was perhaps hinting that he is not "supernatural" and that his amulets do not protect against all forms of harm.

76. Peter Jackson, "Buddhism's Changing Political Roles," in *Political Change in Thailand: Democracy and Participation*, ed. Kevin Hewison (London and New York: Routledge, 1997).

77. *Bangkok Post Weekly Review*, November 12, 1993. Quoted in Jackson, "Buddhism's Changing Political Roles," 84.

Conclusion

1. Nithinand Yorsaengrat, "Talismanic Tales," *The Nation*, February 11, 2007.

2. "Amulet Sends Mixed Blessing," *Bangkok Post*, May 20, 2007.

3. Ibid.

4. Noppawan Bunluesilp, "Thai Amulet craze 'unacceptable face of Buddhism,'" *Reuters*, July 13, 2007.

5. "Abbot recommends a nibble at religion," *The Nation*, July 1, 2007.

6. Ibid.

7. "Cookie Shortage: Jatukam t-shirts, anyone?" *The Nation*, September 3, 2007.

8. I am thinking specifically of the media's portrayal of Jim Bakker as a money-hungry malfeasant who preyed upon the delicate religious sensibilities of the elderly.

9. Sulak Sivaraksa, *Thammakai: Fang San Sudthay Haeng Khwamsueamsalay Khog Sathaban Song Thai* (Bangkok: Kongthun Raktham Phua Kanfunfu Phra Phutthasatsana, 1999).

10. Santikaro Bhikkhu, "Thai Sangha Crisis: The Wat Phra Dhammakaya Case," *Bangkok Post*, March 22, 2000.

11. See Phra Phaisan Wisalo, "Khamnan: Pharakit Lae Phanthamit Khong Satsana (Preface: Mission and Allies of Religion)" in Suwanna Satha Anand, *Ngoen Kap Satsana: Thepyut Haeng Yuk Samai* (Money and Religion: the Godly War of the Era) (Bangkok: Samnakphim Munnithi Komol Keemthong, 1999), 11–21, and a comprehensive call for reform in Sanitsuda Ekachai, *Keeping the Faith: Thai Buddhism at the Crossroads* (Bangkok: Post Books, 2001).

12. Prapasri Osathanon, "A philosophy in decay," *The Nation*, March 24, 1996.

13. "Monkhood in Serious Crisis," *The Nation*, November 20, 2001.

14. Frank E. Reynolds, "Civic Religion and National Community in Thailand, Journal of Asian Studies 36:2 (1977): 274–275.

15. See Sulak Sivaraksa, *Siam in Crisis: Collected Articles* (Bangkok: Komol Keemthong Foundation, 1980); *Thammakai: Fang San Sudthay Haeng Khwamsueamsalay Khog Sathaban Song Thai* (Dhammakāya: The Final Straw) (Bangkok: Kongthun Raktham Phua Kanfunfu Phra Phutthasatsana, 1999); *Wikrit Thammakai* (Crisis of Dhammakāya) (Bangkok: Khana Kammakan Satsana Phua Kanphattana, 2000); Phra Phaisan Wisalo, *Phuttasatsana Thai nai Anakot: Naeo lae Thangok jak Wikrit* (Thai Buddhism in Future: Trends and Solutions for Crisis) (2002); and Phra Payutto (Phra Dhammapitaka), *Phutthasasana Cha Wikrit Tong Kit Hai Klai Ru Hai Than* (Thai Buddhism Will Be in Crisis, We Must Have Forward Thinking) (Bangkok: Buddhist Dhammic Foundation, 2002).

16. Charles Keyes, one of the leading anthropologists of Thai Buddhism, for instance, interprets the numerous religious scandals involving prominent monks in Thailand and the debates surrounding them as a reflection of a "crisis of moral authority" within Buddhism where the power of the saṅgha is no longer axiomatic. Keyes links this "crisis of moral authority" to modernity, to the "ambiguities, uncertainties, and disorientations" that

characterize modern Thai society. See Charles Keyes, "Moral Authority of the Sangha and Modernity in Thailand: Sexual Scandals, Sectarian, Dissent, and Political Resistance," in *Socially Engaged Buddhism for the New Millennium* (Bangkok: Sathirakoses-Nagapradipa Foundation, 1999), 121–147.

17. Anne M. Blackburn, *Buddhist Learning and Textual Practice in Eighteenth-Century Lankan Monastic Culture* (Princeton and Oxford: Princeton University Press, 2001), 8–9.

18. Ibid., 76–77.

19. See "Decline of Thai Buddhism," *The Nation*, September 22, 1989; "The Root Cause of Decline is More Complicated," *Bangkok Post*, March 28, 1993; Chaowanee Tangwongprasert, "A Crisis of Confidence," *The Nation*, February 24, 1994; Prapasri Osathanon, "A Philosophy in Decay," *The Nation*, March 24, 1996; Satchunij Pornphong, "Sincere Bids for Reform Foiled by Complacency," *The Nation*, March 24, 1996; Pravit Rojanaphhruk, "Religion is Now Little More than Convenience, *The Nation*, January 30, 1997; Kamolthip Bai-ngern, "Temples are Open Doors: Everyone is Allowed Inside," *The Nation*, March 24, 1996; Vithamon Pongpairoj, "Shaking the Faith: Scandals Fuel Calls for Reform of Monkhood, *Bangkok Post*, February 19, 1996; and "Reform Urged in Bid to Save Faith in Buddhism," *Bangkok Post*, February 10, 1996.

20. As Talal Asad argues in the case of Islam, textualists and anthropologists alike have tended to view religious debates "as a symptom of 'the tradition in crisis' on the assumption that 'normal' tradition excludes reasoning just as it requires unthinking conformity." Talal Asad, "The Idea of an Anthropology of Islam," Occasional Paper Series (Washington DC: Georgetown University Center for Contemporary Arab Studies, 1986).

21. Pattana Kitiarsa's recent analysis of Buddhism and modernity in contemporary Thai film, for instance, challenges the thesis of a religious crisis by demonstrating how Thai Buddhism, as a syncretic and multivoiced tradition, continues to thrive as it facilitates negotiation with complex global and postmodern forces. Pattana Kitiarsa, "Faiths and Films: Countering the Crisis of Thai Buddhism from Below," *Asian Journal of Social Science*, 34:2 (2006): 264–290.

22. Tessa J. Bartholomeusz, *In Defense of Dharma: Just-war Ideology in Buddhist Sri Lanka* (London and New York: Routledge Curzon, 2002).

Bibliography

Abeysekara, Ananda. *Colors of the Robe: Religion, Identity, and Difference.* Columbia: University of South Carolina Press, 2002.

Acts on the Administration of the Buddhist Order of Sangha of Thailand. Bangkok: Mahāmakuta Educational Council, 1989.

Almond, Philip. *The British Discovery of Buddhism.* Cambridge: Cambridge University Press, 1988.

Alnor, Jackie. "Joel Osteen: The Prosperity Gospel's Coverboy." *The Christian Sentinel,* June 2003.

Anderson, Benedict. "Studies of the Thai State: The State of Thai Studies." In *The Study of Thailand: Analyses of Knowledge, Approaches, and Prospects in Anthropology, Art History, Economics, History, and Political Science,* edited by Eliezer B. Ayal, 193–247. Athens: Ohio University Center for International Studies, 1978.

Anuphap Haeng Bun. Pathum Thani: Dhammakāya Foundation, December 3, 2000.

Anuphap Phra Mahasiriratthat, No. 1. Pathum Thani: Dhammakāya Foundation, 1998.

Anuphap Phra Mahasiriratthat, No. 30. Pathum Thani: Dhammakāya Foundation, 1999.

Apinya Fuengfusakul. "Empire of Crystal and Utopian Commune: Two Types of Contemporary Theravada Reform in Thailand." *Sojourn* 8, no. 1 (1993): 153–83.

Appadurai, Arjun. *Modernity at Large: Cultural Dimensions of Globalization.* Minneapolis and London: University of Minnesota Press, 1996.

———. "The Production of Locality." In *Counterworks: Managing the Diversity of Knowledge,* edited by Richard Fardon, 204–25. London and New York: Routledge Press, 1995.

Appadurai, Arjun and Carol Breckenridge. "Public Modernity in India." In *Consuming Modernity: Public Culture in a South Asian World,* edited by Carol Breckendridge. Minneapolis: University of Minnesota Press, 1995.

Asad, Talal. *The Idea of an Anthropology of Islam,* Occasional Paper Series. Washington DC: Georgetown University Center for Contemporary Arab Studies, 1986.

Associated Press. "Japanese Monks Stage Fashion Show." December 15, 2007.

Aung-Thwin, Maureen and Thant Myint-U. "The Burmese Ways to Socialism " *Third World Quarterly* 13, no. 1 (1992).

Ayal, Eliezer. "Value Systems and Economic Development in Japan and Thailand." *The Journal of Social Issues* 19, no. 1 (1963).

Bailey, Greg and Ian Mabbett. *The Sociology of Early Buddhism*. Cambridge: Cambridge University Press, 2003.

Bainbridge, William Sims. *The Sociology of Religious Movements*. London and New York: Routledge, 1997.

Bangkok Post. "Amulet Sends Mixed Blessing." May 20, 2007.

———. "Panel to Help Probe Temple December 25, 1998.

———. "Phra Dhammapitika Accuses Temple of Doctrinal Distortions " February 19, 1999.

———. "Poor Deserve Free Funeral." *Bangkok Post*, June 5, 1998.

———. "Poor Woman Claims Cold-Hearted Monk Ruined Dad's Funeral." May 23, 1998.

———. "Reform Urged in Bid to Save Faith in Buddhism." February 10, 1996.

———. "The Root Cause of Decline Is More Complicated." March 28, 1993.

———. "Temple Gets B400 Million from Faithful." November 2, 1992.

———. "Thai Sangha Case: The Wat Phra Dhammakaya Case." March 22, 2000.

Barrett, David. *Sects, 'Cults' and Alternative Religions: A World Survey and Sourcebook*. London: Blandford, 1996.

Bartholomeusz, Tessa J. *In Defense of Dharma: Just-War Ideology in Buddhist Sri Lanka*. London and New York: Routledge Curzon, 2002.

Basham, Richard. "'False Consciousness' and the Problem of Merit and Power in Thailand." *Mankind* 19, no. 2 (1989).

Batchelor, Stephen. *Buddhism without Beliefs: A Contemporary Guide to Awakening*. New York: Riverhead Books, 1998.

Beckford, James. "Introduction." In *New Religious Movements and Rapid Social Change*, edited by James Beckford. Paris and London: United Nations Educational, Scientific and Cultural Organization and Sage, 1986.

Bellah, Robert. *Tokugawa Religion: The Values of Pre-Industrial Japan*. New York: The Free Press, 1957.

Berger, Peter. *The Sacred Canopy: Elements of a Sociological Theory of Religion*. Garden City, NY: Anchor Books, 1967.

Best, Steven. *The Politics of Historical Vision: Marx, Foucault, Habermas*. New York: The Guilford Press, 1995.

Bhikkhu Buddhadāsa. "Exchanging Dhamma While Fighting." In *Visakha Puja*. Bangkok: The Buddhist Association of Thailand, 1970.

Blackburn, Anne M. *Buddhist Learning and Textual Practice in Eighteenth-Century Lankan Monastic Culture*. Princeton and Oxford: Princeton University Press, 2001.

Bocock, Robert. *Consumption*. London: Routledge, 1993.

Bond, George. *Buddhism at Work: Community Development, Social-Empowerment and the Sarvodaya Movement*. Bloomfield: Kumarian Press, 2004.

————. "The Contemporary Lay Meditation Movement and Lay Gurus in Sri Lanka." *Religion* 33, no. 1 (2003): 23–55.

————. *The Word of the Buddha: The Tipitika and Its Interpretation in Theravada Buddhism.* Colombo: Gunasena, 1982.

(Phra Maha) Boonthuang. *Phra Thammakai Kap Satthampatirup*, 1999.

Bourdieu, Pierre. *Outline of a Theory of Practice*, Cambridge Studies in Social Anthropology 16. Cambridge: Cambridge University Press, 1977.

Bowie, Katherine. "The Alchemy of Charity: Of Class and Buddhism in Northern Thailand." *American Anthropologist* 100, no. 2 (1998): 469–81.

Brereton, Bonnie Pacala. *Thai Tellings of Phra Malai: Texts and Rituals Concerning a Popular Buddhist Saint.* Arizona State University: Program for Southeast Asian Studies, 1995.

Brown, Peter. *Poverty and Leadership in the Later Roman Empire*, The Menahem Stern Jerusalem Lectures. Hanover: University Press of New England, 2001.

Brown, Sid. *The Journey of One Buddhist Nun: Even Against the Wind* Albany: State University of New York Press, 2001.

Bunnag, Jane. *Buddhist Monk, Buddhist Layman.* Cambridge: Cambridge University Press, 1973.

Carrette, Jeremy and Richard King. *Selling Spirituality: The Silent Takeover of Religion.* New York and London: Routledge, 2005.

Carrithers, Michael. *The Forest Monks of Sri Lanka: An Anthropological and Historical Survey.* Delhi: Oxford University Press, 1983.

Carter, John Ross. *On Understanding Buddhists: Essays on the Theravāda Tradition of Sri Lanka.* Albany: State University of New York Press, 1993.

Chaowanee Tangwongprasert. "A Crisis of Confidence." *The Nation*, February 24, 1994.

Chandler, Stuart. *Establishing a Pure Land on Earth: The Foguang Buddhist Perspective on Modernization and Globalization.* Honolulu: University of Hawaii Press, 2004.

————. "Spreading Buddha's Light: The Internationalization of Foguang Shan." In *Buddhist Missionaries in the Era of Globalization*, edited by Linda Learman, 162–84. Honolulu: University of Hawaii Press, 2005.

Chatsumarn Kabilsingh. *Thai Women in Buddhism.* Berkeley: Parralax Press, 1991.

Chidester, David. "The Church of Baseball, the Fetish of Coca-Cola, and the Potlatch of Rock 'n' Roll: Theoretical Models for the Study of Religion in American Popular Culture." *Journal of the American Academy of Religion* 64, no. 4 (1996): 743–65.

Choluk Wat Phra Thammakai. Pathum Thani: The Dhammakāya Foundation, 1998.

Chryssides, George. *Exploring New Religions.* London: Cassell Academic, 1999.

Cohen, Paul. "Buddhism Unshackled: The Yuan 'Holy Man' Tradition and the Nation-State in the Tai World." *Journal of Southeast Asian Studies* 32, no. 2 (2001): 227–47.

Cohen, Richard S. *Beyond Enlightenment: Buddhism, Religion, Modernity*. London and New York: Routledge, 2006.

Cohen, Yvon. "Some Thais See Economic Hardship as a Boon to 'Traditional Values'." *Christian Science Monitor*, July 24 1998.

Collins, Steven. *Nirvana and Other Buddhist Felicities*. Cambridge: Cambridge University Press, 1998.

———. "On the Very Idea of the Pali Canon." *Journal of the Pali Text Society* 15 (1990): 89–126.

Comaroff, Jean and John Comaroff. "Millenial Capitalism: First Thoughts on a Second Coming." In *Millenial Capitalism and the Culture of Neoliberalism*, edited by Jean Comaroff and John Comaroff, 1–56. Durham and London: Duke University Press, 2001.

Covell, Stephen G. "Buddhism in Japan: The Creation of Traditions." In *Buddhism in World Cultures: Comparative Perspectives*, edited by Stephen C. Berkwitz, 219–43. Santa Barbara: ABC-CLIO, 2006.

———. *Japanese Temple Buddhism: Worldliness in a Religion of Renunciation*. Honolulu: University of Hawaii Press, 2005.

Daily News. "Dhammachayo-Thammakai Mi 50 Lan." February 23, 1999.

Darlington, Susan M. "The Ordination of a Tree: The Buddhist Ecology Movement in Thailand." *Ethnology* 37, no. 1 (1998): 1–15.

Davis, Winston. *Japanese Religion and Society: Paradigms of Structure and Change*. Albany: State University of New York Press, 1992.

(Phra) Dhammachayo. *Anuphap Haeng Bun*, December 3, 2000.

Dhammadāyada: A New Hope for the Thai Nation. Pathum Thani: Dhammakāya Foundation, n.d.

Duang tawan haeng Santiphap (The Sun of Peace) Pathum Thani: Dhammakāya Foundation, 2007.

Dunn, Wayne. "Buddha Bad for Business." *Capitalism Magazine: In Defense of Individual Rights*, April 30, 2004.

Einstein, Mara. *Brands of Faith: Marketing Religion in a Commercial Age*. London and New York: Routledge, 2008.

Elson, Robert E. "International Commerce, the State and Society: Economic and Social Change." In *Cambridge History of Southeast Asia, Vol. Two, Part One: From c. 1800s–1930s*. Cambridge: Cambridge University Press, 1992.

Evans, Bruce. "Contributions of Venerable Prayudh to Buddhism and Society." In *Socially Engaged Buddhism for the New Millennium. Essays in Honor of the Venerable Phra Dhammapitika on His 60th Birthday Anniversary*, 3–14. Bangkok: Santhirakoses-Nagapradipa Foundation, 1999.

Falk, Nancy Auer. "Exemplary Donors of the Pāli Tradition." In *Ethics, Wealth, and Salvation: A Study in Buddhist Social Ethics*, edited by Russell F. Sizemore and Donald K. Swearer, 124–43. Columbia: University of South Carolina Press, 1990.

Faure, Bernard. "The Kyoto School and Reverse Orientalism." In *Japan in Traditional and Postmodern Perspectives*, edited by Charles Wei-hsun Fu and Steven Heine, 245–82. Albany: State University of New York Press, 1995.

Fitzgerald, Frances. "Reflections: Jim and Tammy." *The New Yorker* (1990): 45–87.

Gaza, Stephanie. "Overcoming the Grip of Consumerism." In *Socially Engaged Buddhism for the New Millennium: Essays in Honor of the Venerable Phra Dhammapitika on His 60th Birthday Anniversary*. Bangkok: Santhirakoses-Nagapradipa Foundation, 1999.

Germano, David and Kevin Trainor, eds. *Embodying the Dharma: Buddhist Relic Veneration in Asia*. Albany: State University of New York Press, 2004.

Gernet, Jacques. *Buddhism in Chinese Society: An Economic History from the Fifth to the Tenth Centuries*. Translated by Franciscus Verellen, Studies in Asian Culture. New York: Columbia University Press, 1995.

Gethin, Rupert. *The Foundations of Buddhism*. Oxford: Oxford University Press, 1998.

Goldstein, Melvyn C. and Matthew T. Kapstein, ed. *Buddhism in Contemporary Tibet: Religious Revival and Cultural Identity*. Berkeley, Los Angeles, and London: University of California Press, 1998.

Gombrich, Richard. *Theravada Buddhism: A Social History from Ancient Benares to Modern Columbo*. London and New York: Routledge and Kegan Paul, 1988.

Gombrich, Richard and Gananath Obeyesekere. *Buddhism Transformed: Religious Change in Sri Lanka*. Princeton: Princeton University Press, 1988.

Griswold, A. B. and Prasert ṇa Nagara. "The Inscription of Văt Khemā: Epigraphic and Historical Studies No. 15." *Journal of the Siam Society* 63, no. 1 (1975): 127–42.

Gunawardana, R. A. L. H. *Robe and Plough: Monasticism and Economic Interest in Early Medieval Sri Lanka*, The Association for Asian Studies: Monographs and Papers, No. 35. Tucson: University of Arizona Press, 1979.

Guruge, Ananda, ed. *Return to Righteousness: A Collection of Speeches, Essays and Letters of Anagarika Dharmapala*. Colombo: The Anagarika Dharmapala Birth Centenary Committee, 1965.

Hallisey, Charles. "Ethical Particularism in Theravāda Buddhism." *Journal of Buddhist Ethics* 4 (1996): 32–43.

———. "A Response to Kevin Shilbrack." *Journal of Buddhist Ethics* 4 (1997): 184–188.

———. "Roads Taken and Not Taken in the Study of Theravada Buddhism." In *Curators of the Buddha: The Study of Buddhism under Colonialism*, edited by Jr. Donald S. Lopez, 31–61, Chicago, University of Chicago Press, 1995.

Hallisey, Charles and Anne Hansen. "Narrative, Sub-Ethics, and the Moral Life: Some Evidence from Theravāda Buddhism." *Journal of Religious Ethics* 24, no. 2 (1996): 305–27.

Hanks, Lucian M. "Merit and Power in the Thai Social Order." *American Anthropologist* 64 (1962): 1247–61.

Hannerz, Ulf *Cultural Complexity: Studies in the Organization of Meaning*. New York: Columbia University Press, 1992.

Hansen, Anne. *How to Behave: Buddhism and Modernity in Colonial Cambodia, 1860– 1930* (Honolulu: University of Hawaii Press, 2007).

Harris, Elizabeth J. *Theravada Buddhism and the British Encounter: Religious, Missionary and Colonial Experience in Nineteenth-Century Sri Lanka*. Abingdon and New York: Routledge, 2006.

Harris, Ian. *Cambodian Buddhism: History and Practice*. Honolulu: University of Hawaii Press, 2005.

Heelas, Paul. "Prosperity and the New Age Movement: The Efficacy of Spiritual Economics." In *New Religious Movements: Challenge and Response*, edited by Bryan Wilson and Jamie Coswell. London and New York: Routledge, 1999.

H.R.H. Prince Wan Waithayakon Krommun Naradhip Bongsprabandh. "The Boon of Buddhism to Thailand." *Visakha Puja* (1961).

Hubbard, Jamie. "Embarrassing Superstition, Doctrine, and New Religious Movements." *Journal of the American Academy of Religion* 66, no. 1 (1998): 59–92.

Ingersoll, Jasper. "Merit and Identity in Village Thailand." In *Change and Persistance in Thai Society: Essays in Honor of Lauriston Sharp*, edited by G. W. Skinner and A. T. Kirsch. Ithaca: Cornell University, 1975.

Ishii, Yoneo. *Sangha, State, and Society: Thai Buddhism in History*. Translated by Peter Hawkes. Honolulu: University of Hawaii Press, 1986.

Jackson, Peter. *Buddhadāsa: Theravada Buddhism and Modernist Reform in Thailand*. 2nd ed. Chiang Mai: Silkworm Books, 1987.

———. *Buddhism, Legitimation, and Conflict: The Political Functions of Urban Thai Buddhism*. Singapore: Institute of Southeast Asian Studies, 1989.

———. "Buddhism's Changing Political Roles." In *Political Change in Thailand: Democracy and Participation*, edited by Kevin Hewison. London: Routledge, 1997: 75–93.

———. "The Enchanting Spirit of Thai Capitalism: The Cult of Luang Phor Khoon and the Post-Modernization of Thai Buddhism." *Southeast Asia Research* 7, no. 1 (1999): 5–60.

———. "Royal Spirits, Chinese Gods, and Magic Monks: Thailand's Boom-Time Religions of Prosperity " *Southeast Asian Research* 7, no. 3 (1999): 245–320.

Jayawickrama, N. A., trans. *The Story of Gotama Buddha: The Nidāna-kathā of the Jātakaṭṭhakathā*. Oxford: Pali Text Society, 1990.

———. *The Sheaf of Garlands of the Epochs of the Conqueror: Being a Translation of Jinakālamālīpakaraṇaṁ of Rananapañña Thera of Thailand*. London: Pali Text Society, 1978.

Jory, Patrick "Thai and Western Buddhist Scholarship in the Age of Colonialism: King Chulalongkorn Redefines the Jatakas." *The Journal of Asian Studies* 61, no. 3 (2002): 891–918.

Kamala Tiyavanich. *The Buddha in the Jungle*. Seattle: University of Washington Press, 2004.

———. *Forest Recollections: Wandering Monks in Twentieth-Century Thailand*. Honolulu: University of Hawaii Press, 1997.

Kamolthip Bai-ngern. "Temples Are Open Doors: Everyone Is Allowed Inside." *The Nation*, March 24, 1996.

Kasian Tejapira. "The Postmodernisation of Thainess." In *Cultural Crisis and Social Memory: Modernity and Identity in Thailand and Laos*, edited by Shigeharu Tanabe and Charles F. Keyes. Honolulu: University of Hawaii Press, 2002: 202–227.

Kaufman, H. K. *Bangkhuad: A Community Study in Thailand*, Association for Asian Studies Monograph 10. Locust Valley: J. J. Augustin, 1960.

Kemper, Steven. "Wealth and Reformation in Sinhalese Buddhist Monasticism." In *Ethics, Wealth, and Salvation: A Study in Buddhist Social Ethics*, edited by Russell F. Sizemore and Donald K. Swearer. Columbia: University of South Carolina Press, 1990.

———. *Buying and Believing: Sri Lankan Advertising and Consumers in a Transnational World*. Chicago and London: University of Chicago Press, 2001.

Keyes, Charles. "Buddhism and National Integration in Thailand." *Journal of Asian Studies* 30, no. 3 (1971): 551–67.

———. "Buddhist Economics and Buddhist Fundamentalism in Burma and Thailand." In *Fundamentalisms and the State: Remaking Politics, Economics, and Militance*, edited by Martin Marty and R. Scott Appleby, 367–409. Chicago: University of Chicago Press, 1992.

———. "Buddhist Politics and Their Revolutionary Origins in Thailand." *International Political Science Review* 10, no. 2 (1989): 121–42.

———. "Merit Transference in the Kammic Theory of Popular Theravada Buddhism." In *Karma: An Anthropological Inquiry*, edited by E. Valentine Daniel and Charles Keyes, 261–86. Berkeley: University of California Press, 1983.

———. "Moral Authority of the Sangha and Modernity in Thailand." In *Socially-Engaged Buddhism for the New Millennium*. Bangkok: The Sathirakoses-Nagapradipa Foundation, 1999.

———. "Mother or Mistress but Never a Monk: Buddhist Notions of Female Gender in Rural Thailand." *American Ethnologist* 11, no. 2 (1984): 223–41.

———. *Thailand: Buddhist Kingdom as Modern Nation-State*. Boulder: Westview Press, 1987.

———. "Tug-of-War for Merit: Cremation of a Senior Monk." *Journal of the Siam Society* 63, no. 1 (1975): 44–62.

Kieschnick, John. *The Impact of Buddhism on Chinese Material Culture*. Princeton Princeton University Press, 2003.

Kikuchi, Yuko. *Japanese Modernisation and Mingei Theory: Cultural Nationalism and Oriental Orientalism*. London and New York: Routledge, 2004.

King, Richard. "Orientalism and Religion: Postcolonial Theory, India and 'the Mystic East'." London and New York: Routledge, 1999.

———. "Orientalism and the Study of Religions." In *The Routledge Companion to the Study of Religion*, edited by John R. Hinnells, 275–90. London and New York: Routledge, 2005.

King, Winston L. *Theravada Meditation: The Buddhist Transformation of Yoga*. Delhi: Motilal Banarsidass Publishers, 1992.

Kirsch, A. Thomas. "Economy, Polity, and Religion in Thailand." In *Change and Persistance in Thai Society: Essays in Honor of Lauristan Sharp*, edited by G. William Skinner and A. Thomas Kirsch. Ithica: Cornell University Press, 1975.

———. "Modernizing Implications of Nineteenth Century Reforms in the Thai Sangha." In *Religion and Legitimation of Power in Thailand, Laos, and Burma*, edited by Bardwell Smith. Chambersburg, PA: Anima Books, 1978.

Klima, Alan. *The Funeral Casino: Meditation, Massacre, and Exchange with the Dead in Thailand* Princeton and Oxford: Princeton University Press, 2002.

The Life and Times of Luang Phaw Wat Paknam. Pathum Thani: Dhammakāya Foundation, 1998.

Lopez, Donald S. *Critical Terms for the Study of Buddhism*. Chicago and London: The University of Chicago Press, 2005.

———. *Curators of the Buddha: The Study of Buddhism under Colonialism*. Chicago and London: University of Chicago Press, 1995.

———. *Prisoners of Shangri-La: Tibetan Buddhism and the West*. Chicago and London: University of Chicago Press, 1998.

Loy, David. *Money, Sex, War, Karma: Notes for a Buddhist Revolution*. Boston: Wisdom Publications, 2008.

———. "The Religion of the Market." In *The Religion of the Market: A Buddhist Look at the Global Economy, Consumerism, Development and the Role of Spirituality in Society, Think Sangha Journal* 1, no. 1 (1998): 14–33.

Mackenzie, Rory. *New Buddhist Movements in Thailand: Towards an Understanding of Wat Phra Dhammakāya and Santi Asoke*. London and New York: Routledge, 2007.

Mahathammakai Chedi: Mahachedi Phua Santiphap Lok. Pathum Thani: Dhammakāya Foundation, 2000.

Masuzawa, Tomozo. *The Invention of World Religions*. Chicago and London: University of Chicago Press, 2005.

Matthews, Bruce. "Buddhism and the Nation in Myanmar." In *Buddhism and Politics in Twentieth-Century Asia*, edited by Ian Harris. London: Continuum, 1999.

McCargo, Duncan. "Populism and Reformism in Contemporary Thailand." *South East Asia Research* 9, no. 1 (2001): 89–107.

McDaniel, Justin. "The Curricular Canon in Northern Thailand and Laos." *MANUSYA: Journal of Humanities* Special Issue 4 (2002): 20–59.

McKean, Lise. *Divine Enterprise: Gurus and the Hindu Nationalist Movement*. Chicago: University of Chicago Press, 1996.

Medley, Joseph and Lorrayne Carol. "The Hungry Ghost: IMF Policy, Global Capital-
ist Transformation, and Laboring Bodies in Southeast Asia." In *Postcolonialism
Meets Economics*, edited by Eiman O. Zein-Elabdin and S. Charusheela, 145–64.
London and New York: Routledge, 2004.

Metraux, Daniel A. "The Soka Gakkai: Buddhism and the Creation of a Harmonious
and Peaceful Society." In *Engaged Buddhism: Buddhist Liberation Movements in
Asia*, edited by Christopher S. Queen and Sallie B. King, 365–400. Albany: State
University of New York Press, 1996.

(Phra) Mettanando. "TRT and the Dhammakaya Temple—Perfect Match." *The Nation*, September 27, 2006.

Miles, Steven. *Consumerism: As a Way of Life*. London: Sage Publications, 1998.

M L Pattaratorn Chirapravati. *Votive Tablets in Thailand: Origins, Styles, and Uses*. Oxford, Singapore, New York Oxford University Press: 1997.

Mongkhon Chiwit. Pathum Thani: Dhammakāya Foundation, 1982.

Monier-Williams, Monier. *Buddhism: In Its Connexion with Brâhmanism and Hindûism,
and in Its Contrast with Christianity*. London: John Murray, 1889.

Moore, R. Laurence. *Selling God: American Religion in the Marketplace of Culture*. New
York: Oxford University Press, 1994.

Moore, W. Dinty. *The Accidental Buddhist: Mindfulness, Enlightenment, and Sitting Still,
American Style*. New York: Doubleday, 1997.

Morris, Rosalind. *In the Place of Origins: Modernity and Its Mediums in Northern Thailand*. Durham and London: Duke University Press, 2000.

The Nation. "Abbot Recommends a Nibble at Religion." July 1, 2007.

———. "Abbot Vows to Die in Saffron Robe: Dhammachayo Dares Authorities." May
24, 1999.

———. "Abbot's Lust for Land His Undoing." May 1, 1999.

———. "Cookie Shortage: Jatukam T-Shirts, Anyone?" September 3, 2007.

———. "The Decline of Buddhism." September 22, 1989.

———. "Dhammakaya Beliefs Wrong, Says Monk." February 15, 1999.

———. "Dhammakaya's Marketing Guru Shows His Merit Again." January 15, 1999.

———. "Education Must Teach Virtue, Not Cronyism " 1999.

———. "Former Dhammakaya Monk Threatened." December 29, 1998.

———. "Monkhood in Serious Crisis." November 20, 2001.

———. "Monks Urge Media Chiefs to Meditate." January 5, 1999.

———. "Sun Halo Heats up Temple Critics." November 28, 1998.

———. "Temple Evicted Villagers to Make Room for Gigantic Pagoda." December 12, 1998.

———. "Temple Funds Go Begging in Age of Dud Cheques." September 26, 1998.

———. "Temple Has Exploited Community, Says Banished Disciple." December 17,
1998.

———. "Thai Culture Ministry Mulling Monk Zones in Malls." November 26, 2005.

———. "The Under and Over of Development." 1999.

————. "When Money Guarantees Nirvana." November 29, 1998.,

Nidhi (Nithi) Eosiwong (Aeusrivongse). "Wattanatham Khong Chon Chan Klang Thai." *Journal of Thammasat University* 19, no. 1 (1993).

Nithinand Yorsaengrat, "Talismanic Tales." February 11, 2007.

Noppawan Bunluesilp. "Thai Amulet Craze 'Unacceptable Face of Buddhism'" *Reuters* July 13, 2007.

Norberg-Hodge, Helena. "Buddhist Engagement in the Global Economy." In *Socially Engaged Buddhism for the New Millennium: Essays in Honor of the Venerable Phra Dhammapitika on His 60th Birthday Anniversary*, 34–42. Bangkok: Santhirakoses-Nagapradipa Foundation, 1999.

(Phra) Nyanatiloka. *Buddhist Dictionary*. Colombo: Frewin and Company, 1972.

Obeyesekere, Gananath. "The Great Tradition and the Little in the Perspective of Sinhalese Buddhism." *The Journal of Asian Studies* 22, no. 2 (1963): 139–153.

————. "Theodicy, Sin and Salvation in a Sociology of Buddhism." In *Dialectic in Practical Reason*, edited by E. R. Leach, 7–40. Cambridge: Cambridge University Press, 1968.

O'Connor, Richard. "Urbanism and Religion: Community, Hierarchy, and Sanctity in Urban Thai Buddhist Temples." Ph.D. diss., Cornell University, 1978.

————. "Interpreting Thai Religious Change: Temples, Sangha Reform and Social Change." *Journal of Southeast Asian Studies* 24, no. 2 (1993): 330–39.

Osteen, Joel. *Your Best Life Now: 7 Steps to Living at Your Full Potential*. New York: Warner Faith, 2004.

Paritta Chalermpow Koanantakool. "Thai Middle-Class Practice and Consumption of Traditional Dance: "Thainess" And High Art." In *Local Cultures and The "New Asia:" The State, Culture, and Capitalism in Southeast Asia*, edited by C. J. W. - L. Wee, 217–41. Singapore: Institute of Southeast Asian Studies, 2002.

Paisal Sricharatchanya and Ian Buruma. "Praise the Buddha, and Pass the Baht." *Far Eastern Economic Review* (1987): 53-55.

Pasuk Phongpaichit and Chris Baker. *Thailand's Boom and Bust*. Chiang Mai: Silkworm Books, 1998.

Pattana Kitiarsa. "Beyond Syncretism: Hybridization of Popular Religion in Contemporary Thailand." *Journal of Southeast Asian Studies* 36, no. 3 (2005): 461–87.

————. "Faiths and Films: Countering the Crisis of Thai Buddhism from Below." *Asian Journal of Social Science* 32, no. 2 (2006): 264–90.

(Phra) Payutto. *Korani Santi Asok*. Bangkok: Mulanithi Phutthatham, 1988.

———— (Phra Rajavaramuni). "Foundations of Buddhist Social Ethics." In *Ethics, Wealth, and Salvation: A Study in Buddhist Social Ethics*, edited by Russell F. Sizemore and Donald K. Swearer, 29–53. Columbia: University of South Carolina Press, 1990.

————. *Buddhist Economics: A Middle Way for the Market Place*. Bangkok: Buddhadhamma Foundation, 1992.

———— (Phra Dhammapitaka). *Korani Thammakai: Botrian Phua Suksa Phra Phut-thasatsana Lae Sangsan Sangkhom Thai* Bangkok: Kongthun Wutthitham Phua Kansuksa lae Patibattham, 1999.

————. *Phuthasatsana Cha Wikrit Tong Kit Hai Klai Ru Hai Than* (Thai Buddhism Will Be in Crisis, We Must Have Forward Thinking). Bangkok: Buddhist Dhammic Foundation 2002.

(Phra) Phaisan Wisalo. "Khamnan: Pharakit Lae Phanthamit Khong Satsana (Preface: Mission and Allies of Religion)." In *Ngoen Kap Satsana: Thepyut Haeng Yuk Samai* (Money and Religion: The Godly War of the Era), edited by Suwanna Satha-Anand. Bangkok: Samnakphim Munnithi Komol Keemthong 1999.

————. *Phutta Satsana Thai Nai Anakot: Naeo Lae Thangok Jak Wikrit* (Thai Buddhism in Future: Trends and Solutions for Crisis), 2002.

————. "Spiritual Materialism and the Sacraments of Consumerism: A View from Thailand." *The Religion of the Market: A Buddhist Look at the Global Economy, Consumerism, Development and the Role of Spirituality in Society, Think Sangha Journal* 1, no. 1 (1998): 34-39.

Prakobpong Panapol. "Santi Asoke, Dhammakaya Show Contrast." *The Nation*, March 15, 1999.

Prapasri Osathanon. "A Philosophy in Decay." *The Nation* March 24, 1996.

Pravit Rojanaphhruk. "Religion Is Now Little More Than Convenience " *The Nation*, January 30, 1997.

Prawase Wasi. *Suan Mokh, Thammakai, Santi Asok*. third ed. Bangkok: Mo Chaoban Publishing, 1998.

————.*Latthi Thammakai: Kap Botbat Khong Sanghkom Thai*. Bangkok: Samakhom Sitkao Mahachulalongkornratchawitthayalai, 1999.

Preecha Changkhwanyuen. "Buddhist Analysis of Capitalism." *The Chulalongkorn Journal of Buddhist Studies* 3, no. 2 (2004): 247-59.

Prentiss, Craig R. "The Power of Positive Thinking." In *Religion in the United States in Practice*, edited by Colleen McDannell. Princeton: Princeton University Press, 2001.

Queen, Christopher S. and Sallie B. King, ed. *Engaged Buddhism: Buddhist Liberation Movements in Asia*. Albany: State University of New York Press, 1996.

(Somdet Phra Maha) Rajmangkalajahn. "Foreward." In *The Heart of Dhammakāya Meditation*, edited by Phra Ajahn Maha Sermchai Jayamanggalo. Bangkok: Dhammakaya Buddhist Meditation Foundation, 1991.

Reader, Ian and George J. Tanabe. *Practically Religious: Worldly Benefits and the Common Religion of Japan*. Honolulu: University of Hawaii Press, 1998.

Reynolds, Craig J. "The Buddhist Monkhood in Nineteenth Century Thailand." Ph.D. diss., Cornell University, 1972.

————. "Power." In *Critical Terms for the Study of Buddhism*, edited by Jr. Donald S. Lopez. Chicago and London: University of Chicago Press, 2005.

Reynolds, Frank E. "Ethics and Wealth in Theravāda Buddhism: A Study in Comparative Ethics." In *Ethics, Wealth, and Salvation: A Study in Buddhist Social Ethics*, edited by Russell F. Sizemore and Donald K. Swearer. Columbia: University of South Carolina Press, 1990.

———. "Civic Religion and National Community in Thailand." *Journal of Asian Studies* 36, no. 2 (1977): 267–82.

———. "The Several Bodies of Buddha: Reflections on a Neglected Aspect of Theravada Tradition." *History of Religions* 16, no. 4 (1977): 374–89.

Reynolds, Frank E. and Mani B. *Three Worlds According to King Ruang: A Thai Buddhist Cosmology*, Berkeley Buddhist Studies Series 4. Berkeley: University of California Press, 1982.

Rhys Davids, T.W. *Buddhism: Being a Sketch of the Life and Teachings of Gautama, the Buddha.* Revised Edition ed. London: Society for Promoting Christian Knowledge, 1912.

Roberts, Richard H., ed. *Religion and the Transformations of Capitalism: Comparative Approaches.* London and New York: Routledge 1995.

Roof, Wade Clark. *Spiritual Marketplace: Baby Boomers and the Remaking of American Religion.* Princeton: Princeton University Press, 1999.

Said, Edward W. *Orientalism.* 1st ed. New York: Pantheon Books, 1978.

Sanitsuda Ekachai. "It's Exploitation That's Intolerable " *Bangkok Post,* September 3, 1999.

———. *Keeping the Faith: Thai Buddhism at the Crossroads.* Bangkok: Post Books, 2001.

———. "Photirak May Have the Last Laugh." *Bangkok Post,* March 26, 1997.

———. "Prosecutors Let Monk Off the Hook." *Bangkok Post,* August 24, 2006.

———. "Sale of Amulets Is Not So Charming." *Bangkok Post,* November 26, 1997.

Santikaro Bhikkhu. "Thai Sangha Crisis: The Wat Phra Dhammakaya Case." *Bangkok Post,* March 22, 2000.

Sarkisyanz, E. "Buddhist Backgrounds of the Burmese Socialism." In *Religion and Legitimation of Power in Thailand, Laos, and Burma,* edited by Bardwell Smith. Chambersburg, PA: Anima Books, 1978.

Satchunij Pornphong. "Sincere Bids for Reform Foiled by Complacency" *The Nation,* March 24, 1996.

Satianpong Wannapok. *Suan Thaang Nipphan.* Bangkok: Sormafai Publishers, 1998.

———.*Botrian Chawphut Chak Korani Thammakai.* Bangkok: Sahathammik, 1999.

Sayadaw U. Pandita. *In This Very Life.* Sri Lanka: Buddhist Publication Society, 1992.

Schober, Julianne. "Religious Merit and Social Status among Burmese Buddhist Lay Associations." In *Merit and Blessing in Mainlaind Southeast Asia in Comparative Perspective,* edited by Cornelia Ann Kammerer and Nicola Tannenbaum, 197–211, 1996.

———. "The Theravāda Buddhist Engagement with Modernity." *Journal of Southeast Asian Studies* 26, no. 2 (1995).

Schopen, Gregory. *Bones, Stones, and Buddhist Monks: Collected Papers on the Archaeology, Epigraphy, and Texts of Monastic Buddhism in India*. Honolulu: University of Hawaii Press, 1997.

————. *Buddhist Monks and Business Matters: Still More Papers on Monastic Buddhism in India*. Honolulu: University of Hawaii Press 2004.

Scott, David. *Formations of Ritual: Colonial and Anthropological Discourses on the Sinhala Yaktovil*. Minneapolis: University of Minnesota Press, 1994.

Scott, Rachelle M. "A New Buddhist Sect?: The Dhammakāya Temple and the Politics of Difference." *Religion* 36, no. 4 (2006): 215–30.

Seager, Richard Hughes. *Buddhism in America*. New York: Columbia University Press, 2000.

Seneviratne, H. L. *The Work of Kings: The New Buddhism in Sri Lanka*. Chicago: University of Chicago Press, 1999.

(Phra Maha) Sermchai Jayamanggalo. *The Heart of Dhammakāya Meditation*. Bangkok: Dhammakāya Buddhist Meditation Foundation, 1991.

Sirikul Bunnag. "Famous Temple Faces Probe over Teachings and Fund-Raising Methods." *Bangkok Post*, November 27, 1998.

Sizemore, Russell F. and Donald K. Swearer. "Introduction." In *Ethics, Wealth, and Salvation: A Study in Buddhist Social Ethics*, edited by Russell F. Sizemore and Donald K. Swearer, 1–24. Columbia: University of South Carolina Press, 1990.

Snodgrass, Adrian. *The Symbolism of the Stupa*, Studies on Southeast Asia. Ithica: Cornell University Press, 1985.

Solomon, Robert L. "Saya San and the Burmese Rebellion." *Modern Asian Studies* 3, no. 3 (1969): 209–23.

(Phra) Somchai Thanawuttho. *Nipphan Pen Atta Ru Anatta* (Nibbāna is Self or Not-Self). Pathum Thani: Dhammakāya Foundation, 1999.

Somkiet Meethum. *Chik Nakak Thammakai* Bangkok: Reunkeaw, 2000.

(Phra) Somsak Duangsisen. "Consumerism, Prostitution, and Buddhist Ethics." *The Chulalongkorn Journal of Buddhist Studies* 2, no. 1 (2003): 107-14.

Spiro, Melford. "Buddhism and Economic Action in Burma." *American Anthropologist* 68, no. 5 (1966): 1163–1173.

————. *Buddhism and Society: The Great Tradition and Its Burmese Vicissitudes*. New York: Harper and Row, 1978.

Sri Dao Ruang. *Matsii*. Bangkok: Love and Life Press, 1990.

Strange, Paul "Religious Change in Contemporary Southeast Asia." In *The Cambridge History of Southeast Asia*, edited by Nicholas Tarling, 201–56. Cambridge: Cambridge University Press, 2000.

Strengs, Irene. "Millenial Transitions." In *Millenial Capitalism and the Culture of Neoliberalism*, edited by Jean Comaroff and John Comaroff, 57. Durham and London: Duke University Press, 2001.

Strong, John. *Relics of the Buddha*. Princeton: Princeton University Press, 2004.

———. "Rich Man, Poor Man, Bhikkhu, King." In *Ethics, Wealth, and Salvation: A Study in Buddhist Social Ethics*, edited by Russell F. Sizemore and Donald K. Swearer. Columbia: University of South Carolina Press, 1990.

Sukanya Sae-Lim. "Winning's Easy, Just Rub Any Old Tree." *The Nation*, September 16, 1999.

Sulak Sivaraksa. "Buddhism with a Small 'b'." In *Seeds of Peace: A Buddhist Vision for Renewing Society*, edited by Tom Ginsburg. Berkeley: Parallax Press, 1992.

———. *A Buddhist Vision for Renewing Society: Collected Articles by a Concerned Thai Intellectual*. Bangkok: Thai Inter-Religious Commission for Development, 1994.

———. "The Religion of Consumerism." In *Seeds of Peace: A Buddhist Vision for Renewing Society*, edited by Tom Ginsburg. Berkeley: Parallax Press, 1992.

———. *Siam in Crisis: Collected Articles*. Bangkok: Komol Kheemthong Foundation, 1980.

———. *Thammakai: Fang San Sudthay Haeng Khwamsueamsalay Khog Sathaban Song Thai*. Bangkok: Kongthun Raktham Phua Kanfunfu Phra Phutthasatsana, 1999.

———. "The Think-Big Strategy of Development." In *Seeds of Peace: A Buddhist Vision for Renewing Society*, edited by Tom Ginsburg. Berkeley: Parallax Press, 1992.

———. *Wikrit Thammakai* (Crisis of Dhammakāya). Bangkok: Khana Kammakan Satsana Phua Kanphattana, 2000.

Suthon Sukphisit. "The Bigger the Better." *Bangkok Post*, August 20, 1998.

Suwani Srisopha, *Chotmay Thueng Nanglek* Pathum Thani: Dhammakāya Foundation, 1996.

Suwanna Satha-Anand. *Ngoen Kap Satsana: Thepyut Haeng Yuk Samai (Money and Religion: The Godly War of the Era)*. Bangkok: Samnakphim Munnithi Komol Keemthong, 1999.

———. "Religious Movements in Contemporary Thailand: Buddhist Struggles for Relevance." *Asian Survey* 30, no. 4 (1990): 395–408.

Swearer, Donald K. *Me and Mine: Selected Essays of Bhikkhu Buddhadāsa*. Albany: State University of New York Press, 1989.

———. *The Buddhist World of Southeast Asia*. Albany: State University of New York Press, 1995.

———. *Becoming the Buddha: The Ritual of Image Consecration in Thailand*. Princeton and Oxford: Princeton University Press, 2004.

———. "Dhammic Socialism." In *Dhammic Socialism*, edited by Donald K. Swearer. Bangkok: Thai Inter-Religious Commission for Development, 1986.

———. "Fundamentalistic Movements in Theravada Buddhism." In *Fundamentalisms Observed*, edited by Martin Mary and R. Scott Appleby. Chicago: University of Chicago Press, 1991: 628–690.

———. "The Worldliness of Buddhism." *The Wilson Quarterly* 21, no. 2 (1997): 81–93.

——— and Sommai Premchit. *The Legend of Queen Cāma: Bodhiraṃsi's Cāmadevivaṃsa, a Translation and Commentary*. Albany: State University of New York Press, 1998.

————, Sommai Premchit, and Phaithoon Dokbuakaew. *Sacred Mountains of Northern Thailand and Their Legends*. Chiang Mai: Silkworm Books, 2004.

Tambiah, Stanley J. *Buddhism and the Spirit Cults in Northeast Thailand*, Cambridge Studies in Social Anthropology 5. Cambridge: Cambridge University Press, 1970.

————. *The Buddhist Saints of the Forest and the Cult of Amulets: A Study in Charisma, Hagiography, Sectarianism, and Millenial Buddhism*, Cambridge Studies in Social Anthropology. Cambridge: Cambridge University Press, 1984.

————. *World Conqueror and World Renouncer : A Study of Buddhism and Polity in Thailand against a Historical Background*, Cambridge Studies in Social Anthropology 15;. Cambridge and New York: Cambridge University Press, 1976.

————. *Buddhism Betrayed?: Religion, Politics, and Violence in Sri Lanka*. Chicago: University of Chicago Press, 1992.

————. "The Ideology of Merit and the Social Correlates of Buddhism in a Thai Village." In *Dialectic in Practical Religion*, edited by Edmund R. Leach. Cambridge: Cambridge University Press, 1968: 41–121.

————. "Buddhism and This-Worldly Activity." *Modern Asian Studies* 7, no. 2 (1973): 1–20.

————. "Sangha and Polity in Modern Thailand." In *Religion and Legitimation of Power in Thailand, Laos, and Burma*, edited by Bardwell Smith, 111–33. Chambersburg, PA: Anima Books, 1978.

(Phra) Tattacheevo. *Blueprint for a Global Being*. Pathum Thani: Dhammakāya Foundation, 2000.

Taylor, James L. *Forest Monks and the Nation-State: An Anthropological and Historical Study in Northeastern Thailand*. Singapore: Institute of Southeast Asian Studies, 1993.

————. "New Buddhist Movements in Thailand: An 'Individualistic Revolution,' Reform and Political Dissonance." *Journal of Southeast Asian Studies* 21, no. 1 (1990): 135–54.

————. "Thamma-Chat: Activist Monks and Competing Discourses of Nature and Nation in Northeastern Thailand." In *Seeing Forest for Trees: Environment and Environmentalism in Thailand*, edited by Philip Hirsch. Chiang Mai: Silkworm Books, 1997: 37–52.

————. "(Post)-Modernity, Remaking Tradition and the Hybridisation of Thai Buddhism." *Anthropological Forum* 9, no. 2 (1999): 163–87.

Terwiel, B. J. *Monks and Magic: An Analysis of Religious Ceremonies in Central Thailand*. London: Curzon Press, 1979.

Thongchai Winichakul. *Siam Mapped: A History of the Geo-Body of a Nation*. Honolulu: University of Hawaii Press, 1994.

Trainor, Kevin. *Relics, Ritual, and Representation in Buddhism: Rematerializing the Sri Lankan Theravāda Tradition*. Cambridge: Cambridge University Press, 1997.

Tweed, Thomas. *The American Encounter with Buddhism, 1844–1912: Victorian Culture and the Limits of Dissent*. Chapel Hill: University of North Carolina Press, 2000.

———. *Crossing and Dwelling: A Theory of Religion.* Cambridge: Cambridge University Press, 2006.

(Phra Mahasupha) Utto. *Wiphak: Wat Phra Thammakai* Bangkok: Amy Printing, 1999.

(Somdet Phra Mahā a Samana Chao Krom Phrayā) Vajirañānavarorasa. *Navakovāda.* Compiled by Somdet Phra Mahā Samana Chao Krom Phrayā Vajirañānavarorasa and translated by Bhikkhu Paññāvaḍḍho. Bangkok: Mahamakuta Buddhist University, 1993.

Vithamon Pongpairoj. "Shaking the Faith: Scandals Fuel Calls for Reform of Monkhood." *Bangkok Post*, February 19, 1996.

Walshe, Maurice. *The Long Discourses of the Buddha: A Translation of the Dīgha Nikāya* Boston: Wisdom Publications, 1995.

Watts, Jonathon. "Is the Crisis Just Economic." In *The Religion of the Market: A Buddhist Look at the Global Economy, Consumerism, Development and the Role of Spirituality in Society, Think Sangha Journal* 1 (Winter 1998): 3–6.

Webb, Andrew. "The Temple of Benz." *Bangkok TimeOut*, January 2001, 22–25.

Weber, Max. *The Protestant Ethic and the Spirit of Capitalism.* London: Unwin University Books, 1970.

———. *The Religion of China: Confucianism and Taoism.* New York: The Free Press, 1951.

———. *The Religion of India: The Sociology of Hinduism and Buddhism.* New York: The Free Press, 1958.

Wenk, Klaus. *The Restoration of Thailand under Rama I 1782–1809*, The Association of Asian Studies 24. Tucson: University of Arizona Press, 1968.

Williams, Paul. *Mahāyāna Buddhism: The Doctrinal Foundations.* London: Routledge, 1989.

Yamaguchi, Mari. "Japanese Monks Stage Fashion Show." *Associated Press*, December 15, 2007.

Zehner, Edwin. "Reform Symbolism of a Thai Middle-Class Sect: The Growth and Appeal of the Thammakai Movement." *Journal of Southeast Asian Studies* 21, no. 2 (1990): 402–26.

Index